$R \pm \sigma_1$

ENGLISH FOR CROSS-CULTURAL COMMUNICATION

ENGLISH FOR CROSS-CULTURAL COMMUNICATION

Edited by

Larry E. Smith

St. Martin's Press   New York

ISBN 0–312–25423–7

Library of Congress Cataloging in Publication Data

Main entry under title:

English for cross-cultural communication.

Bibliography: p.
1. English language—Social aspects—Addresses,
essays, lectures.   2. English language—Study and
teaching—Foreign students—Addresses, essays, lectures.
3. Intellectual cooperation—Addresses, essays,
lectures.   4. Language, Universal—Addresses, essays,
lectures,   I. Smith, Larry E.
PE1073.E54   1979   420   79–11303
ISBN 0–312–25423–7

087978

Contents

List of Tables and Figures   vii
Foreword   ix
Notes on the Contributors   x
Introduction
     Braj B. Kachru and Randolph Quirk   xiii
Overview   xxi

1. Forms of English: an Analysis of the Variables
     Peter Strevens   1
2. The Pragmatics of Non-Native Varieties of English
     Braj B. Kachru   15
3. Norm and Variability in Language Use and Language Learning
     Jack C. Richards and Mary W. J. Tay   40
4. Unity and Diversity in L2 Teaching: English in Non-Native Settings from a Canadian Perspective
     H. H. Stern   57
5. Teaching English for International and Intranational Purposes: the Philippine Context
     Aurora L. Samonte   74
6. Will EIIL Succeed where ESL and EFL Fail?
     M. L. Boonlua Debyasuvarn   83
7. English in Malaysia
     Irene F. H. Wong   94
8. Asian Student Attitudes towards English
     Willard D. Shaw   108
9. Questions in the Negotiation for Understanding
     Ruth Crymes and William Potter   123
     Appendix 9.1. Questionnaire—Pedagogical Practices in ESL   134
     Appendix 9.2. Excerpts from the Transcripts   135
10. International Communication and the Concept of Nuclear English
     Randolph Quirk   151
11. Discoursal Patterning and the Equalizing of Interpretive Opportunity
     Christopher N. Candlin   166
12. Via-Drama: an Answer to the EIIL Problem
     Richard A. Via   200

13. English as an International Language: an Attitudinal
    Approach
        Gregory Trifonovitch   211
14. Crossing the Cultural Threshold: a Challenge to Users
    of EIL
        Mayuri Sukwiwat   216

    Bibliography
    Index   225
                                                                245

List of Tables and Figures

TABLES

1.1. Parameters of variety   5
8.1. The frequency of use of English in an average span of two
    months   113
8.2. The use of English in the future   114
8.3. The rankings of the four skills   116
8.4. Variety of English presently spoken by educated speakers   119
8.5. The variety that we should learn to speak   120
8.6. Comparison of percentages choosing native and
    non-native standards   120

FIGURES

3.1. Models of development   42
3.2. Language learning as a developmental continuum   44
3.3. Language learning as a non-developmental lectal
    continuum   46
9.1. Cline from softened assertion to no-assertion   129
9.2. Form/function correlations   129
9.3. Questioner roles and question functions   131

Foreword

For several years the Culture Learning Institute of the East–West Center in Hawaii arranged a series of multinational "workshops" which were attended by professionals in the field of teaching English to persons whose mother-tongues are other than English. A wide variety of topics was discussed by the members of these workshops but four questions proved to be of common interest and were raised again and again. Who uses the English language today? In what circumstances is it used? What varieties of the language are used for what purposes by individuals within a country, that is, *intranationally*? What varieties of the language are used by individuals for purposes of *international* communication?

In 1978, at a conference sponsored by the Culture Learning Institute, a group of scholars from 16 countries gave particular attention to such questions and identified a number of related issues which they felt needed to be explored further. Some of these issues are addressed in this selection of conference papers. Others will be examined at the Institute in Honolulu and elsewhere, for example, at a forthcoming conference on varieties of English to be held at the Regional Language Centre, Singapore.

It was in the *Regional Language Centre Journal* (Volume 7, No. 2, December 1976) that the editor of the present volume, Mr Larry Smith, first argued for the "denationalization" of English and suggested that, "since English belongs to the world and every nation which uses it does so with different tone, color and quality", the Teaching of English as a Second Language and the Teaching of English as a Foreign Language should give way to the Teaching of English as an International "Auxiliary" (later Intranational) language. In this book a further attempt is made to determine whether or not it is valuable to make such a distinction when English is taught to help people to communicate effectively across both cultural and national boundaries.

Director   VERNER BICKLEY
East–West Culture Learning Institute

Notes on the Contributors

Christopher N. Candlin, Director, Institute for English Language Education, University of Lancaster, teaches undergraduate and graduate courses in linguistics, sociolinguistics, discourse analysis, and curriculum design in language teaching. He has directed several research projects in doctor–patient communication skills, language testing for overseas doctors, engineering discourse and listening comprehension. His major publications and editorial works include *The Communicative Teaching of English*, *English for Special Purposes*, and *Challenges* (with Brian Abbs, Malcolm Sexton, Terry Moston, and Christoph Edelhoff).

Ruth Crymes, Professor of English as a Second Language, has taught ESL and trained teachers at the University of Hawaii since 1958. Her areas of interest are teacher training, materials development, and English syntax. She is now the President of the Association of Teachers of English to Speakers of Other Languages (TESOL).

M. L. Boonlua Debyasuvarn is a member of the Higher Education Commission in Thailand and Professor of English and Thai at Chulalongkorn University and Silpakorn University, Thailand. Formerly Dean of the Faculty of Arts, Silpakorn University, and Chairman of the National Committee for the Co-ordination of English Instruction (with RELC, SEAMEO), she has taught English and Thai and has published numerous teaching materials, books and articles on the subjects of education, language and literature.

Braj B. Kachru is Professor and Head of the Department of Linguistics, University of Illinois, Urbana. He was the director of the Linguistic Institute of the Linguistic Society of America in 1978; has served as consultant to various linguistic research projects; and has published articles, reviews and books on Indian English, bilingualism, stylistics, sociolinguistics and Kashmiri literature. Two of his forthcoming publications are *Some Aspects of Sociolinguistics in South Asia* and *Kashmiri Literature*.

William Potter, Jr. taught English in Japan for three years before entering Harvard University for post-graduate work in East Asian Studies. He is presently teaching in Honolulu, Hawaii.

Randolph Quirk is Quain Professor of English, Department of English, University College, London, Fellow of the British Academy, and

Chairman of the English Studies Advisory Panel of the British Council. Since 1960 he has directed a major on-going research project called the *Survey of English Usage*.

Jack C. Richards is a Specialist at the SEAMEO Regional Language Centre, Singapore. He was formerly a Visiting Professor at Sakjawacana University, Indonesia, and Associate Professor at Université Laval, Quebec, Canada. He is presently involved in designing curriculum and textbooks for Japan, Indonesia, and Thailand. Included in his publications are numerous articles on error analysis, second language learning and Singapore English.

Aurora L. Samonte teaches graduate courses on second language teaching at the Graduate School of Education, University of the East, Manila. Formerly Chairman of the Department of Language Teaching, University of the Philippines, and Specialist in TESL/TEFL at the SEAMEO Regional Language Centre, Singapore.

Willard D. Shaw worked in Asia for eight years as a volunteer and training consultant for the Peace Corps and as an English teacher and programme director. He is presently doing research with the Culture Learning Institute of the East–West Center and the Department of ESL, University of Hawaii.

H. H. Stern is Professor and Director of the Modern Language Centre, Ontario Institute for Studies in Education, Toronto, Canada. He has taught graduate courses and directed the research programme of the Modern Language Centre on many aspects of second language teaching and learning, applied linguistics, and psycholinguistics. His publications include the UNESCO Studies on *Foreign Languages in Primary Education* and *Languages of the Young School Child*.

Peter Strevens is Director of the Bell Educational Trust, Cambridge, and Fellow of Wolfson College, Cambridge University. He was formerly Professor of Applied Linguistics and Director of the Language Centre, University of Essex. He has served as consultant to a number of research projects in applied linguistics, testing, description and analysis of languages. He was joint editor with Mr. R. Mackin of the Oxford University Press series on *Language and Language Learning* and Editor of the Collier-Macmillan (London) *Special English Series*.

Mayuri Sukwiwat was formerly Director of the Central Institute of English Language, Bangkok, Thailand and Secretary to the National Committee for the Co-ordination of English Instruction (with RELC, SEAMEO). She is currently a Visiting Research Fellow at the Culture Learning Institute, the East–West Center, and mainly involved in the study of the role of culture in language teaching materials.

Mary W. J. Tay, Senior Lecturer at Nanyang University, Singapore, is presently in charge of the developing, designing and teaching of English Language courses. She has also served as consultant to the English Language section of the Ministry of Education in Singapore in curriculum development, teaching techniques and examinations. Her main areas of interest are language learning, phonetics, phonology and sociolinguistics.

Gregory Trifonovitch is Assistant Director for Program Affairs, Culture Learning Institute, East–West Center. He has more than twenty years of experience as an educator in the Pacific and the Middle East. He often serves as a consultant and/or seminar leader on culture learning.

Richard A. Via, Educational Specialist with the Culture Learning Institute, East–West Center, Hawaii. He was for twenty-three years an actor, stage manager and director in the professional theatre. While in Japan as a Fulbright lecturer he became interested in the use of drama techniques for language teaching and learning. He has written many journal articles but is perhaps best known for his book, *English in Three Acts*.

Irene F. H. Wong, Associate Professor, the Department of English University of Malaya, Malaysia, teaches linguistics and trains teachers of English for the school and university levels. Her areas of interest are in transformational syntax and English and Malay structure.

Introduction

Braj B. Kachru and Randolph Quirk

In April 1978, the Culture Learning Institute of the East-West Center, Honolulu, invited a small group of scholars for a two-week conference on English for international and intranational purposes, probing issues opened up in Smith (1976a). It was a unique learning experience, where examples of the object under discussion were audibly and automatically used as the medium itself in which it was discussed. There were almost as many varieties of English—native and non-native, western and non-western—as there were participants, including voices from Bangladesh, Singapore, Malaysia, Thailand, India, the Philippines, New Zealand, Britain, Germany, and the USA. Numerous cultural, linguistic, ideological and other differences could be found among the participants, but they all had this one thing in common: all of them used the English language to debate, discuss, and argue questions which concern both native and non-native users of English, as well as the global uses of English in various sociolinguistic contexts in different parts of the world.

This two-week conference was unique in many respects, but one stood out among these. The deliberations of the participants demonstrated the international implications—and consequences—of a linguistic prophecy made on 23 September 1780 by John Adams, the second President of the United States (*Life and Works*, IX:50940). In his far-sighted statement, Adams proclaimed that

> English will be the most respectable language in the world and the most universally read and spoken in the next century, if not before the close of this one.

His time schedule was only a little optimistic, and he was quite correct in visualizing that English (Mathews, 1931:42) was

> destined to be in the next and succeeding centuries more generally the language of the world than Latin was in the last or French is in the present age. The reason of this is obvious, because increasing population in America, and their universal connection and

correspondence with all nations will . . . force their language into general use.

Perhaps at that time his fellow Americans did not share his linguistic enthusiasm for English in the same measure; at any rate, in the "succeeding centuries" the American contribution toward fulfilling his prophecy was in fact rather lukewarm. But, in the 19th century, Great Britain powerfully contributed to raising English to the status of an international language. Not all of this was the inadvertent exercise of empire: in 1835, for example, a decision by Thomas Babington Macaulay on the teaching of English in India (so that Indians could have "ready access to all the vast intellectual wealth" available in that language) had a purposeful and profound effect (Quirk, 1968).

It was almost two centuries after the Adams prophecy that at this conference representatives from a wide range of English-using countries were debating its linguistic, educational, and political implications. The aim of the group was to discuss in what sense, after several generations' experience of the use of English around the world, there was need for a new direction and a new orientation in the teaching and learning of English. The emphasis was on considering the implications of English as a language of *cross-cultural* and *cross-national* understanding.

The factors for the spread of English have been varied, but the result has been unprecedented in the linguistic history of the world. During the period since Adams, English has attained a status which other natural languages such as French, Spanish or Arabic have never matched and to which artificial languages such as Novial, Occidental, Interlingua, Volapük, Ido, or Esperanto could scarcely be imagined even aspiring. This status was primarily attained because of the control which English-speaking Britain had over vast areas in Africa and Asia. Since the 1950s the political arms of the *Raj* have slowly been withdrawn, and now in the 1970s the political climate of the world has changed and the sun does now set on the once mighty empire. But the empire has left behind the legacy of the English language, on which the sun shows no sign of setting. In its various forms and functions English is used by well over 500 million people on the four continents of the world. In becoming something close to a universal language English has accomplished something close to a linguistic miracle. In 1582, as Richard Mulcaster put it, the English language was "of small reach", extending "no further than this Island of ours, nay not there over all". But by now we have almost 120 million non-native users of English in practically every part of the world. And (it is especially significant to note) bilingualism in English is being spread especially by those who are themselves non-native users of the language. As a consequence, the native speakers of English may well come to be outnumbered by the non-native speakers. On the scale concerned, this is an unprecedented linguistic phenomenon and therefore raises questions never asked before: questions with implications that could scarcely have been even conceivable to Adams.

During the two weeks of the conference, the participants set their minds to issues such as the following:

1. What is the position of English in the glotto-political and socio-political context of the countries where it is used as a non-native language?

2. What factors motivated the retention of English after the end of the colonial period?

3. What are the functional and pragmatic contexts in which the new varieties are used?

4. What is the sociolinguistic profile of each variety and how does it contribute to the development of varieties within a variety?

5. What are the linguistic and contextual parameters which result in *nativization* at various levels and in the development of "interference" varieties?

Such issues arise through the extent to which English has its *native* and *non-native* speakers geographically dispersed in practically every linguistic and cultural area of the world. It is one of the world's most important languages, because of the "vehicular load" it carries as a medium for science, technology and literature. And it continues to be associated with those nations which are "powerful", not only in political spheres, but as leaders in technology and science (Quirk et al., 1972: 2–3).

One must, however, emphasize that this diffusion of bilingualism in English does not necessarily imply that there are *intrinsic* linguistic characteristics which entitle English to this enviable linguistic status. It is unfortunate that in many writings on the subject such claims have been made both by linguists and popular writers. For example in Jespersen's justly well-known book *Growth and structure of the English language*, we are told that

> The English language is a methodical, energetic, business-like and sober language, but does not care much for finery and elegance, but does care for logical consistency . . . It must be a source of gratification to mankind that the tongue spoken by two of the greatest powers of the world is so noble, so rich, so pliant, so expressive, and so interesting.

In Laird (1970:480) roughly the same position is adopted. While observing that the language "is triumphing because American culture is advancing on a broad front", he is prepared to assume that it is "spreading through the world partly because it is a good language with a simple grammar and a vast and highly flexible vocabulary". Equally controversial beliefs are presented as facts by Barnett (1964:9) who claims that:

contrary to popular supposition, languages evolve in the direction
of simplicity. English, being a highly evolved, cosmopolitan,
sophisticated language, has been refined and revised, planed
down and polished through centuries of use, so that today it is far
less complicated than any primitive language.

In any case, irrespective of what truth there may be in assertions that
English possesses characteristics such as *logical consistency, simplicity*
and *refinement*, we have little reason to believe that these qualities
contributed to its spread.

The outstanding factor in extending the use of English has undoubtedly been the political power and influence of the English-speaking
nations and the superiority they attained in various fields of commerce,
technology, military affairs, and the pure sciences. Political power was
especially effective during the colonial era, strongly contributing to the
position of English as a non-native language. English became a symbol
of power, prestige and superiority, and the non-native users of English
valued what it did for them socially, attitudinally, nationally and
internationally (see Fishman et al., 1977, especially Chapters 1 and 2).

In looking at English in a global perspective, we should note that the
use of English around the world does not entail the global emergence of
a single, homogeneous and mutually intelligible English-speaking
community. Far from it. The users of English differ in their goals
regarding their uses of English, in the model of English at which their
aim is directed, and in their degree of achieving competence, irrespective of model. There is thus a cline of formal and functional competence
across varieties of English throughout the world, and the varieties
themselves range from educated standard forms to creolized and pidgin
types. But, in spite of this variation, what is striking is not only the extent
of bilingualism involving English, but also the mutual intelligibility of
the educated non-native varieties of English. This is a vital linguistic fact
of modern times to which critical and informed attention must be paid
(see the papers by Kachru and by Richards and Tay in this volume).

If we look at the demographic distribution of English, it is clear that
its non-native use is not restricted to the erstwhile colonies and
dependencies, though it is true that users of English in these territories
constitute the largest number of non-native speakers of English. In
Asia, there are 60 million; in Africa, almost 20 million; in the Soviet
Union, 10 million; in Western and Central Europe, 15 million; and in the
Western Hemisphere, 10 million. The Indian subcontinent is one of the
areas of special interest where English has attained the status of an
adopted language, with almost 25 million people making regular use of
it in the course of their daily lives: India (18 million), Bangladesh (3.8
million), Pakistan (1.8 million), and Sri Lanka (1.2 million). The largest
of these countries presents an arresting picture of the kind of impact that

English can have in a non-native context, even when compared statistically with countries in which English is the mother-tongue. In India the speakers of English amount to 8.4 per cent of the population of the United States, 32.4 per cent of the population of Great Britain, and 139 per cent of the population of Australia.

In the profession of English teaching, a fundamental and compelling distinction has long been established between

(1) English as a mother-tongue; and

(2) English for speakers whose mother-tongue is other than English. More recently, but with gathering insistence over the past thirty years, (2) has been itself subdivided as between

(2a) English as a Foreign Language (e.g. in Germany or Japan); and

(2b) English as a Second Language (i.e. where English has major functions in daily life, as in India or Nigeria).

The Honolulu conference raised the question as to whether this latter distinction, between (2a) and (2b), adequately grappled with the pragmatic facts of language use—in, for example, ignoring (or tacitly accepting) traditionally established relations between English standards in the countries where English is the mother-tongue (1), and those in countries where it is not (2). Of these latter, those in (2b), where English has unique functions, uniquely related to non-native social, cultural and industrial contexts, we have the phenomenon that is becoming known as "nativization"—a concept with vitally important pedagogical implications, as well as an inherent interest for linguistic theory.

The issue of models in English acquisition was therefore very much on the conference agenda as members focused attention on the new demands being made on English as an *international* and *intranational* language, a reorientation of the distinction between (2a) and (2b) which has far from purely academic interest. There are serious theoretical and pedagogical implications.

The deliberations at the conference resulted in the following statement:

1. As professionals, members of the Conference felt that the stimulus given to the question of English used as an international or auxiliary language has led to the emergence of sharp and important issues that are in urgent need of investigation and action.

2. These issues are seen as summarized in the distinction between the uses of English for international (i.e. external) and intranational (i.e. internal) purposes.[1] This distinction recognizes that, while the teaching of English should reflect in all cases the sociocultural contexts and the educational policies of the countries concerned, there is a need to distinguish between (a) those countries (e.g. Japan) whose requirements focus upon international comprehensibility and (b) those countries (e.g. India) which in addition must take account of English as it is used for

their own intranational purposes. This distinction need not of course supersede the useful terms "foreign language" and "second language", but provides a broader perspective within which we can view the dynamics of the language situation of a wide range of countries.

3. So far as we know, no organization exists that takes account of any language in the light of this fundamental distinction, and we congratulate the East–West Center on having provided the initial thinking that has led to its recognition. The Culture Learning Institute constitutes a very good base for embarking on activities in this area.

4. It is not for us to define or prescribe the policies to be adopted, but the papers and discussions at the Conference have identified a number of fundamental issues. These issues can be considered under four headings:
   (a) Basic Research
   (b) Applied Research
   (c) Documentation, Dissemination, and Liaison
   (d) Professional Support Activities

5. *Basic Research*: e.g. descriptive and empirical studies of English in different settings; fact-finding (supported by relevant statistics) at international, national, regional, and local levels, in relation to roles, functions, attitudes, expectations, achievement, etc.; studies in the feasibility of devising a core English for international use; development of research techniques appropriate to such investigations as those listed above.

6. *Applied Research*: e.g. studies of the implications of the international–intranational distinction for language learning/teaching; arising from such studies, the elaboration of a framework of concepts and data, leading first to a re-appraisal of goals, approaches, methods, materials, tests, examinations, and teacher training, and subsequently to the necessary curriculum development, with appropriate modes of evaluation.

7. *Documentation, Dissemination, and Liaison*: e.g. promoting and creating resource centres for descriptive linguistic data and acting as a clearing house for the results of such other research as listed in 5 and 6; the interpretation and dissemination of research findings and other relevant information appropriate to specific countries and regions; liaison with relevant institutions, organizations and professional associations.

8. *Professional Support Activities*: the understanding of the findings and consequences of the foregoing research and development activities will require the institution of a well coordinated programme of workshops and conferences as well as advisory and training programmes. These would focus upon particular intra-

national, international and professional questions, and should be organized with flexibility in the choice of location. Meetings should have two crucial aims: (a) assisting in professionalizing the teaching force, and (b) enabling policy-makers and administrators to become familiar with all these developments and to elaborate ways of implementing them in their situations. Future support activities will need increasingly to reflect the new orientation that has emerged.

This statement clearly shows not only the shift in emphasis that we saw as necessary; it also goes some way towards outlining the new directions that are required in the teaching of English on a global basis.

The grounds on which the statement was based emerge equally clearly, we trust, from the selection of Conference papers presented in this volume. Richly representative of the Conference's thinking, these fourteen papers will show the widely ranging consideration that was given to many acutely important issues. It has not been possible to include all the papers presented at the Conference, nor could it have been possible to print the lengthy, provocative and fruitful discussions that followed each; still less the informal but informed talk that flourished outside the Conference sessions.

It is obvious now that English has become a part of the cultural heritage of great populations in Asia and Africa. The uses of English in these areas will differ from the uses of English in America and Britain. The emergent forms of English are creating a *distance* between the native varieties of English on the one hand and the non-native varieties on the other. This naturally raises questions of "intelligibility"—both linguistic and contextual—which have been too much ignored or treated with gross inadequacy. The linguistic implications of using English in non-native *linguistic* and *cultural* contexts are significant and it is encouraging that several studies are already available. The fast-growing lexicon of English is open to the influence not merely of classical Greek and Latin, nor yet of French and Spanish and the other familiar western languages. The impact of Hausa, Yoruba, Hindi, Arabic and Persian is also growing, particularly of course on non-native varieties of English in the relevant areas of the world. The steadily continuing hybridization of the English lexicon is one obvious linguistic manifestation of the uses of English in the international context. The time is therefore ripe to look at the linguistic and cultural processes which are "de-Anglicizing" or "de-Americanizing" the English language as it responds to cultural and linguistic forces in Asia and Africa. But it is not only a question of English being "nativized". The contact of English with other languages has had a wider effect than influencing the English language alone. It has also "Anglo-Americanized" a number of major indigenous languages in Asia and in Africa. After all, linguistic and cultural contact for a century must take its toll, and linguistic "purity" has been the first sacrifice.

The Conference marked a genuinely new phase in the study of English in the international context. In part, it raised issues which had earlier been fudged if not entirely ignored. In part, the reorientation in international/intranational terms released new insights. Not least, problems previously suppressed were brought into the open through the growing confidence of the fast-increasing numbers of non-native users of English, and of course through the atmosphere of frankness in the face of intractable difficulties that is so characteristic of East–West Center meetings.

No conference was needed to demonstrate that the English language carries the weight of British and American experience; nor that it now also carries an increasing weight of African and Asian experience; nor that this has given birth to new Englishes which are "in communion with [their] ancestral home but altered to suit [their] new . . . surroundings" (Achebe, 1965:222)—new surroundings which include the sociocultural and linguistic contexts of Africa, Asia, and the Caribbean nations. But the Conference blazed the trail for a new approach which provides a realistic framework for looking at English in the global context, and for relating concepts such as appropriateness, acceptability and intelligibility to the pragmatic factors which determine the uses of English as an international or intranational language.

NOTES

1. At the beginning of the Conference, "auxiliary" was used in the sense proposed by the Culture Learning Institute, as a language used within a country. In the course of the Conference it was found that the term can be misinterpreted and it was replaced by "intranational".

Overview

The papers in this book can be grouped into three sections:

1. "Varieties of English for cross-cultural communication." The seven papers within this section attempt to clarify the parameters of English for cross-cultural communication, offer perspectives from several different countries, and state some of the general problems involved.

2. "Frequently expressed concerns about English as a language for cross-cultural communication." The two papers within this section deal with empirical studies on topics which are frequently mentioned as special problems in the use of English for cross-cultural communication.

3. "Possible solutions to the problem of using English for cross-cultural communication." The five papers in this section offer suggestions for possible solutions to the problem of using English for cross-cultural communication.

VARIETIES OF ENGLISH FOR CROSS-CULTURAL COMMUNICATION

Since there are many acceptable native and non-native varieties of educated English, it may be helpful to think of English as being a galaxy rather than a star. Peter Strevens, in beginning this section, makes this point clearly as he describes the features that define and differentiate between local forms of English (LFE). The following paper by Braj Kachru includes the four functions of English which result in the nativization of English. Jack Richards and Mary Tay[1] point out that because of the local forms of English and the nativization of English many of the terms we have taken for granted like "native speaker", "English as a first language", "English as a second language", and "English as a foreign language" may no longer be adequate. H. H. Stern suggests that the concept of English for international and intranational purposes (EIIP), which was proposed at an East–West Center conference on English in April 1978, may be more relevant to the present situation in English education and that EIIP should be added to the concepts of EFL and ESL. Aurora Samonte and Boonlua Debyasuvarn state how this concept, sometimes called English as an international and intranational language (EIIL) will affect English language teaching in their countries—the Philippines and Thailand respectively. Irene Wong's paper completes this section on *Varieties* by describing English in Malaysia and calling for universal acceptance of non-native varieties of English for international and intranational purposes.

FREQUENTLY EXPRESSED CONCERNS ABOUT ENGLISH AS A LANGUAGE FOR CROSS-CULTURAL COMMUNICATION

In discussions about English as a language for cross-cultural communication, I have heard two concerns expressed most frequently:

1. What are the motivations for students to learn English for cross-cultural communication?

2. What are the rules of discourse when English is used for cross-cultural communication?

The papers in this section report studies in reference to these questions. There is no claim that the questions have been answered, but the papers do provide insights into the questions and information towards the answers. Willard Shaw's study on student attitudes suggests that instrumental motivation may be more important than we once thought and that we can doubt the hypothesis that integrative motivation is essential for achievement in second language learning. The Crymes/Potter study suggests that different groups of speakers, using the same linguistic resources, shape the discourse in different ways according to features in the context. No doubt such information about what is happening at the discourse level has significance for the teaching and learning of English for both native and non-native speakers.

POSSIBLE SOLUTIONS TO THE PROBLEM OF USING ENGLISH FOR CROSS-CULTURAL COMMUNICATION

The papers by Randolph Quirk and Christopher Candlin offer alternative suggestions for increasing the likelihood of cross-cultural communication when using English. Quirk suggests that the code (English) be simplified while Candlin suggests the learner be made more sophisticated. Whichever direction is chosen, the suggestions from Richard Via, Gregory Trifonovitch, and Mayuri Sukwiwat will be of assistance. Via stresses the communication of ideas and emotion through language rather than the study of language itself. He points out that language is not culturally neutral but we need not emphasize the native cultural context. It should be possible for any speaker to express his own cultural heritage through the medium of any language. Via-drama appears to provide a way to do this. Trifonovitch feels that if English is to be successfully used for cross-cultural communication, the attitude of most native speakers of English must change and Sukwiwat states that for genuine cross-cultural communication to take place, a person must become more consciously aware of his own culture and also more aware of the culture of the people with whom he is attempting to communicate.

NOTES

1. This paper, at the request of the editor, is a single shorter version of two papers originally presented separately at the Conference on English as an International Auxiliary Language, East–West Center, Honolulu, Hawaii: Jack C. Richards, "The Dynamics of English as a Second, Foreign, International and Auxiliary Language" and Mary W. J. Tay, "The Uses, Users and Features of English in Singapore".

ACKNOWLEDGEMENTS

I would like to thank the following people for their help in the preparation of this volume: Charlene Fujishige, Jenny Ichinotsubo, Bill Potter, and Mayuri Sukwiwat.

L. E. S.

1 Forms of English: an Analysis of the Variables

Peter Strevens

I INTRODUCTION: THE NATURE OF THE PROBLEM

It is commonly accepted that the English language is vastly more used nowadays than it was in the past, and that the expansion of its use continues apace. Yet paradoxically, as this one single language expands, the diversity of forms within the total envelope of "English" also increases: "more use of English" is accompanied by "more different kinds of English". The increase in diversity of forms brings in its wake a number of new anxieties and problems for the users of English, especially for non-native speakers of the language, and above all for those concerned with language education.

These anxieties are related to doubts about criteria for the acceptability of different forms of English, about the maintenance of international mutual intelligibility in English, about value-judgments on various "non-native" forms, about technical problems of description and typology, and about problems of the educational suitability of some forms of English.

In this paper, having discussed these problems in further detail we shall describe ten parameters of variation and will end by suggesting certain kinds of public and professional enlightenment that are needed.

II THE EXPANSION OF ENGLISH AND SOME CONSEQUENTIAL PROBLEMS

1. The Expansion of English
Three kinds of expansion need to be recognized, i.e. expansion in.
  (a) number of users;
  (b) range of uses; and
  (c) number of local forms of English.

Each of these contributes to the circumstances under discussion, but in differing ways.

(a) *Expansion in number of users of English*. It is estimated (Bowen, 1975) that the number of those who use English now exceeds 600 million, of whom about 300 million are native speakers while another 300 million are users who have "picked up" the language or have learned it through formal instruction, to a level where they can use it for some purpose or other, however limited and instrumental. These figures make it likely that English has the biggest number of non-native users of any language.

(b) *Expansion in the range of uses of English*. All languages display a range of uses employed by its native speakers; in the case of the majority of languages, when they are taught to (or acquired by) foreigners, only a restricted sub-set of these uses are transferred, and no new ones are likely to appear. In the case of English, by contrast, a major difference can be seen, in that English serves in many countries as a vehicle for science, for the mass media (press, radio, television) and some kinds of international entertainment and to some extent for literature. Of course, a very large number of languages other than English serve as vehicles for these activities, too, but *only in their own country* and for native speakers, whereas English serves these purposes for non-native speakers in most of the countries where it is used. In addition, the use of English for purely local purposes (e.g. certain uses of English in India) creates new circumstances unknown in the "mother tongue" situation.

(c) *Expansion in the number of local forms of English*. By this is meant quite categorically the proliferation of identifiable forms of English, embraced in preference to all others, by a major section of a particular English-using community. Thus, for example, the existence of Singapore English, Malta English, Zambian English, Hong Kong English, etc. are all examples of this trend. It should be noted that whereas 25 years ago the existence of these forms of English would have been conceded defensively, if not defiantly, by those who use them, nowadays they are accepted as being in a certain sense the manifestation of local cultural identity, even though English is not the mother tongue of any but an atypical handful of the inhabitants.

2. New Causes for Concern

In using this heading "causes for concern" it is essential to make the point that these are concerns actually felt and expressed by users of English, both native speakers and non-native speakers. It is not that there exists some generalized state of emergency that threatens the language: rather that quite specific reasons for anxiety, doubt or uncertainty nowadays face people who previously had no dubieties about English. Leaving aside the professional aspects of such problems, as expressed by educational specialists and Anglists (these problems are discussed in section 3 below) two types of concern may be distinguished, relating respectively to: (a) *international intelligibility*, and (b) *value-judgments about acceptability*.

(a) *Concern over international intelligibility*. A form which this concern often takes is the question: "Will other speakers of English understand us?" One of the strongest virtues of English as an international language is that those who use it for purposes of international communication can comprehend each other, in both its written and its spoken forms. But the extent of variation that can exist without impairing mutual intelligibility is by no means obvious; many people jump to the extreme and unwarranted conclusion that local variation is inherently undesirable for this reason, regardless of whether it may have other advantages.

(b) *Concern over value-judgments of acceptability*. The myth of a single "golden" or "pure" form of English dies hard. Echoes of the past, when only native-speaker varieties—the English of those for whom it is the mother tongue—were acceptable among educated speakers, are still to be heard; the irrational view that since Shakespeare (or Wordsworth, Dickens, etc.) was the greatest writer in the English language, and since he came from England, therefore only the English of England is acceptable, is still expressed in some places. Even among communities where it is recognized that a local form of English (especially a locally identifiable accent) is a desirable means of expressing social and cultural identity, there remains a widespread apprehension that variation from mother tongue forms may lead to judgments that these variations embody a "second-class" English, at least in the eyes of some English-users.

3. Professional Problems

The concerns touched on above are those often articulated by the non-specialist public. But those engaged in academic studies of English, too—including those in the teaching of English as a foreign language, in teacher training and other apposite branches of education, in applied linguistics and sociolinguistics—acknowledge new problems as a result of the expansion of English and the proliferation of new forms of the language. These problems can be summarized as being related to *description*, *typology*, and *educational suitability*.

(a) *Problems of description*. With few exceptions, only native-speaker forms of English have been described in a tolerably comprehensive way, and although much effort within sociolinguistics is currently being devoted to the description and explanation of diversity, it seems that the proliferation of forms of English is taking place faster than the description of them. It is of course extremely difficult to produce a comprehensive description of *any* form of language: the sheer quantity, intensity and stamina of intellectual effort involved can be divined from a study of e.g. Quirk et al., *A grammar of contemporary English*. To produce even a tiny proportion of that massive achievement for each of a score of other forms of English would be a hefty undertaking. Nevertheless, once a form of English is identified as having an existence it cries out to be described, at least in its essential or differential features.

(b) *Problems of typology.* Beyond the questions of describing each individual form there arises the question of relationships between different "Englishes": similarities, differences, reasons for common or divergent features, etc. At the present time some local forms of English are being considered in terms of typology, particularly from the standpoint of studies of *creolization* and pidginization. Such studies are valuable in their own right but they do not by any means exhaust the inventory of forms requiring to be described, and indeed it seems that the spread of criteria that have to be handled puts the task beyond the scope of sociolinguistics alone, or of any other single discipline.

(c) *Problems of educational suitability.* The emergence of a newly-identified form of English brings with it problems as to its suitability for use as a model (Strevens, 1978). If "Educated Nigerian English" exists as a recognizable, identifiable entity, should that form become the model and target used in the teaching of English in the Schools of Nigeria? If so, what steps are needed in the production of teaching materials, in teacher training, in testing and examining? If a local form is *not* used, what attitudes towards it should teachers adopt, and how could and should they justify the use of a model derived from elsewhere? These and many other problems of great difficulty and yet of prime importance are raised by the proliferation of forms of English.

4. An Approach to these Concerns and Problems
It is not realistic to suppose that all these difficulties can be solved by a single, simple solution. A first step towards at least the understanding of the underlying nature of the difficulties, however, is the analysis of the principal parameters of variety. These are summarized in Table 1.1 and discussed in detail in Section III of this paper.

III PARAMETERS DEFINING AND DIFFERENTIATING LOCAL FORMS OF ENGLISH

A Terminological Question
The expression "local form of English" has been used in this paper without explanation thus far. It is intended as a technical term to refer to an identifiable version of English associated with a given community of English-users. It may not be immediately obvious why the terms "dialect" and "accent" are inadequate for this purpose, but we shall see

in the detailed discussion of the variables at work that although these two terms are already used in the descriptive apparatus, an additional term is required in order to designate the particular profile or mixture of five distinct variables.

Two Kinds of Parameter

Local forms of English vary in two ways: first, according to a profile of variables that describes their nature in linguistic terms; second, according to their use and function, broadly interpreted. In the analysis that follows these two kinds of parameter are labelled "defining" and "differentiating" respectively. The former set determines a particular local form of English (LFE); the latter set differentiates one LFE from another.

Table 1.1 Parameters of variety
Group A: Defining Parameters
(i.e. Parameters defining particular Local Forms of English)

1. Dialect and Accent
2. Range of Varieties
3. Discoursal Rules
4. Existence of 'Standard' and Non-Standard Forms
5. Primary-language and Secondary-language Forms (L1/L2)
6. Foreign Language/Second Language Forms: (FL/SL)

Local Forms of English derive from Profiles of A1–6

Group B: Differentiating Parameters
(i.e. Parameters that differentiate between different Local Forms of English)

1. Status and Uses in the Community
2. Whether the vehicle for:
   (a) Public Education
   (b) Science and Technology
   (c) International News, Entertainment, Publicity
   (d) Literature
3. Attitudes of the Local Intellectual and Educational Leaders
4. Sociocultural Affinities and Aversions:
   (a) Geographical
   (b) Historical
   (c) Sociopolitical
   (d) Cultural

Group A: Defining Parameters

1. Dialect and Accent

Differences of *accent* are phonological in nature; differences of *dialect* are grammatical and/or lexical. In the great majority of cases, dialects and accents are paired, so that local dialect X is always spoken in accent X, dialect Y in accent Y, and vice versa; never dialect X with accent Y, and so forth. However, it is a characteristic of English (and I believe it occurs also in other international languages of widespread currency) that one dialect at least ("Standard English": see below) is not localized and is observed to be spoken with virtually any accent. Within most English-using communities one is likely to find individuals using each of the following:

(a) Local dialect with local accent
(b) Standard English with local accent
(c) Standard English with a non-localizable accent (e.g. "R.P." in Britain, "General American" in the US)

And probably the majority of people will have competence in more than one of these combinations. The central point is that a local form of English is defined in part by the particular mixtures of dialect and accent which it displays.

2. Range of Varieties

Strictly speaking, variety theory, as it is used in this paper, already incorporates dialect and accent. The justification for giving them a separate section of the discussion is that it seems quite clear that in normal social intercourse dialect and accent are used by all English-users as a first and primary defining criterion: "I know where you come from and I make some conclusions about your social and educational background, on the basis of your dialect and accent". Nevertheless, other dimensions of variety exist, notably *register* (roughly, variety according to topic and subject matter, which may be manifested in phonology, in grammar, in lexis and in rhetoric, and is usually visible in a mixture of all three) and a *formality–familiarity* dimension (in which the degree of formality of the communicative situation and the degree of personal and social familiarity between the participants jointly affect the choice of language actually employed). As far as LFEs are concerned, two points have to be noticed: (a) every LFE displays a range of varieties which can be analysed in the foregoing way, but (b) the particular set of varieties actually employed is specific to a given LFE.

3. Discoursal Rules

Local forms of English differ from each other in their discoursal rules. The pragmatics of discourse seem to be prone to display features transferred from local culture, in the same way as pronunciation does. This is perhaps not surprising: the pragmatics of discourse constitute a major part of our rules for regulating both inter-personal relations in general and at the same time the subtle ways in which we express our own requirements and understand what other human beings are doing. Such rules are learned within our particular culture from a very early age—certainly before mastery of language—and over a long period, perhaps one's entire lifetime. Yet they are made explicit only very rarely. Consequently we tend, as learners of a foreign language, to be only dimly aware, if at all, that the rules of discourse for using a foreign language in its cultural setting will be different from those of our native language. As teachers of a foreign language, we have only recently begun to describe, and hardly at all as yet to incorporate into teaching materials, the rules for constructing discourse, for taking and ceding a turn, for producing with our language a desired effect through choice and manipulation of illocutionary force, and so forth. The point at issue is that local forms of English vary in the detail of their discoursal rules; the appropriate set of detailed rules is an essential defining feature.

4. Existence of "Standard" and Non-Standard Forms

Languages used by very large populations with great geographical dispersion frequently exhibit a tendency to develop one dialect (possibly two over a whole continent) which breaks free from the normal localized nature of dialects and their paired accents, and which assumes a role as a "standard" dialect. This role is social in its origin; the language of a dominant clan, or social class, or educational/intellectual community, becomes accepted as a kind of reference point or norm. In the case of English—and it must be stressed that we are referring to the language in a global sense, not simply to British English—one dialect, and only one, uniquely possesses the following characteristics:

(a) it is spoken with any accent and has no "paired" accent of its own;

(b) it is encountered with only trivial variation throughout the English-using world (we are referring to grammar and lexis, it should be recalled, and not to pronunciation);

(c) it is almost universally accepted by native speakers of English as a suitable model of English for teaching their own young and for teaching foreign learners. This dialect is the one known to linguists and the English language teaching profession as "Standard English".

In this definition, "Standard English" is the name for that which is constant and similar in the written usage—although obviously it exists in speech also and can be made plain by transliterating spoken discourse into written form—of educated English-users in every country: it is the label for those features that enable, for example, British and Americans to understand each other and to exhibit in their grammar and lexis only trivial differences (Strevens, 1972).

Within American English there is a special case to be observed: "Black English". In the language of the black community in the United States, Black English occupies a place rather similar to that of Standard English within English as a whole, on the foregoing analysis, since Black English is a non-local dialect that is spoken with local accents. In Black English, the dialect is distributed ethnically but the accents in which it is spoken are distributed geographically. The local accents used by black speakers are very similar to, yet crucially different from, the local accents of whites. Thus, when they have the necessary experience to do so, people immediately recognize from an accent, even when the dialect is Standard English, not only where the speaker comes from but also whether he or she is white or black. (The matter is complicated by other general ethnic differentiations such as characteristic voice quality.)

A high proportion of users of Standard English, black or white, are bi-dialectal or multi-dialectal—they switch from one dialect to another and from one accent to another, without conscious decision, according to the social situation within which they find themselves.

Note that "standard" here does *not* imply "imposed", nor yet "of the majority". One interesting aspect of Standard English is that in every English-using community those who habitually use *only* Standard English are in a minority: over the global population of English-users mono-dialectal Standard English users are in a very small minority.

The phenomenon of Standard English exists and maintains itself without any conscious or coordinated programme of standardization—unlike the position for French, which has its Académie Française as the presumed guardian of the purity of language. I surmise that Standard English, like "standard" forms in other languages, is one product of fundamental psycho-social mechanisms by means of which both the cohesion and the hierarchies of society are roughly paralleled within language.

However that may be, local forms of English have to be considered in relation to Standard English as well as to their own nature. In many places, the outcome is very like that which exists in e.g. Britain or North America: an "internationally high-valued form" occurs, consisting of Standard English spoken with an identifiable local accent, with a small admixture of local expressions and vocabulary; in addition, the majority of the English-using population uses a dialect of more or less local type, with local accents. It is presumably the former, an "internationally high-valued form", that was referred to by Tongue (1974):

Singapore's Representative to the United Nations, T. T. B. Koh, recently pointed out: " . . . when one is abroad, in a bus.or train or aeroplane and when one overhears someone speaking, one can immediately say this is someone from Malaysia or Singapore. And I should hope that when I'm speaking abroad my countrymen will have no problem recognising that I am a Singaporean."

5. Primary/Secondary Forms

This variable relates to the status of the language for the individual user. The *primary language* (L1) of an individual is the one (or, rarely, more than one) first acquired; all others ever acquired or learned by that individual are *secondary languages*. It is a remarkable feature of English that probably more communication takes place between L2 users than between L1 users. As Kachru (1976a) says, referring to "Third World countries such as the Indian sub-continent, the West Indies or Africa": "In these countries English is used to teach and maintain the indigenous patterns of life and culture, to provide a link in culturally and linguistically pluralistic societies, and to maintain a continuity and uniformity in educational, administrative and legal systems." That being so, it seems obvious that different attitudes towards the language will be appropriate among L2 users, compared with L1 users, including attitudes towards English in education.

6. Foreign Language/Second Language Forms

Where the L1/L2 distinction relates to the individual user of English, the foreign language/second language (FL/SL) distinction applies to communities of English-users. The distinction is a sociolinguistic one, generally with historical origins. Thus, where English is a *foreign* language it has no special status in the community; where it is a *second* language it does have special status, which may take any of several forms (accepted as an official language in administration or the courts of law; the medium of instruction for some parts of the public education system; given major time allocations in local broadcasting systems; etc).

This distinction is reflected in the acronyms used in British English, in relation to the teaching of English in L2 countries: EFL means "English as a foreign language", ESL means "English as a second language". This makes sense in the context of the British-based profession, since its historical experience has been overwhelmingly overseas. However, the American experience has been overwhelmingly in teaching immigrants within the United States (though there have been important exceptions to this generalization). Bearing in mind that FL and SL refer to English-using *communities*, it is clear that the United States is an L1 community, therefore by definition neither FL nor SL, and consequently the label TEFL as used in America does not bear the same meaning as the British usages of EFL and ESL.

The FL/SL distinction has very real practical importance for the teaching of English (Strevens, 1977). In FL countries it is usual for the educational model to be an L1 form (e.g. British, American, Australian, etc.) and for only a small proportion of learners to reach a high standard; in SL countries there is a tendency for a much higher proportion of learners to reach a level of "local practical communication" and for a local form of English to be increasingly acceptable as the educational model and target (Strevens, 1978). Furthermore, the importance accorded to evidence of the learner's L1 showing through into his learning of English ("interference errors") is often much greater in EFL—and more heavily penalized—than in ESL conditions.

The nature of any local form of English is defined by the profile of particular values of the five foregoing variables. But in addition to their description, forms of English are differentiated from each other by a further set of variables relating to uses, attitudes and affinities within the English-using community.

Group B: Differentiating Parameters

1. Status and Uses in the Community

Here we are thinking of the general public, rather than just of the intellectual and educational community. It is obvious that English possesses different status and uses in e.g. Quebec and Nairobi, although in both cases English is a *second* language. In Quebec the average standard of performance in English may be higher than in Nairobi and the range of uses for which English is employed may be more extensive; the public status of the language is very different in the two cases. In Nairobi, English is an acceptable instrument of communication within a multicultural community, as well as outwards to other countries in Africa and the rest of the world. In Quebec, English is the focus of bitter emotions and political passions, and for many people it has become the symbol of the domination within Canada of French-speakers by English-speakers. Every English-using community has its own particular range of uses and status within that community.

2. Whether English is the Vehicle for Certain Uses

Among L2 English-using communities both SL and FL in type, English may or may not be used to a significant extent as a vehicle for certain uses: *education, science and technology, the mass media, international entertainment and publicity,* and *literature.* The first of these is somewhat different from the others: nevertheless the four seem to make up a coherent set.

(a) *As a vehicle for public education.* This relates not solely to whether English is the medium of instruction in university, secondary or primary public education, but also to whether major public lectures, seminars, conferences, broadcasts etc. are customarily offered in English, in the certainty that a sufficient audience of local people can and will attend or understand them.

(b) *As a vehicle for science and technology*. It is a feature of Western science and technology that although many of the world's languages serve as a vehicle for expressing and discussing matters of science, not all of them do so. English is one of those which does, probably to a greater extent than any other. A consequence of this state of affairs is that in many countries the scientific community switches into English when serving scientific purposes. In other countries, French, German, Spanish, Portuguese, Russian etc. may serve the same purpose. In the context of an analysis of forms of English we note that one differentiating feature is whether or not English forms the vehicle for science and technology.

(c) *As a vehicle for the mass media, international entertainment and publicity*. Somewhat analogous to the case of science is what occurs with the press, radio, television and the cinema. Although of course there exists in virtually every community a well-developed media industry operating in the country's own language or languages, at the same time an international, English-language extension of that multi-headed industry also exists. As the level of public command of English rises, so English is used more and more for these purposes. Indeed, the two feed each other: more English-language magazines etc. lead to greater competence in English, and vice versa. The same applies to certain international entertainment and to some branches of advertising, publicity and marketing.

(d) *As a vehicle for literature*. What is referred to here is not simply the use of English by academic specialists in English literature, but its use either for creative literature or for critical discussion among L2 English-users. In Nigeria, for example, and also in India, there has grown up an important literary profession working entirely in English yet created by and for a readership who are not English L1 speakers. Some English-using communities have developed in this way, others have not.

3. Attitudes of the Local Intellectual and Educational Community
It is not unknown for these to be in conflict with, or at any rate different from, the attitudes of the general public. For instance, there is a considerable use of English in France, including great quantities of linguistic borrowing into the French language, yet intellectual attitudes firmly reject the principle of using English or even borrowing it, partly on the grounds that French, too, is an international language, a vehicle for science and literature, with an expansionist political history and therefore with L1/L2 and FL/SL variants in existence overseas, and so forth. At all events, the attitudes of the intellectual and educational community affect to a considerable extent the nature of a local form of English.

4. *Sociocultural Affinities and Aversions*

L2-using communities belong to a great range of cultural traditions, all of them different in crucial ways from the traditions, history, institutions, attitudes, aspirations, of any and all of the English L1 communities. In some ways, then, we must expect to observe the consequences of these differences made manifest through certain affinities and aversions. For example, West Indian English (which is in any case a simplification: there are many West Indian Englishes) although located on the American side of the Atlantic and although containing some linguistic similarities with (American) Black English, seems to exhibit rather more affinity with British Isles English. The influence of Black English is greater upon (white) American forms of English through entertainment and the media, whence the influence is felt in British English, too, at least in the ephemeral usage of teenagers, young adults and middle-aged disc-jockeys.

The sources of these affinities and aversions are of four main kinds:

(a) Geographical
(b) Historical
(c) Sociopolitical
(d) Cultural

(a) *Geographical.* This is an obvious source of affinity, but not an over-riding one, since e.g. political aversion can be stronger than geographical affinity.

(b) *Historical.* Ultimately most of the present LFEs of L2 communities have historical roots. But the course of history is convoluted, and present affinities may wrestle with past aversions, or vice versa, as for example in Malaysia (over the future role of English) or Morocco (over the future role of French).

(c) *Sociopolitical.* The youngest Peace Corps volunteer quickly discovers that in L2 English-using communities both the status of English and the choice of a particular branch of English (British or American) is much affected by social and political philosophies and preferences, which in turn may be very different in neighbouring countries.

(d) *Cultural (including Religious).* The demand for English for 'instrumental' purposes may compete with, or be supported by, cultural and religious affinities and aversions. This is particularly true in areas of the world where the ideological temperature is high, or where major religious ideas are on the march, e.g. Islam, or communism.

This concludes our survey of the two Groups of principal parameters relating to the definition of local forms of English and to the differentiation between them.

IV SOME CONSEQUENCES FOR LANGUAGE EDUCATION AND TEACHER TRAINING

1. General

The complex set of phenomena reported and analysed in this paper represent the outward signs of massive sociolinguistic change and development. Their consequences for language education and teacher training are correspondingly great and can only be touched on here in brief outline. In the most general terms, what is required is an increase in public and professional enlightenment about language, about variety, about English in particular, and especially about the existence and interaction of the parameters outlined in preceding sections of this paper. This enlightenment is needed in order to combat prejudice and ignorance, since matters of language are sorely liable to accrete myths, legends and old wives' tales, which in turn can lead to social action being taken on totally erroneous grounds.

2. Professional Enlightenment

That there should be a need for a major campaign of enlightenment for *professionals*, as well as for the public, reflects the continuing inadequacies in the preparation of teachers, teacher trainers, educational administrators and decision-making officials. In particular, more understanding is needed, among the categories of occupation noted above, of *language*. Not, it should be noted, of *literature* nor of *linguistics*—or rather, only peripherally of linguistics: more centrally, an understanding of the nature of language in terms of the individual, of society, of literacy and education, of literature, of philosophy, of science, of pedagogy, of national development and language planning.

These are difficult prescriptions, but they are not impossible and are already being approached in some countries. They entail, first, a basic change in the nature of the first degree normally required of an intending teacher of English, so that this shall no longer be solely concerned with literature but should bring out in the student a sensitive awareness of the nature of language in general and of English in particular, including some familiarity with its phonetic/phonological, grammatical/syntactic, lexical and semantic mechanisms; second, a basic change in the nature of the specialist initial training given to a teacher, so as to include an understanding of the ways in which teaching can and cannot be helpful, and the ways in which the community's sociolinguistic ideas and conditions affect the learning and teaching of languages; and third, a great increase in the availability of further, specialist training for experienced teachers, to give them a deeper understanding of the related disciplines and to help them to be ready for service as advisers, syllabus designers, materials writers, teacher trainers, and so forth. In short, this is a plea for more "language" in the

BA degree, more "language education" in the teacher-training course, and more "applied linguistics" in the higher degree courses.

As for *popular* enlightenment, this is equally important. Language teaching policy derives its ultimate sanction and justification from the "public will" (see Strevens, 1977); consequently the more rapidly change occurs the more essential it is that the public will should be informed and enlightened in matters of language. One of the basic duties of the professionals is to keep the public informed: hence the interlaced importance of these two aspects of enlightenment.

V CONCLUSION

The general thesis of this paper, then, is that English has increased vastly in the quantity and range of its use, that this increase has been accompanied by a proliferation of forms of English, that these events have produced doubts and anxieties among professionals and the general public alike, that the manifold forms of English can best be grasped by an analysis of the multiple variables that define and differentiate them, and that there are great tasks ahead of us in the further and continuing enlightenment of our fellow professionals and of the general public of which we are part.

2 The Pragmatics of Non-Native Varieties of English

Braj B. Kachru

INTRODUCTION

The distinction proposed in this paper between the NATIVE Englishes and NON-NATIVE Englishes is not motivated by an urge to foster linguistic divisiveness in the English-using speech community, nor is the aim to identify varieties of English on the spectrum of colours, with black, brown and yellow on one side, and white English on the other.

This paper attempts to present an overview of the pragmatics of the new Englishes which have developed in new contexts, and to initiate linguistic, attitudinal and functional realism about their uses. It seems that such an approach has become important, since in the fast-growing body of literature on the English language, and its expansion as an international language, there still is a lack of studies which focus on the pragmatic or functional aspects of these varieties and distinguish these varieties from those Englishes which are used primarily as native languages in, for example, North America, Australia, Britain, Canada and New Zealand.[1] The non-native Englishes are the legacy of the colonial period, and have mainly developed in "un-English" cultural and linguistic contexts in various parts of the world, wherever the arm of the western colonizers reached.

In earlier studies the native speakers of English have essentially studied these varieties from a pedagogical angle, sometimes demonstrating linguistic tolerance, at other times showing amusement, and often expressing irritation at the "linguistic flights . . . which jar upon the ear of the native Englishman" (Whitworth, 1907:6). There are very few studies in which a distinction is made between the functions of the non-native Englishes and those of the native varieties of English, a distinction which would take into consideration formally and functionally relevant questions such as the following:

1. The factors which introduced English in new non-native roles in Asia and Africa;

2. The reasons which contributed toward retention of English after the independence of the colonies;

3. The functional and pragmatic contexts in which the new varieties are used;

4. The linguistic and contextual parameters which contributed to the nativization and development of so-called "interference varieties";

5. The sociolinguistic context which contributed to the development of varieties within a variety; and

6. The current linguistic interaction between the users of the new Englishes and native speakers of English.

It is with reference to these questions that one can study the pragmatics of the new Englishes. I do not claim that all these questions are raised or answered in the following pages—far from it. But there is an awareness of these questions in the discussion.

TYPES OF ENGLISHES

In the literature (Bell, 1976:152–7; Kachru, 1969; Quirk et al., 1972:13–32; Richards, 1974:64–91; Strevens, 1977:119–28), several dimensions have been used to distinguish various types of Englishes, but in this study we are primarily concerned with the distinction between *Native Englishes* and *Non-Native Englishes*. It is obvious that this dichotomy is too broad since it gives the impression of a homogeneity within these two types. That is not how language actually works. Among the *non-native* speakers one must make a distinction between those who use English as a *second language* and those who use it as a *foreign language*. In the use of English as a *second* or *foreign* language there is, of course, substantial variation in competence. I have earlier used the concept of *cline of bilingualism* to account for this variation (Kachru, 1965:393–6).

In studies on the uses of English in new contexts, various euphemistic and metaphorical terms have been used to refer to their special characteristics; for example, *transplanted* English, *transported* English, and *twice-born* English. The underlying rationale for the use of such metaphorical terms is to show that the context in which these Englishes function is not the same as that of Britain, though historically all these varieties are related to *mother English*, which is generally termed *English English* or *British English*. These terms have been used not only to designate the non-native varieties, but also for all those Englishes which function in the non-native contexts, in the sense that the context of these Englishes is different from British English. Thus, Turner (1966) and Ramson (1970) used the term "English transported" for Australian and New Zealand English, and Mukherjee (1971) used the term "twice-born" for the English in Indian fiction since it is " . . . the product of two parent traditions . . ." (p.11), the Indian and British.

The largest English-using population is now using a *transplanted, transported* or *twice-born* variety of the language; it includes a substantial number who use it as their first language. Our concern is, however, with a smaller number, specifically those who are not its native users.

At this point, therefore, a minor digression into some statistical data might provide a factual basis for this general discussion. The speakers of the *transplanted* native varieties of English are spread on two continents, the largest group being speakers of American English (182 million), followed by the speakers of Australian and Canadian varieties of English who are equal in number (13 million each), and the smallest group being the users of New Zealand English (3 million). We did not include in this list the speakers of mother English (British English), who number 55 million.

The users of non-native varieties show a wide range of competence, varying from a pidginized variety to what may be called ambilingualism. The figures given below are, however, based on enrolments in classes for formal English instruction. This figure is very impressive, and divided in terms of geographical areas, it gives us the following distribution: Asia (excluding the USSR), 60 million; Africa, 20 million; western and central Europe, 15 million; Soviet Union, 10 million; The Western Hemisphere, 10 million.

The following twenty-five countries have the largest enrolments in English.[2]

Country	Millions of students
India	17.6
Philippines	9.8
USSR	9.7
Japan	7.9
Nigeria	3.9
Bangladesh	3.8
Republic of South Africa	3.5
West Germany	2.5
Malaysia	2.4
France	2.4
Indonesia	1.9
Mexico	1.9
South Korea	1.8
Pakistan	1.8
Kenya	1.7
Ghana	1.6

Brazil	1.6
Egypt	1.5
Quebec	1.5
Thailand	1.3
Taiwan	1.2
Sri Lanka	1.2
The Netherlands	1.1
Iran	1.0
Tanzania	1.0

Thus, in South Asia alone, 24.8 million people are users of English, followed by Africa, which has 20 million English users. If we add up the users of English (excluding Britain), we have 211.2 million who speak transplanted native varieties of English, 58 per cent of the total number of English speakers. And the non-native users of English add up to 85.6 million, about 26 per cent of the total English-using population.

The major non-native varieties of English have a history distinctly different from the transported varieties used in North America, Australia or Canada. There was no significant population of English speakers who settled down in, for example, South Asia or West Africa and then used their language in those countries (for South Asia see Kachru, 1969 and for Africa see Spencer, 1971a, b). The English language came to the vast areas of Asia and Africa with the expansion of the Empire, with the spread of Christianity by zealous missionaries, and with eventual "imposition" of the language due to local linguistic and cultural pluralism. However, during almost three hundred years of contact with Africa and Asia, English has been completely embedded in the local contexts and has slowly gone through the process of *nativization*.

The manifestations of nativization and the development of sub-varieties within a non-native variety have resulted in two types of reactions. One type we find in, for example, Prator (1968) who claims that the process of nativization should be curtailed, since it reduces intelligibility with the native speakers of English. Therefore, a non-native learner's model should be a native variety of English. The other type of reaction is that these varieties should be viewed with respect to their typical functions in the context in which they are used. In addition, these Englishes are viewed as going through a normal historical development, as did Latin and Sanskrit in the past,[3] therefore nativization and "local models" should be recognized as part of the total *Variety Repertoire* of the international Englishes (Kachru, 1976a; 1977a; Perren and Holloway, 1965:39 and Strevens, 1977). This approach emphasizes that in establishing the criteria for concepts such as *communicative competence* one must take into consideration the *Context of Situation* of each non-native English-speaking community.[4]

What marks the members of the speech community is certain shared features in their use of a language. But it is equally important to emphasize the non-shared culture-bound features which each variety has developed, and which make these varieties and sub-varieties distinct from each other. It is these characteristics which make these varieties " . . . capable of expressing the socio-cultural reality of that country" (Richards, 1974:87).

The range of *Verbal Repertoire*, which forms an essential part of communicative competence, is determined by culture-bound parameters, and the concept of *acceptability, appropriateness*, and *intelligibility* cannot be used independently of this context. Therefore, the appropriateness and congruence of a speech act in English has to be related to the specific variety, for example, *Indian* English, *Nigerian* English, or *West Indies* English.

Language is essentially a social activity and the contexts for the use of language are determined by various parameters in the context of situation. It is, therefore, important that the non-native varieties of English be studied in the context of situation which is appropriate to each variety, its uses and user.

We shall present some restricted data here about the uses of non-native Englishes in four broad functions. Following Bernstein we shall term these the *Instrumental* function, the *Regulative* function, the *Interpersonal* function, and the *Imaginative/Innovative* function and discuss some cultural and linguistic processes which have contributed toward nativization of English in these functions.[5]

NATIVIZATION: FUNCTIONAL

There are various ways of defining the above four functions. In culturally and linguistically pluralistic societies, *Instrumental* function implies the status given to English in the educational system, in which it functions as an instrument of learning at various stages. *Regulative* function entails the use of English in, for example, the legal system and administration. *Interpersonal* function provides a clue to how a non-native language is used as a *link* language for effective communication between speakers of various languages, dialects, ethnic groups, and religions, thus providing a code of communication for diverse linguistic and cultural groups. In addition to providing a code, in the interpersonal function, English may also symbolize élitism, prestige, and modernity. The more attitudinal benefits a language provides to a user, the more its uses are stabilized and expanded. At present in several countries where English is a non-native language, it provides various status-marking advantages for which one prefers to become part of this speech community (see, e.g. K. Sridhar, 1978a). This reminds one of the status-providing advantages of Persian during the Islamic rule in India, French in parts of Africa, and Sanskrit in parts of South Asia. The *Imaginative/Innovative* function of English has resulted in the development of a large body of writing in English in different genres in various parts of the world. It is the use of English in creative contexts that has now resulted in a fast-growing body of, among other, Indian English literature, West African literature, and Caribbean literature.

Let me now elaborate on these four functions with some data from India to illustrate the point. As an instrument of higher education, English continues to hold a dominant position in 83 Indian Universities (which include specialized institutes, considered "deemed" universities by the University Grants Commission). Of these, 12 universities in the Hindi region (*madhya desa*) have introduced Hindi as a medium of instruction. In addition, 4 universities in Gujarat and 1 in Rajasthan use the regional language at the BA and MA levels for instruction. In all, 19 universities continue to use English exclusively as the medium of instruction.

Instructional materials for the humanities are locally produced, often at the state level, and the majority of these focus on India as opposed to the West, which was the case during the colonial days. In post-independence textbooks, it is normal now to include text materials from Indian English writers such as R. K. Narayan and Mulk Raj Anand. Thus, English is used not only as a tool to impart education to linguistically and ethnically pluralistic groups, but it is also primarily through textbooks in English that attempts are being made towards imparting what Indians call *all-India awareness*, and consciousness of the underlying cultural unity of the country. The situation in West Africa is not much different from that in India.

The regulatory function basically involves the legal system and the administrative network. Over the last five or six centuries, the legal system, especially the high courts, have traditionally used two non-Indian languages: earlier, Persian and later, English. In 1965, when attempts were made to use regional languages in the high courts and lower courts, the Indian Bar Council opposed the resolution, claiming that "deep study and felicity in the use of one common language are vital to the existence of an all-India Bar, each of which is in turn indispensable to national integration" (Shah, 1968:168). As in education, in the legal system the claim is made that for "national integration", and "all-India" standards, English must continue as a regulatory language, though there are very vocal groups who do not support this view.

In administration, different languages are used at various levels, but there is no national consensus on policy. The discussion in favour of Hindi and regional languages, or in favour of the continuation of English, is an on-going debate which provides both entertainment for people and an issue for politicians. In the meantime, however, English has the upper hand. During the period 1969–73, the central and state governments released 398 publications, of which 50.4 per cent (191) were in English and 21 per cent (81) in Hindi. There are other indications, too, which demonstrate the dominance of English in the regulatory function; for example, 50 per cent of the total amount spent on various types of advertisement by the government during this period was used for English-language newspapers, and the Ministry of Education sent 2,662 telegrams, of which only 20 were in Hindi (K. Sridhar, 1978b).

These figures are only indicative of the use of a language, and may not necessarily interest a linguist or a language teacher, but thereby hangs a linguistic tale. More interesting is to see how this regulatory use of English in the Indian setting has linguistic implications, namely, development of typically Indian registers of English in the legal system, administration, education, and advertising. And, after all, *Babu English* is a manifestation of such uses.

There are only two languages which are used for interaction all over India, English and Hindi—in various varieties—but the symbolic and attitudinal implications of English are greater than that of Hindi. A variety of English which ranks low on the cline of bilingualism is still preferred to the use of Hindi in many roles. The result is code-mixed conversation where linguistically there is no need for the fusion of English and Hindi (see, e.g. Kachru, 1978a; 1978b and S. Sridhar, 1978). In national communication book production has an important role. The UNESCO *Statistical yearbook* (1975:462) provides very informative data on this. The comparison of the years 1969 to 1973 shows that, of the 14 major Indian languages (English included), book production in English has not only been the highest but has been increasing every year.

The same study reveals that, of the 47 countries included in the study, India produced more books in English than, for example, Canada, New Zealand, Japan, South Africa and the USSR. Though in the USSR English is the major foreign language, it published only 0.02 per cent of its books in English, while the percentage in India is 39.9. In Ghana, Kenya, Nigeria, Pakistan and Sri Lanka, to name a few of the countries using English as a non-native language, the number of books published in English is out of proportion to the percentage of English-using population. But then one can easily understand the reason for this.

In the production of professional journals English is understandably far ahead. During 1971, 94 out of 127 scientific journals were published in English (74 per cent). This is again true of journals in engineering and technology. In 1971, out of 208 journals, 172 (83 per cent) were published in English.

The above figures refer mainly to specialized professional journals. If we compare the number of newspapers and news magazines in India,

English is among the five major languages, along with Hindi, Urdu, Tamil and Marathi, according to figures for 1973. In terms of the reading public, English-language newspapers commanded the highest circulation (23.7 per cent). English-language newspapers are published in 27 of the 29 states and union territories. (The two parts which have no newspapers in English are Arunachal Pradesh and Dadra and Nagar Haveli.)

In broadcasting, English and Hindi are the only two pan-Indian languages used by the All India Radio (AIR). AIR does, however, broadcast in other languages and dialects as well. In 1971 AIR had 18 bulletins each in Hindi and English per day. The number in other languages was substantially lower: Assamese—3, Bengali—3, Dogri—2, Gorkhali—1, Gujarati—1, Kannada—3, Kashmiri—2, Marathi—3, Malayalam—3, Nefa-Assemese—1, Oriya—3, Punjabi—3, Sindhi—2, Telugu—3, Tamil—3, and Urdu—3 (see Chatterjee, 1973:78).

In a sense, the creative use (in Bernstein's terms the imaginative or innovative function) incorporates the earlier three functions, and I must introduce it with a minor digression. In the rich literary tradition of the English language it was usual to point to Joseph Conrad as the lone writer who excelled in his creativity using English as a second language. One after-effect of colonization has been that the list of such writers has not only swelled, but an array of non-native English literatures has developed all over the globe. This fast-growing body of writing provides impressive evidence for linguistic and contextual nativization of the English language. The result is the development of English literatures with areal modifiers such as *West African* English literature, *Indian* English literature, *Caribbean* English literature, and so on. These are not only modifiers conveying geographical variations, but cultural and sociolinguistic attitudes, too. These literatures are one manifestation of the national literatures in multilingual and multicultural non-Western English-using nations. In India, for example, one can claim that there are only three languages in which pan-Indian literature is produced with an *all-India* reading public, namely English, Sanskrit and Hindi. Therefore, Iyengar (1962:3) is right when he says that " . . . Indian writing in English is but one of the voices in which India speaks. It is a new voice, no doubt, but it is as much Indian as others." The African situation is not different. "If you take Nigeria as an example, the national literature, as I see it, is the literature written in English; and the ethnic literatures are in Hausa, Ibo, Yoruba, Effik, Edo, Ijaw, etc., etc." (Achebe, 1965:217). (For further discussion see Kachru, 1969 and 1976b; Mazrui, 1973; Ramchand, 1973).

It is, therefore, these four functions of English, in situations diametrically opposed to those of the native varieties of English, which have resulted in the nativizations of English.

NATIVIZATION: FORMAL

One can also claim that the distinctive uses of English in, for example, America, and resultant nativization in American sociocultural (and linguistic) contexts contributed to its Americanness and make it in some respects separate from British English. This claim is justified and has been made both aggressively, for example by Mencken (1919), who claimed the status of an independent *American language* for it, and moderately by, for example, Mathews (1931) and Marckwardt and Quirk (1964). The Australianness of Australian English has formed part of several studies (e.g. Baker, 1945; Morris, 1898; Ramson, 1966 and 1970 and Turner, 1966). Their aim again was to demonstrate how the new cultural and linguistic contexts have initiated linguistic changes in Australian English which make it distinct from mother English.

The nativization of phonology and lexis have formed part of several earlier studies.[6] I would therefore like to elaborate on one particular aspect, that of the influence of multilingual and multicultural contexts on the non-native Englishes. In order to illustrate this point I shall consider three types of linguistic evidence, namely hybridization, collocations and larger formations which are culture-determined.

In a hybridized item there is at least one lexical item of English and another item from the native language. There are various structural variations possible, but we shall not go into that discussion here.[7] The hybridized lexical items are used in all the non-native varieties. Consider for example, *ahimsa soldier, police wala* and *lathi charge* from Indian English (Kachru, 1975) and *dunno drums, bodom bead,* and *Awerba lamps* from Ghanian English (Sey, 1973:63).

On the other hand, a specifically non-native English collocation has no lexical item from a native language but there are other reasons which make it specifically non-native. It may be a transfer ("translation") from the native language of a non-native user of English, it may show semantic restriction or extension, and it may be culture-specific and therefore have to be defined with special reference to, say, the African, Caribbean or Indian sociocultural context. In West African English, the following examples have one or more of the above characteristics, *chewing-sponge,* or *chewing stick* ("twig used for cleaning teeth"), *cover-shoulder* ("a blouse"), *to destool* or *enstool* ("to depose or install a chief"), *hot drinks* ("alcoholic drinks"), *knocking fee* ("fee paid by a man to a woman's family for initiating negotiations about marriage"), *outdooring* ("first appearance of a baby in public"), *sleeping cloth* ("cloth on which one sleeps at night"), *small room* ("toilet") and *tight friend* ("close friend") (see Sey, 1973:75–91). Bamgbose (1971:43ff) gives interesting examples of semantic change, for example *branch* in the sense of *call* ("I am going to branch at my uncle's house") or *globe* used for *electric light* ("we had no light because she broke the globe"), and *cup* used for a drinking glass ("he drank a cup of water"). In Indian English there is a large number of such collocations discussed in Kachru (1965, 1966, and 1969). Consider, e.g. *forehead marking, stranded thread*, and *dining leaf*. The transfer to the non-native English speaker's native linguistic and cultural elements is not restricted to lexical items—hybrid or non-hybrid. It shows in sentences and clauses, too, and in several cases results in unintelligibility with the native speakers, particularly in those formations which are used in the interpersonal and creative contexts, for example in creative writing. Let us consider the following:

1. *May we live to see ourselves tomorrow.*
2. *He has no chest.*
3. *He has no shadow.*
4. *Where does your wealth reside?*
5. *What honourable noun does your honour bear?*

It is obvious that from a native speaker's point of view these five examples are not only contextually deviant, but the lexical selection also is odd and unintelligible. On the other hand, from the point of view of the non-native speakers of English—in this case, African and Indian—the native speaker's point of view is not necessarily relevant because these formations do form part of the *Communicative Repertoire* of specific non-native varieties. It is easy to show the contextual equivalence of these formations with the formations which a native speaker might use. An African user of English, whose native language is Ijaw, might say that *may we live to see ourselves tomorrow* is the equivalent of *good night* in western societies. And sentences 2 and 3 above are equivalents of *He is timid*. Okara (1963:15) further comments on these formations: "Now a person without a chest in the physical sense can only mean a human that does not exist. The idea becomes clearer in the second translation. A person who does not cast a shadow of course does not exist. . . ."

The other two sentences (4 and 5) were used by the Indian creative writer Khushwant Singh in his *Train to Pakistan*. It is not necessary that Indian English users use these in their daily speech; they are in fact author-bound and used by Singh for developing a typical Panjabi character in a Panjabi context. The contextualization of language, through the device of translation, is one process of language nativization (Kachru, 1966). At first, these formations are unacceptable, as are any other linguistic innovations. Those of us interested in lexicography should be familiar with the lexicographer's dilemma: whether or not to include formations of low frequency in a lexicon. But, as such formations gain currency, they become more acceptable, as for example, in West Africa, have formations such as *bone-to-flesh-dance* ("denotes a man dancing with a girl, in contrast to the 'bone-to-bone' style"); *long legs* ("for using influence in high places to secure a service"), and *been-to* ("been [to] overseas") (Kirk-Greene, 1971:138).

The above-mentioned examples of linguistic units are only a part of what results in a distinct style. Let us now consider how one's idea about what constitutes impressive (*grand*) style in English is also determined by native literary traditions and culture-bound notions about style. South Asian (Kachru, forthcoming (b)) and West African (see Sey, 1973) perception of good style is diametrically opposite to the view of (at least some) native speakers of English. In Ghana (Sey, 1973:7)

> . . . flamboyance of English prose style is generally
> admired . . . and the speaker or writer who possesses this style is
> referred to in the vernaculars in such terms as "the learned
> scholar who, from his deep mine of linguistic excellence, digs up
> on suitable occasions English expressions of grandeur, depth and
> sweetness".

In Fante, for example, there is an expression *Br fo ye dur* meaning "English is weighty, powerful".

Raja Rao, (1947:10) himself a creative writer, puts it more forcefully:

> After language, the next problem is that of style. The tempo of
> Indian life must be infused into our English expression even as
> the tempo of American or Irish life has gone into the making of
> theirs. We, in India, think quickly, we talk quickly, and when we
> move we move quickly. There must be something in the sun of
> India that makes us rush and tumble and run on.

Achebe (1965:222) asks the question: "Can an African ever learn English well enough to be able to use it effectively in creative writing?" And his answer is: "certainly yes". But then, he qualifies it: "if on the other hand you ask: 'can he [an African] ever learn to use it like a native speaker?' I should say, 'I hope not. It is neither necessary, nor desirable for him to be able to do so.'" And, as a linguistic realist he adds, ". . . I feel that the English language will be able to carry the weight of my African experience. But it will have to be a new English, still in communion with its ancestral home but altered to suit its new African surroundings."

But to a native speaker such style may appear full of "verbosity" and "preciosity" (Sey, 1973:124ff). According to Goffin (1934) the attributes of Indian style of English are "Latinity" (e.g. preference for *demise* to *death*, *pain in one's bosom* to *pain in one's chest*), "polite diction", "phrase mongering" (e.g. *Himalayan-blunder, dumb-millions*) and a "moralistic tone" (in the sense that Indians cannot keep God out of it). In Kindersley's study (1938:26) the use of "clichés" is one of the stylistic features of Indian English (e.g. *do the needful, better imagined than described*).

THE CLINE OF VARIETIES: VARIETY WITHIN VARIETY

It would be misleading to say that the non-native varieties of English are homogeneous and the users of these varieties are intelligible among all the users of each variety, and across the various sub-varieties. As we know, linguistic homogeneity is the dream of an analyst, and a myth created by language pedagogues. In reality, linguistic variation is the fact which realists have accepted, though slowly, and with rewarding results.

The variation within a non-native variety of English is perhaps much more exasperating and bewildering than it is in a native variety. There are reasons for it, one reason being as Quirk (1972:26) appropriately says, that the English language has developed what he terms "interference varieties . . . that are so widespread in a community and of such long standing that they may be thought stable and adequate enough to be institutionalized and regarded as varieties of English in their own right rather than stages on the way to a more native-like English". And he particularly refers to ". . . India, Pakistan and several African countries, where efficient and fairly stable varieties of English are prominent in educated use at the highest political and professional level". The interference is not only linguistic but sociocultural as well.

The primary varieties of each non-native variety are again to be distinguished on the basis of the *users* and the participants in a speech act. We have varieties of English which are essentially used for local needs and consumption, say for example, Indian English, which is used primarily in the *Indian* contexts, with *Indian* participants for typically *Indian* situations. All these uses may be incorporated under the term national uses. The appropriateness and role of an American or Britain native speaker is not necessarily relevant to such contexts. In fact, if it were culturally, linguistically and politically expedient, India would have opted to use a language of *Indian* origin in such contexts. Not that I purposely mentioned a language of Indian *origin*, and not an Indian language since in the Indian linguistic context it is now appropriate to consider English as an Indian language though not of Indian origin.

There is, however, a small group of Indians who use English for international communication. It is in this context that the participants have the need for what may be termed international English. The Indians who function in these contexts will then use educated Indian English, which may provide approximations to various degrees of, for example, British English or American English. But the Indians who function in international contexts form only a small number out of the total English-using population of India. Statistics can be deceptive, and in this case are misleading. If one accepts the present language statistics of India, almost 3 per cent of the Indian population are English-using bilinguals. But in numerical terms these account for almost 18 million people. In other words, this number is equal to 8.4 per cent of the population of the United States, 139 per cent of the Australian population, and 32.4 per cent of the population of Great Britain. If we add the figures of the whole Indian subcontinent to these figures the picture changes substantially: there are 3.8 million users of English in Bangladesh, 1.8 million in Pakistan, and 1.2 million in Sri Lanka. And this adds up to 24.8 million. These figures do not include Bhutan and Nepal, for which no reliable figures are available.

The distinction between *national* and *international* Englishes has a crucial importance in our understanding of the concept of English as an *international* language and as an *intranational* language I shall return to this point later.

The varieties within the national varieties of non-native Englishes also provide a spectrum. Let us consider a specific variety, namely Indian English, from this point. One can intuitively say that there is significant deviation among the users of Indian English, as there is among the users of native Englishes. This intuitive impression is verified by empirical evidence presented by Schuchardt as early as 1891 when English was used in India as a highly restricted *foreign* (not *second*) language.[8] In later studies more evidence has been presented (see Kachru, forthcoming(a)).

Schuchardt develops a cline of "Indo-Englishes" and attempts to provide the formal exponents for each type. The isoglosses with reference to areas which he sets up for each sub-variety are no longer applicable, but they do provide some insight into the uses of English in India almost a century ago. The varieties he lists are *Indo-English*; *Butler English* (Madras); *Pidgin English* (Bombay); *Boxwala English* (itinerant peddlers, upper India); *Cheechee English* (or *chi-chi*, spoken by Eurasians) and *Baboo (Babu) English* (Bengal and other places.).

Thus, we find here an attempt towards explaining the varieties in terms of the speaker, and in terms of the use. This is perhaps the first attempt towards structuring the variation in Indian English. Schuchardt's paper, as Gilbert (1977) says, shows

> . . . great interest in problems associated with languages-in-contact, the nature of borrowing, the process of language "mixture", and the linguistic structures produced by imperfect, socially stabilized second language acquisition. He points out the premature nature of many of the claims being made by linguists of his day (cf. his running feud with the neo-grammarians) and urges that the study of language be put on a more experimental basis, in the sense of field observation in a social context.

I shall briefly discuss these sub-varieties. The term INDO-ENGLISH is roughly equivalent to the use of the term *educated* Indian English. In order to explain what we mean by an *educated* Indian we must of necessity use a circular definition, for example, an Indian who has a degree in English, say at the Bachelor's level. This is the type of approach Quirk et al. followed in their description of *educated* British English,[9] and Sey (1973) adopted for defining *educated* Ghanian English (EGE). It may sound circular, but in reality it is not so confusing, since description of such a corpus eventually resulted in a monumental description of English entitled *A grammar of contemporary English* (1972) by Quirk et al.

The best example of BUTLER ENGLISH is provided by Yule and Burnell (1886:133–4) in the following explanation:

> . . . the broken English spoken by native servants in the Madras Presidency which is not very much better than the Pigeon-English of China: It is a singular dialect; the present participle (e.g.) being used for the future indicative, and the preterite indicative being formed by *done*; thus *I telling* = "I will tell"; *I done tell* = "I have told"; *done come* = "actually arrived".

In Schuchardt we have additional examples:

> Butler's yevery day taking one ollock for own-self, and giving servants half half ollock; when I am telling that shame for him, he is telling, Master's strictly order all servants for the little milk give it—what can I say mam, I poor ayah woman? (*The Times*, 11 April 1882:8)

> . . . an English man wishing to assure himself that an order has been duly executed, asks, *Is that done gone finished. Yes, sare all done gone finished whole.* (Ibid.)

The term CHEE-CHEE ENGLISH is used both by Yule and Burnell (1886) and Schuchardt (1891) with reference to the speech of Eurasians or Anglo-Indians and applies both to group and ". . . also to their manner of speech. The word is said to be taken from *chi* (Fie!), a common (S. Indian) interjection of remonstrance or reproof . . .". A citation of 26 August 1881 from *St James's Gazette* says:

> There is no doubt that the "chee chee twang", which becomes so objectionable to every English before he has been long in the East, was originally learned in the convent and the Brothers' school, and will be clung to as firmly as the queer turns of speech learned in the same place.[10]

This sub-variety is marked by its "mincing accent" and "hybrid minced English", and specifically noticeable in pronunciation. But certain formations have been marked as peculiar to this sub-variety by Schuchardt. The following are illustrative:

CCE	English
to blow one's self	*to hit one's ownself*
to get tossed	*to be thrown from a horse*
to cover	*to sleep under a sheet or a blanket*
to roll a bird	*to hit a bird with a stone or pellet*

There are also alternate lexical items used, e.g. hall-room for British English *parlour*. The use of this term is also attitudinally marked since it refers to both an ethnic group and their variety of English.

The most talked about variety, however, is *Baboo (Babu) English*. The word *bābū* has several uses in Indian languages. It is, however, primarily used for a clerk who could use various Indian registers of English. Since originally Calcutta was the main centre of business and administration it was, as Yule and Burnell suggest, used for a Bengali, who was "often effeminate". The main characteristic of Babu English is its extreme stylistic ornamentation and ". . . in Bengal and elsewhere, among Anglo-Indians, it is often used with a slight savour of disparagement, as characterizing a superficially cultivated, but too often effeminate, Bengali". Babu (Baboo) English has provided inexhaustible resources for linguistic entertainment and has resulted in several volumes, for example, *Baboo Jabbarjee* (1898), *Honoured Sir from Babujee* (1931), and *Babuji writes Home* (1935).

In the Indian context, as in the West African context, there developed what may be called PIDGIN ENGLISH. In a sense the pidginization of English was initiated with the first contact of Indians and the Englishmen during the earliest phase of the activities of the East India Company, especially in the eastern parts of India. It has continued ever since in various degrees and forms. One might use the term pidginization as a cover term for the sub-varieties such as *Butler English* and *Box-wallah English* (see below) too, these then being two functional varieties in the range of pidginization.

The last sub-variety is termed *Box-wallah English*. In 1891 when Schuchardt collected his data perhaps *Box-wallah English* was restricted to what he calls upper India. This variety is used by the itinerant pedlars, who habitually carry a box containing their wares to the houses of foreigners and affluent Indians, or to hotels frequented by such people. The wares vary from antiques to *papier-mâché*, wood carving and silk and jewellery. Their command of English is restricted to what may be termed a type of trade language. In addition to *Box-wallah* English, there has also developed a *Box-wallah* Hindi, which such pedlars—for example, Kashmiri traders—use in selling their wares in the plains during the winter months when the tourist trade comes to a standstill in the highlands.

In another non-native English-using continent, Africa, the picture is not different. In Ghana, Sey (1973) distinguishes primarily between three distinct types. The first type is *Educated Ghanaian English*. This includes ". . . any Ghanian who has at least completed a course of formal instruction in the primary and middle schools in Ghana" (p. 1). This does not entail competence in speaking RP since ". . . the type that strives too obviously to approximate to RP is frowned upon as distasteful and pedantic". In educated Ghanaian English there are various degrees of competence varying from "sub-Basic type" to ambilingualism which is "rare in Ghanian context".

The second sub-variety is *Broken English*, which is closer to what in the South Asian context has been called *Butler English* or *Box-wallah English*, e.g.,

I come go: I am going away, but I'll be back.
One man no chop: Eating is not the privilege of only one person.
This good, fresh sixpence: This is good and fresh, it's only sixpence.
He thief me: He robs, robbed, etc. me.

Broken English has several characteristics of child language and given the context, and the participants in the contexts, it is not only intelligible but it is also functional (cf. Ferguson and DeBose, 1977: 107–10).

The third type is *Pidgin English*, which is associated with labourers who come from other parts of Africa, namely Northern Ghana, Nigeria, Sierra Leone and Liberia (Sey, 1973: 3).

In another part of West Africa, Nigeria, we find again the South Asian and Ghanian situation repeated; the variation ranges from " . . . the home-grown pidgins and creoles at one end of the spectrum to the universally accepted formal written registers of standard English . . ." (Spencer, 1971a:5). As in Ghana or in India, in Nigeria, too, it is " . . . agreed that the aim is not to produce speakers of British Received Pronunciation: (even if this were feasible!) . . . Many Nigerians will consider as affected or even snobbish any Nigerian who speaks like a native speaker of English" (Bamgbose, 1971:41); so will many Indians, and Ghanians. Even in Pidgins there exists considerable variety in terms of area and functions (For details see Schneider, 1966 and Mafeni, 1971).

The Caribbean variety of English has its well-defined sub-varieties; Allsopp uses the following terms for them, *free vernacular, vernaculars of subculture, elevated vernacular, creolized English* and *formal Caribbean English*.

In our discussion of the varieties within varieties, we cannot ignore the development of code-mixed varieties in South Asia (Kachru, 1978a and b; S. Sridhar, 1978); Africa (Ansre, 1971), the Philippines (Bautista, 1977), Thailand (Warie, 1977) Puerto Rico (Nash, 1977) (also see Paradis (1978) especially Section V). Code-mixing is a result of language-contact and code-switching, and has to be distinguished from just lexical borrowing. By code-mixing we mean ". . . the use of one or more languages for consistent transfer of linguistic units from one language into another, and by such a mixture developing a new restricted—or not so restricted—code of linguistic interaction."[11] The implications of code-mixing are important from the point of view of language attitude, elitism and language change. I have discussed this in detail elsewhere with reference to code-mixing of Hindi and English (Kachru, 1978a and b).

The range of varieties, and varieties within varieties, discussed above should not give us the mistaken impression that there are no common shared features in the educated varieties of these Englishes. In spite of the range of variation there are many shared and transparent features. That is why we find that cover-terms such as Caribbean English (Allsopp, 1972), South Asian English (Kachru, 1969 and Kachru, forthcoming(b)), and West African English (Spencer, 1971:7) have been used in the literature. But such labels have to be used with caution, since if we look for homogeneous speech communities, or identical functions of varieties of English with differing cultural contexts, we will be disappointed. As we have seen, even more specific modifiers, such as *Ghanian, Indian* and *Nigerian* with English do not imply non-variability. As Quirk (1972:13) appropriately warns us,

> The properties of dog-ness can be seen in both terrier and al-satian (and, we must presume, equally) yet no single variety of dog embodies all the features present in all varieties of dog. In a somewhat similar way, we need to see a common core or nucleus that we call "English" being realized only in the different actual varieties of the language that we hear or read.

The concept of dog-ness is an abstract concept and so is the concept speech community. The beholder is not only the judge, but he also has preconceived notions which are reflected in his language attitudes. From a native speaker's point of view, perhaps the range and variation in non-native varieties is alarming. A native speaker tends to have a protective attitude toward his language, and the more educated he is, the more ways he finds to show it. There are already several studies which express this alarming attitude toward the other Englishes. We might find it therefore more useful to recognize the distinction which Firth (1959:208) suggested between ". . . a close *speech fellowship* and a wider *speech community* in what may be called the language community comprising both written and spoken forms of the general language." This distinction is useful to show the pluralism of social roles and functions of each sub-variety, and the varying degrees of poly-dialectism which non-native varieties have developed, in the same way as have the native varieties of English.

These varieties within varieties, marked with reference to various speech fellowships, are not actually competing with each other. In West Africa, for example, ". . . in the life of the individual they usually have complementary roles" (Spencer, 1971: 5). That is also true of South Asia or the West Indies. This point has been well illustrated by Strevens (1977:140) with reference to Indian English. He argues that the term "Indian English" in a sense is a misleading one,

> since it refers not to a single variety but to a set of many varieties across the whole spectrum. The Indian (or Pakistani) doctor who communicates easily in English with professional colleagues at an international medical conference is using a type of "Indian English" . . . the Indian clerk who uses English constantly in his daily life for communicating with other Indians, by correspondence or telephone, may employ an "Indian English" in which the dialect is not standard English and the accent is regional or local. The lorry-driver who uses English occasionally, as a lingua franca, may be using an "Indian English" which is for all practical purposes a pidgin.

Strevens then asks whether the criticism of the teaching profession (e.g. that of Prator, 1968) is justified in criticizing the above-mentioned second type of Indian English. Then he rightly answers: "The ultimate test of effectiveness of a variety of a language is whether it meets the communication needs of those who use it" (p. 140). Indian English seems to pass that test.

NON-NATIVE ENGLISHES AND NATIVE LANGUAGES

The nativization of English presents only one aspect of the Janus-like faces of the non-native varieties of English. The other face, which is equally important, is that of the process of *Englishization* of the native languages and literatures in those parts where there is a long tradition of contact with and use of English, especially in parts of Asia and Africa.

The two-way process has further embedded the English language into the cultural and linguistic traditions of these areas, and become a part of the linguistic and literary context. In West Africa (Ansre, 1971:149)

The languages of the former colonial masters continue to play important roles, not only as independent languages but in the way in which elements from them continue to find their way into the indigenous languages; and there is no reason to believe that this process will terminate in the near future.

In earlier studies it has been demonstrated that this contact has deeply influenced the phonologies and lexicons of these languages (see, e.g. for Hindi, Bhatia, 1967). The influence is much deeper and of vital structural importance. A casual look, as Ansre says (1971:160)

at any given piece of a West African language that has been influenced by English leaves one with the impression that it contains many English lexical items but hardly any influences relatable to the grammatical categories of structure, system or class. Closer examination however shows that the grammar is also more deeply affected than is realised.

In Kachru (1977b) it has been shown that contact with English has initiated several syntactic changes and innovations in Hindi such as the introduction of impersonal constructions, a tendency toward change of word order from SOV to SVO, use of indirect speech, use of passivization with agent, and also introduction of certain types of post-head modifiers.

This influence of English language and literature is reflected also in the native literatures of Asia and Africa. In the South Asian context, all the literary languages demonstrate the influence of English. There are a large number of studies devoted to this aspect: among others, Latif (1920) discusses the impact of English on Urdu literature; Sen (1932), Das Gupta (1935), Bhattacharya (1967) on Bengali; Misra (1963) on Hindi, and Walatara (1960) on Sinhalese. Gokak (1964:3) summarizes it well with reference to South Asia when he says that, "It is no exaggeration to say that it was in the English classroom that the Indian literary renaissance was born." The African case is almost identical to the South Asian situation, if not stronger. Colonialism, says Achebe (1965:218), gave Africans ". . . a language with which to talk to one another. If it failed to give them a song, it at least gave them a tongue, for singing."

NEW ENGLISHES AND THE BATTLE OF ATTITUDES: WHO IS TO JUDGE?

We have mentioned earlier various ways in which members of a speech community may be marked as different from one another. In the case of

English, even though no academy was entrusted with the task of language standardization, the battle of attitudes was waged when the transplanted varieties developed their distinct characteristics in North America or in Australia (see Heath, 1977; Kachru, forthcoming (a); Kahane and Kahane, 1977). In this case the opponents in argument were native speakers using English on two different continents.

But with respect to non-native varieties, the attitude of native English speakers has not necessarily been one of acceptance, or recognition. It is a story of a long battle of attitudes which has yet to be fully studied. Often positions are taken which are not linguistically realistic, or do not show understanding of the reason why a particular country chooses English as a preferred second language. As we know, such attitudes are not essentially based on linguistic value judgment but various other factors play an important role, one being a native speaker's fear of seeing *his* language disintegrate in the hands of (or shall we say, on the lips of) non-native users.

In the literature (e.g. Prator, 1968) it is claimed that there are two broad views among the native speakers of English towards the non-native varieties. The two attitudes are said to be those of the users of American English and of British English. I have elsewhere shown (Kachru, 1976a) that like all generalizations, this generalization is misleading, and what is more important, is based on wrong attitudes which result in *seven attitudinal sins* which may be summarized as:

1. The sin of ethnocentrism
2. The sin of wrong perception of the language attitudes on the two sides of the Atlantic
3. The sin of not recognizing the non-native varieties of English as culture-bound codes of communication
4. The sin of ignoring the systemicness of non-native varieties of English
5. The sin of ignoring linguistic interference and language dynamics
6. The sin of overlooking the "the cline of Englishness" in language intelligibility
7. The sin of exhibiting language colonialism

I do not propose to embark on a long discussion on how native users of English have reacted to each non-native variety of English. However, a brief digression may not be out of place here. I find that there are six attitude types shown towards the Indian (or South Asian) variety of English. They are tentatively labelled as follows:

1. Descriptive (attitudinally *neutral*)
2. Cynical (attitudinally *sceptical*)
3. Puritanical (attitudinally *norm-obsessed, élitists*)
4. Realistic (attitudinally *positive*)
5. Prescriptive (attitudinally *pedagogical*)
6. Functional (attitudinally *pragmatic*)

Since a detailed discussion of these six attitude types is the topic of another paper, I shall not elaborate on them here.[12] The last one, however, is important since the functionalist or pragmatic view is the topic of this study. I shall discuss it in the following section.

PRAGMATIC PARAMETERS FOR NON-NATIVE ENGLISHES

A pragmatic view of language use implies that language must be considered an integral part of the meaning system in which it functions, and related to the contexts in which it is used. There is a relationship between a *speech-event* and a parallel *social event* which takes place in English within the context of, for example, West Africa or South Asia. This brings us back to viewing language function within a theoretical framework such as Firth's *Context of Situation* or Hymes' *Ethnography of Communication* (see Hymes, 1964, 1972 and 1974). In the Firthian view (see Firth, 1952:13) meaning is more than "sights" and sounds. It is ". . . intimately interlocked not only with an environment of particular sights and sounds, but deeply embedded in the living processes of persons maintaining themselves in society." It is these "living processes" which result in the *newness* or the *non-nativeness* in non-native Englishes. The *newness* is not only due to *interference* (or *transfer*) from the native language(s) of the user, but also due to the new cultural context in which English has been assigned various roles. There is thus a situation of an "alien" language functioning in "un-English" contexts. The result is development of *new* sub-varieties, *new* styles, and *new* registers. As English undergoes thorough acculturation in non-native contexts, it shows various degrees of culture-boundness. The more culture-bound it becomes, the more distance is created between it and the native varieties.

The formal manifestations of contextualization have been discussed in some earlier studies. In understanding the functions of the *new* Englishes, and relating these to the pragmatics of each variety, one has to consider at least three important parameters within the *context of situation*.

1. *Cline of Participants in a Speech Event*: *Speech-fellowships* within the larger *speech community* is a useful concept and provides a framework for understanding the role of sub-varieties such as *Babu English* and *Box-wallah English*. We may also find a spectrum of Pidgins each having its place on the continuum. On the other hand, for example, *Educated Indian English* or *Educated South Asian English* has its role in the national context. The code-mixed varieties too have their function, and so have the sub-varieties, since a speaker may "switch" within sub-varieties according to the role and context.

2. *Cline of Intelligibility*: In *intelligibility* too there is a cline, and this

concept cannot be used exclusively from a native speaker's point of view. A speaker of an educated non-native variety has a repertoire of sub-varieties which vary in their *Englishness*. Note, for example, how effectively the West African novelist Chinua Achebe uses code-switching, introducing a blend of Pidgin and educated West African English in the following conversation.

> "Good! See you later." Joseph always put on an impressive man-
> ner when speaking on the telephone. He never spoke Igbo or
> Pidgin English at such moments. When he hung up he told his
> colleagues: "That na my brother. Just return from overseas. B.A.
> (Honours) Classics." He always preferred the fiction of Classics to
> the truth of English. It sounded more impressive.
> "What department he de work?"
> "Secretary to the Scholarship Board."
> "E go make plenty money there. Every student who wan' go
> England go de see am for Rouse."
> "E no be like dat," said Joseph. "Him na gentleman.
> No fit take bribe."
> "Na so," said the other in disbelief.
>
> (*No Longer at Ease*, 1960)

3. *Cline of Roles*: The use of sub-varieties is role-dependent, and each sub-variety of English performs a specific role or roles in a given context. A number of these roles are *un-English*, since they are not typically American or British. Thus, the factor of acculturation is an important one, and results in what I have termed *culture-bound* linguistic innovations.

In several roles the English language is preferred to a native language for attitudinal reasons. That explains why even semi-literate Indians use a sprinkling of English lexical items to demonstrate that they are in the "in-group" or working towards attaining a certain status, for English signifies modernity, elitism and prestige. This factor cannot be ignored, as it is part of sociolinguistic reality. The difficulty is that however long a native speaker's arm may be he cannot standardize and codify such functions. Therefore the argument that native models be presented to *all* non-native speakers, for *all* contexts, and for *all* sub-varieties is a constraint which is pragmatically undesirable, since human languages do not work that way.

CONCLUSION

The intent of this paper has been to present a synthesis of some of the issues raised concerning the non-native varieties of English. I have argued in favour of what may be termed a "pragmatic" or "functional" view of the uses of these *Englishes*. These functions have to be seen at various levels and in various contexts to make each variety within a variety pragmatically "meaningful". Such an approach should give us a new perspective in understanding several crucial issues, the following being some of these.

First, the much discussed question of "communicative competence" in a second language, in this case English. It seems to me that in communicative competence one might make a distinction between the uses of a variety of English for *local* uses, *national* uses and *international* uses. It is with reference to these uses that one can then see at what level or levels we have to consider the native speaker as a relevant participant in a communicative act. It might turn out that for certain communicative acts a native speaker may have to learn certain characteristic features of a *national* or a *local* variety of English. Thus, an Englishman may have to "de-Englishize" himself, and an American "de-Americanize" himself in order to understand these national varieties. The second question is more pedagogically oriented: it relates to the concept of "model". In discussing English as an *international* and *intranational Language* it is appropriate to raise the question of choice of model. The local, national, and international uses of English discussed in this paper raise questions about the validity of DIDACTIC models, those which emphasize a *monomodel* approach to the teaching of English. One has to be realistic about such questions and aim at a DYNAMIC approach, based on a *polymodel* concept (Kachru, 1977a). The choice of a model cannot be separated from the functions of the language. And naturally *appropriateness, acceptance* and *intelligibility* cannot be isolated from the total pragmatic context.

While discussing English in the international context, one might also wonder whether we have not buried *Basic English* too soon, before it had a chance to demonstrate its relevance and usefulness. We might find that Basic English or Quirk's concept of *nuclear* English[13] would form a core on which one could further build, at various linguistic levels, *English for Special Purposes* (ESP). In a sense, ESP is closely related to the British concept of *Register* (cf. Ferguson and DeBose, 1977:100–107). And these two cut across the boundaries of varieties and sub-varieties. By recognizing a distinction between English for *international* and *intranational* purposes, we are rightly focusing on two types of functions of English. First, on the shared functions of English in various international contexts by the users of native and non-native varieties of the language. Second, on the cline of uses of a large number of Englishes which range from localized varieties to national varieties. At this point it may be appropriate to quote the following statement (1957:137) of Firth, which shows typical Firthian exaggeration, but is very close to the actual situation.

English as an expression of English life is of little importance—
what matters is English in relation to the national languages in
the changing Asian ways of life.[14]

But then he agrees that,

> Whatever the media of instruction, auxiliary English or plain con-
> temporary English with a practical bias would be desirable in
> schools and other institutions at the pre-University stage and
> possibly also in the Universities.
>
> (*Ibid*: 133).

It seems that Firth is making a case here for English as an international
language.

In an earlier paper Firth has rightly argued for what I have termed a
"pragmatic" or "functional" view toward the uses of English in non-
native contexts (1956:97)

> English is an international language in the Commonwealth, the
> Colonies and in America. International in the sense that English
> serves the American way of life and might be called American, it
> serves the Indian way of life and has recently been declared an
> Indian language within the framework of the federal constitution.
> In another sense, it is international not only in Europe but in
> Asia and Africa, and serves various African ways of life and is in-
> creasingly the all-Asian language of politics. Secondly, and I say
> "secondly" advisedly, English is the key to what is described in a
> common cliché as "the British way of life".

If we view the issue in the Firthian perspective, we are close to a
pragmatic approach to the understanding of the non-native varieties of
English.

NOTES TO CHAPTER 2

I am grateful to the Center for International Comparative Studies and the
Research Board of the Graduate College, both of the University of Illinois at
Urbana, for their support of this and my other language-related research.
  1. However, I am aware of some exceptions to this generalization, for example
     Richards, 1972 (Reprinted in Richards, 1974: 82–7), Quirk et al. 1972 (25–
     7) and Strevens, 1977 (129–46).
  2. See William W. Gage and Sirarpi Ohannessian, 'ESOL enrollments
     throughout the World', *Linguistic Reporter*, November 1974. Reproduced
     in *English Teaching Forum*, July 1977. See also Fishman et al., 1977.

3. There is a large body of literature on how Latin changed under the influence of local languages; much less has been written on the changes of Sanskrit. For Latin consider, for example, W. von Wartburg, *Die Entstehung der romanischen Völker*, 2nd ed., Tübingen: Niemeyer, 1951; *La fragmentation linguistique de la Romania*, Paris: C. Klincksieck, 1967; C. Tagliavini, *Le origini delle lingue neolating*, 5th ed., Bologna: R. Patron, 1969. The above authors have taken an explicit position on the influence of the local linguistic context on Latin. Also see W. D. Elcock, *The Romance Languages*, London: Faber & Faber, 1960; R. Posner, *The Romance Languages: a linguistic introduction*, New York: Anchor Books, 1966. I am grateful to Ladislav Zgusta for suggesting these references.

4. For a detailed discussion of Firth's concept of the "Context of Situation" see his *Speech*, 38–45 (London, 1930); *The Tongues of Men*, 126–30 (London, 1937; Reprinted 1966 London: Oxford University Press); 'Synopsis of Linguistic Theory 1930–55', 1957, reproduced in Palmer (ed.) 1968. Also see Kachru, 1966.

5. See Basil Bernstein, *Class, Codes and Control I: Theoretical studies towards a sociology of language*. London: Routledge and Kegan Paul, 1971. My use of these terms is slightly different from that of Bernstein.

6. For phonology see, for example, Ansre, 1971: 158–60; Bansal, 1969; Sey, 1973:143–53. For lexis see Allsopp, 1972; Kachru, 1973 and 1975; Rao, 1954; Wilson, 1940; and Yule and Burnell, 1886.

7. For a discussion on hybridization in Indian English see Kachru, 1975.

8. This work of Hugo Schuchardt was brought to my attention by Glenn Gilbert of Southern Illinois University at Carbondale, who has translated it into English. I am grateful to him for sending me the manuscript of his translation. The references are to this unpublished manuscript.

9. See his 'The Survey of English Usage', *Transactions of the Philological Society*, 1960.

10. Quoted in Schuchardt, 1891.

11. See Kachru, 1978.

12. See Kachru, forthcoming (a), 'Indian English: a history of attitudes'. A preliminary version of this paper was presented to the Linguistics Club of the Central Institute of English and Foreign Languages, Hyderabad, India, on 2 August 1977.

13. See his paper presented to English as an *international auxiliary language* (EIAL) Seminar, Hawaii, 1–15 April 1978.

14. This paper was written by Firth after his return from a conference in Karachi, Pakistan, and a brief visit to India.

3 Norm and Variability in Language use and Language Learning

Jack C. Richards and Mary W. J. Tay

INTRODUCTION

Two basic distinctions concerning language use and language learning underlie the concepts of English as a second and foreign language. On the one hand there is the distinction between native speakers of a language and foreign learners of a language, made use of with reference to foreign language learning. The two are usually contrasted using a model of proficiency as a basis for comparison, and the goal of one (the foreign language learner) is said to be to approximate the speech usage of the other. A further distinction is the contrast between native users of English and non-native users, or between native varieties of English and non-native varieties. This distinction is not based on differences in proficiency but on different norms of English usage in native and non-native settings. This paper examines the concepts of language proficiency, of second and foreign language, of native and non-native speakers, and considers such distinctions with reference to the status of English in the Republic of Singapore.

1 ASPECTS OF PROFICIENCY

We will begin by considering models of language proficiency and relate these to different contexts for the use and learning of English. Four aspects of proficiency will be considered: grammatical well-formedness, speech-act rules, functional elaboration, and code diversity.

1.1 Grammatical well-formedness

Much of the recent research into the nature of second and foreign language learning has centred on the nature of the grammatical variability of second and foreign language data (Hatch, 1978).

Such research has led to syntactic measures of proficiency (Burt, Dulay and Hernandez, 1975). There has also been an attempt to determine an index of second language development, comparable to say, the mean length of utterance used in first language studies (Larsen Freeman and Strom, 1977). For our purposes here it is sufficient to note that second language users are sometimes compared for evidence of differing degrees of mastery of the target language rules.

1.2 Speech-act rules

A speech act we will loosely define as the production of language for the realization of a certain intention. Searle (1969) states that there are over 1000 verbs in English such as *state, assert, describe, warn, remark, comment, order, request, approve, criticize, apologize, censure, welcome, promise, approve, disapprove,* etc, which mark speech acts. Communication conflict and communication breakdown can result from the transfer of speech-act rules from one language to another, or from misinterpretation of speech-act rules in the target language (Clyne, 1975a). The ways in which speech-act rules differ from one culture to another are sometimes dramatic, yet extremely subtle. Different cultures may have institutionalized functions for particular speech acts. In one society, as Clyne points out, persuasion may be realized by the promise of a bribe, or by a threat of a complaint to a higher authority. Apologizing and joking are also areas where there are often marked cross-cultural differences of this sort. The domain of speech-act rules has been much less researched than that of grammatical development in second language learning, yet clarification of the role of speech-act rules is vital to our understanding of second language proficiency.

1.3 Functional elaboration

In considering proficiency from a functional perspective the focus is on the ways in which the functions assumed by the target language for the language user determine the form of his or her language.

In initial stages of second language learning, the target language serves only a narrowly communicative function; as a consequence, it is acquired in a highly deviant form that exhibits all the characteristic features of pidginization; emphasis on content words, invariable word order, elimination of functors, etc. As the target language's range of functions increases, the learner's inter-language progressively expands and complexifies.

(Valdman, 1977:2)

Valdman compares two dimensions along which language learning may be compared, the grammatical and the functional. He proposes that "the key to interlanguage development lies in an understanding of the relationship between the two systems" (Valdman, 1977:7). In one situation for example, the interlanguage may be relatively well-formed grammaticaly, but have a low degree of functional elaboration. This may be particularly true of classroom-acquired foreign languages, where the emphasis is often on grammatical correctness—on form, rather than on content, or on what Widdowson calls rules of use rather than rules of usage (Widdowson, 1975b; compare also, Krashen et al., 1977). Other learners, such as immigrant workers (Clyne, 1975b) may acquire a language primarily as a functional tool in a non-classroom setting. Their interlanguage may be relatively efficient functionally, but lack grammatical well-formedness. Alternatively a language learner may progress in a balanced way along several directions of proficiency: the grammatical, the speech-act and the functional. Valdman, consider-ing just the grammatical and functional dimensions illustrates three different models of development for an interlanguage (Fig. 3.1).

FIGURE 3.1. Models of development

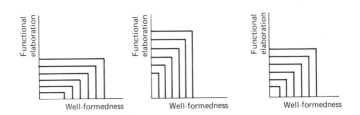

The degree of functional elaboration and development also affects a related dimension, that of topic and content diversity of the in-terlanguage, which can be measured by type token density, availability, (Mackey, 1965) lexical density (Linnarud, 1975) and related measures. A language-user's interlanguage may be relatively well developed grammatically, but deficient in the range of topics which he or she can comfortably talk about. This may lead to topic avoidance, paraphrase, and other strategies of communication which shape the interlanguage in particular ways. Where there is a functional differentiation between languages in bilingual communities, certain topics may generally be discussed in one language (e.g. business, politics, education) and other topics in a different language (home life, religion).

1.4 Code diversity

In addition to proficiency being defined in terms of grammatical and speech-act well-formedness and range of functional elaboration, the degree to which the interlanguage reflects code distinctions must be accounted for. This refers to whether variation is possible in the interlanguage along formal–informal, standard–colloquial, written–spoken dimensions, and whether the learner possesses rules allowing for variation in the interlanguage according to participant-role and setting factors. Speaker–receiver roles, for example, reflect dimensions such as age, sex, social proximity and occupation. Studies of native-language communication have attested the importance of role factors on the form of speech events (Hymes, 1968). Observations of mother-talk to young children have demonstrated that mother-talk is different from adult-directed language (Snow, 1972). Mother-talk is more explicit and relies more on the immediate observable environment than adult talk. Even young children use different speech styles according to the age of the addressee (Sachs and Devin, 1976). However the speech of foreign language users, even when quite a high degree of grammatical competence has been achieved, may be relatively inflexible in terms of code variation. This inability to adjust to role factors may be a cause of frustration and anxiety among second and foreign language users. Certain roles require specific types of speech acts. Children of immigrant workers in Australia have been observed to switch from a type of worker-pidgin when they speak to their parents, and to use a dialect of English closer to standard Australian English when speaking to their peers. Here the child would appear to be adjusting his or her speech in the case of child–adult talk, so as not to downgrade the parent's status by a demonstration of superior language ability, and to vary his or her speech repertoire towards Standard English when speaking to a peer, so as not to downgrade the child's own status vis-à-vis a peer.

Setting factors may also influence the foreign or second language code. Sampson (1971) has noted how phonological features in immigrants' English vary according to whether the setting is the classroom or the playground. Likewise, a public rather than a private setting may require a different code in the foreign language.

2 MODELS OF PROFICIENCY

2.1 Language learning developmental continuum

Two distinct models of proficiency are needed in considering English for cross-cultural communication. The first is a model of proficiency based on comparisons between learner uses of a language, and those of a norm, the norm generally being the native-speaking speech community. This model is appropriate, however, only for situations where learners can be regarded as being situated on a continuum of differing degrees of mastery of the target language rules. We will call such a continuum a language learning developmental continuum. The differences between the way individual learners speak English in, for example, Japan, Norway, Germany etc, are illustrative of particular stages in the language learning developmental continuum which encompasses varying degrees of language mastery. Individual learners can be placed at different stages along this continuum of knowledge of target language rules. In each particular case, the learner is viewed as being in a transitional stage of learning. Further use, practice and exposure will enable him or her to gradually approximate closer and closer to the target language norm. Variation in individual proficiency is seen to reflect different stages of a developmental continuum that encompasses norm-oriented British or American rules of grammatical well-formedness, speech-act rules, functional elaboration and code diversity. The developmental continuum may be thought of as a process of re-creation, or of progressive complexification, and is illustrated in Figure 3.2. The vertical lines represent differing degrees of progress along the continuum of development, which culminates in mastery of the target language norms.

FIGURE 3.2. Language learning as a developmental continuum

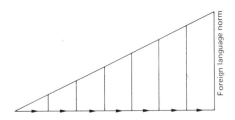

2.2 Non-developmental model of proficiency

In contrast to the model discussed above we need to consider situations where internal (rather than external) norms for the use of English are taken as models for language learning. Such is typically the case in countries where English may be said to have *indigenized*.

By indigenization we mean the evolution of distinct varieties of English as a result of the widespread use of English in new social and cultural contexts (Kachru, 1965, 1969, 1976b; J. Richards, 1977; Tongue, 1974). This is the situation of countries such as Singapore, India and the Philippines.

What characterizes contexts where English has indigenized is that distinct internal norms have emerged for the use of English, according to the socioeconomic and educational background of members of the community and according to the functions played by English in their daily lives. Basilectal, mesolectal and acrolectal speech varieties of English have thus emerged. Through taking on internal functions within a society and through becoming institutionalized within a new cultural environment, English is thus required to exhibit variability according to such dimensions as educational background, economic standing, region, ethnic group and so on. When English is used for such functions we may speak of a *non-developmental lectal continuum* (Corder, 1978). Different lects can be described in terms of rules for basilectal, mesolectal and acrolectal speech varieties, each with their own rules for grammatical well-formedness, speech acts, functional requirements and code marking.

Movement along the continuum is not seen as a process of re-creation, but of *restructuring*, and the different lects are not regarded as progressively more complex or elaborate but as functionally differentiated. Acquisition of the acrolect is thus not related to length of exposure or motivation but depends on the degree to which the speakers' socioeconomic position, and occupation, requires him or her to use the basilectal, mesolectal or acrolectal variety. This may be represented by Figure 3.3.

The functions of English in a multilingual community lead to distinct codes within the speech community, marking variation according to participant role, setting, and social factors. While ethnic identity may be expressed through the mother tongue, there may still be a need to mark this dimension in inter-ethnic communication. English may be spoken in Singapore with features that distinguish Malay, Chinese or Tamil speakers. Formal versus informal registers will also be needed to mark different participant roles.

The process of indigenization of English can be seen to influence the four dimensions of language we noted above, encompassing rules for

FIGURE 3.3. Language learning as a non-developmental lectal continuum

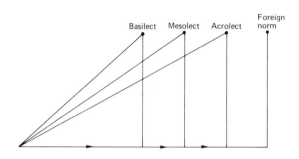

grammatical well-formedness, speech acts, functional distribution, and code marking. Let us consider the case of Singapore.

3 THE STATUS OF ENGLISH IN THE REPUBLIC OF SINGAPORE

Singapore is a multi-ethnic and multilingual country. Its population of about 2.25 million is composed of 76 per cent Chinese, 15 per cent Malays, 7 per cent Indians, and 2 per cent others including Eurasians, Europeans and Arabs (Arumainathan, 1973). The linguistic situation is even more complicated than these ethnic categories suggest. It may be described as one involving "a variety of unrelated languages each with its own literary tradition" (Rustow, 1968:102). These languages are: Hokkien, Teochew, Cantonese, Hainanese, Hakka, Foochow and Mandarin (all with a common Chinese literary tradition but mutually incomprehensible when spoken), Malay (traditionally identified as the language of the Malays), Tamil (the language of the majority of Indians) and English.

3.1 Uses of English

In recent years, English has become an important language in the Republic. Five main uses of English may be identified.

3.1.1 English as an official language
When Singapore became independent in 1965, the Government decided that there would be four official languages: Malay, Mandarin, Tamil and English. In practice, this has meant that newspapers, radio and TV programmes, important public notices issued by the Government and

the addresses of Government bodies such as the Ministry of Education are in all four languages.

In countries where English is used as an official language, it should not be considered a "foreign" language because it has been indigenized. In the Singapore context, English is never referred to as a "foreign" language. Foreign languages are such languages as Japanese and French which are now taught in some schools in addition to English and one of the other three official languages.

3.1.2 English as a language in education

Since Independence, the national policy has been to give equal treatment to all the four official languages in its educational structure. Thus, education is available in English-medium, Chinese-medium, Malay-medium and Tamil-medium schools up to the secondary level. In addition, all four languages are available as second languages at both primary and secondary levels.

The place of English in education is best understood in the context of the bilingual policy. "Bilingualism" has a special meaning in the Singapore educational system. It does not mean the learning of any two languages, but of English and one of the other three official languages. English is taught right from the first year in primary school either as a first or second language.

In the context of education in Singapore, the term "English as a first language" does not necessarily mean that it is the "first" language of the student either in terms of the order of acquisition (the first language learnt in childhood) or of proficiency (his best language), but that it is the English taught in English-medium schools. Similarly, the term "English as a second language" is used to refer only to the English taught in non-English-medium schools.

With the implementation of the bilingual policy, English has come to occupy a unique position in the educational system. In future years, English is likely to become even more important as a language in education for two main reasons. First, student enrolment in the English-medium schools has more than doubled in the past 30 years. In 1947, 31.6 per cent of all the school-going children in Singapore were in English-medium schools; in June 1975, the percentage had increased to 69.4 (Ministry of Education Reports; Yearbook of Statistics, Singapore 1975–76). Secondly, the switch in the medium of instruction from Mandarin to English at Nanyang University in 1975 is an indication of the growing importance of English in tertiary education.

3.1.3 English as a working language

English is the dominant working language in Singapore. It is the language of Government administration and legislation. Thus, on documents such as the Singapore identity card, driving licence, and vehicle registration book, only English is used. Legal contracts are also written only in English.

With the possible exception of some Chinese firms, English is the only language used at job interviews regardless of whether the job is in the civil service or in the private sector. Thus competence in English is an important criterion in recruitment and even in promotion.

3.1.4   English as a language for intra-ethnic and inter-ethnic communication

As the majority of the educated Singaporeans can speak at least two languages, they have a choice of what languages to use in intra-ethnic and inter-ethnic communication. English is just one of several languages available to the educated Singaporean in such communication.

The patterns of intra-ethnic communication have changed noticeably in the last twenty years. Today, English and Mandarin are much more widely used than Hokkien in intra-ethnic communication among the Chinese. In fact, many of the young Chinese in Singapore cannot speak the so-called Chinese "dialects" with any degree of fluency. Among the Malays, Malay continues to be used in intra-ethnic communication although English has also come to be used alongside Malay. Among the Indians, English is beginning to replace Tamil as the language used in intra-ethnic communication.

The patterns of inter-ethnic communication also show interesting changes. Traditionally, when a Chinese spoke to an Indian or a Malay, he used English or Bazaar Malay (a pidginized form of Standard Malay). Today he is likely to use English more often. The same change in the pattern of inter-ethnic communication is observable among the other ethnic groups.

Because of the increasing use of English and Mandarin in the schools, and the fact that a number of Indian and Malay parents are beginning to send their children to schools where English is taught as a first language and Mandarin as a second, we can expect that in the future, English and Mandarin will be the most commonly used languages both in intra-ethnic and inter-ethnic communication, at least among the more highly-educated. Hokkien and Bazaar Malay may continue to be used in intra-ethnic and inter-ethnic communication but their use will be more widespread among the less well-educated.

3.1.5   English as a language for the expression of national identity

While ethnic identity is expressed by the use of one of the Chinese languages for the Chinese, Malay for the Malays, and Tamil for the Indians, national identity is usually expressed in some other language which is not associated with any of the three major ethnic groups in Singapore. This "national identity" by which a Singaporean identifies himself as "Singaporean" rather than as "Chinese", "Malay" or "Tamil" is best expressed through the use of English.

The desire to be recognized as a Singaporean probably explains why the average educated Singaporean, including the language teacher, considers it important to aim at a standard indistinguishable from Standard British English in the area of syntax but not in the area of phonology (pronunciation, rhythm, stress and intonation) and vocabulary. It is the phonology, and vocabulary, rather than the grammar, that identifies a speaker as distinctly Singaporean. The use of English as a language for the expression of one's national identity also explains why the English of some Singaporeans is considered "near-native" rather than "native". Their speech is characterized by stress and intonation patterns which do not conform to those of the "well-established" varieties of English such as British English and American English.

3.2 Users of English

In Singapore, English has not only become a more widely used language in many spheres of life; it has also come to be used by many more speakers of diverse linguistic origins, differing proficiency and so on.

Let us now look at some of these user-variables which influence the "variety" of English that is used.

3.2.1 Age

The age of the user of English is an important variable. The 1970 census shows that there is an inverse correlation between age and literacy in English: in the 15–19 age group we find about 50 per cent literate in English whereas in the 40–44 age group, the rate is only 19 per cent. The 1975 "Survey Research Singapore" survey also revealed that in the 15–20 age group, 87.3 per cent could understand English whereas in the over-40 age group the percentage of those who could understand English was only 27.5.

Not only is the younger generation more literate in English than the older generation but there is reason to believe that the age of the participant influences the variety of English that is spoken by him and to him. Among Singaporeans who are over 25 years of age, (i.e. those who finished secondary education before the implementation of the bilingual policy in 1966), there is a marked difference in the English used by those who studied in English-medium schools and those who studied in non-English-medium schools. The former are generally more proficient in English, where proficiency is defined not just in terms of grammatical well-formedness but also of speech-act rules, functional elaboration, and code diversity. It is particularly in the area of code diversity that the English-educated group is considered more proficient than the non

English-educated. Among Singaporeans who are below 25, however, this difference, though still observable, is less marked. This is probably due to the fact that with the implementation of the bilingual policy, there is equal or near-equal emphasis on two languages—English and another language, and so proficiency does not vary too much between those who learnt it as a first school language and those who learnt it as a second school language. In fact, some students are more proficient in their second school language than in their first school language.

3.2.2 Sex
This variable influences the speaker's language in the area of vocabulary. Some vocabulary items used in "Singapore English" may be described as being characteristic of male speakers only. These are items acquired by the boys during military training and are usually "hybrids" of English and Hokkien. For instance, the word *kuning* meaning "sleeping" is a hybrid of the Hokkien *kun* meaning "sleep" and the English -*ing* ending used to mark the present continuous tense. As girls in Singapore do not as yet have to enlist for military service (or "be called up for National Service" according to the Singapore idiom), those items are usually outside their vocabulary. Whether they will eventually pass into common use remains to be seen, but at present there is a considerable number of "army vocabulary" items which are understood and used only by male speakers who have recently completed National Service.

3.2.3 Proficiency
In a multilingual society like Singapore, proficiency often determines not only which language will be used for communication but also the amount of switching from one language to another. For instance, a Singaporean who is "bilingual" in English and Mandarin will choose to speak Mandarin to someone if he knows that this person is proficient in Mandarin but not in English. If they are both "bilingual" they will probably switch from one language to the other many times in the course of their conversation.

Proficiency also determines which variety of a language will be used. For instance, a speaker who has a command of the whole range of the Singapore speech continuum (from the acrolectal to the basilectal varieties) will choose to use only the basilectal variety when speaking to someone who can speak only this variety. On the other hand, a speaker who has a command of only the basilectal variety will, of course, have to use it all the time, irrespective of what he is talking about and to whom. This explains why a speaker with a command of the acrolectal variety uses it in speaking to a foreigner or if he does not expect the foreigner to understand the basilectal variety. If he thinks the foreigner understands the basilectal variety and if the situation is an informal one, he will still switch from one lect to another. A speaker who does not have the same "lectal" range is, of course, unable to do this.

Proficiency determines what topics will be discussed in which language. For instance, most Singaporeans are able to discuss academic topics in either Mandarin or English but not in their first language, (first in order of acquisition) which may be Hokkien, Malay, Tamil or some other "ethnic" language. They will therefore choose Mandarin or English and avoid using their first language for this purpose. On the other hand, they may be proficient in speaking on other topics, such as family life or religion, only in their first language.

3.2.4 Attitudes

A person's attitude towards the language he uses and the way that other people use it is an important variable that affects not only his own motivation in learning and using the language but also the particular variety of English that he speaks or chooses to speak.

The general language attitude of the Singapore population is seen in the desire to become bilingual (and this means the use of English and one other language). English is generally accepted as a useful language to know as it opens the door the employment, further studies and inter-ethnic communication.

Most Singaporeans recognize the fact that they speak English differently from the so-called "native speakers" of English. They are, of course, exposed to some of these "native" varieties, particularly British and American English in the film world. They accept these differences but are quite content to speak English their "own" way as long as they can be understood by fellow-Singaporeans *and* foreigners.

3.2.5 Role

Differences in the role of the participants affect both the choice of language used and the variety of language used. As an example of the former, take the case of a teacher of English in a classroom situation. He uses English in his teaching because he is playing the role of "English teacher". He and/or his students may be equally conversant in another language but that language would be the "wrong" one to use in his role as "English teacher". Outside the classroom, however, he might use another language with his pupils, especially if these pupils have difficulty expressing themselves in English. There his role is that of a "friend" and this switch in the language used might be an indicator of the change in role. There are, of course, those who carry their role as "English teacher" beyond the classroom and feel that they should talk to their pupils in English under all circumstances to encourage them in their use of English.

As an example of the influence of role on the variety of language used, take the case of the same English teacher. In the classroom, he will be very careful about the "variety" of English that he uses in teaching English. He will use the highest variety that he can speak. He remembers the role he is playing as "English teacher". However, when he is not teaching English he may drop to the basilectal variety in his attempt to establish rapport with his pupils, for his role is now that of a friend.

3.2.6 Linguistic background

The linguistic background of the user of English influences the variety of English that he/she uses in a number of important ways.

First, interference from the speaker's first language to his second language (for those who have a definitely clear-cut first and second language) explains why Malay, Indian and Chinese speakers of English have different features in their pronunciation.

Secondly, as many Singaporeans learn two or more languages simultaneously, it is difficult to state in which direction interference occurs. English could be the speaker's L1, L2 or L3 in terms of proficiency and even L7 in terms of order of acquisition.

Thirdly, as English is so widely used among many speakers who come from diverse linguistic backgrounds and who are bilingual, if not trilingual, the variety of English spoken is affected not only by the speaker's own linguistic background but also by the linguistic background of the other people in that community. For example, an English speaker in Singapore may not be able to speak Tamil but his/her English will probably show characteristic influences from Tamil if he/she learns English from someone who speaks English with Tamil features of pronunciation.

3.3 How should we label English in Singapore?

Which of the following terms best describes the uses and varieties of English in Singapore: ESL or EFL?

Let us take the term EFL first. English cannot be considered a "foreign" language because of its internal status, and the fact that it has indigenized. It is now widely used in many spheres of life by many speakers of diverse linguistic backgrounds, proficiency and so on. When a Singaporean learns English, he is learning it both to communicate with other English-speaking people outside his country (English for international purposes) *and* to communicate it with people within the country (English for intranational purposes).

Singapore has often been described as an ESL country. This term is used to distinguish it from countries like the USA, UK, Australia and New Zealand where English is spoken by the majority of the people as a "native" language. The distinction between a "native" and a "second" language creates a number of difficulties in a multilingual country and needs clarification. The precise definition of "native" varies and is not always clear. However, one can say that two main factors are usually borne in mind in the definition of the term. The first is priority of learning. Thus a language to be called "native" must have been the "first-learnt" language. Priority of learning, however, is not always easy to determine in a country like Singapore which is characterized by polyglossia *and* multilingualism. A child may learn two or more languages simultaneously. Are we then to talk of "childhood acquisition of two or more native languages"? (Diebold, 1961:99). There are difficulties here because one of these languages, such as Mandarin, may be further developed by formal education while the other, such as Hakka, may be forgotten in adult life through disuse. Both languages are therefore not equally "native" in adult life. What is even more disturbing is the fact that absolute priority of learning may not even be needed for a speaker to achieve "native fluency" in the language. Many of the Singaporeans who are able to speak English with "native fluency" did not learn it as their first language. However, English has become their dominant language as a result of education in English and constant use in social interaction. Of course, there are also those who learnt it as their first language in childhood and have continued to use it as their dominant language in adult life.

The second assumption underlying the definition of a "native" or "first" language is the lack of interference from other languages. In a multilingual community, this assumption may be seriously questioned because, although a first language tends to influence a second-learnt, it is equally true that a second-learnt language can also influence the first.

In spite of these difficulties in the definition of "native" language, however, there is one aspect of its use which is particularly relevant to the Singapore context. Where "native" is equated with "first" language in the sense of "dominant" language or "primary" language—the language of its speaker's intimate daily life—(Catford, 1959:165), it serves as a useful definition to distinguish between those for whom it is a "dominant first language" and those for whom it is essentially a "second language".

Our definition of the "native speaker" will therefore be modified as follows:

1. A "native speaker" of English is not identified only by virtue of his birthright. He need not be from the UK, USA, Australia, New Zealand, or one of the traditionally "native English-speaking" countries.

2. A "native speaker" of English who is not from one of the countries mentioned above is one who learns English in childhood *and* continues to use it as his dominant language *and* has reached a certain level of fluency in terms of grammatical well-formedness, speech-act rules, functional elaboration and code diversity. All three conditions are important. If a person learns English late in life he is unlikely to attain "native fluency" in it; if he learns it as a child but does not use it as his

dominant language in adult life, his "native fluency" in the language is also questionable; if he is fluent in the language, he is more likely one who has learnt it as a child (not necessarily before the age of formal education but soon after that) and has continued to use it as his dominant language.

4 GOALS FOR ENGLISH TEACHING

In general, two different sets of factors operate with respect to determining goals for English teaching. Where English is being taught either for use with speakers of other languages (lingua franca) or with native speakers of English, the choice of norm is made by the learner. There are no societal functions for particular norms or for particular levels of proficiency. While the model for *teaching* is usually the native speaker's model as proficient language user, the *learner's model* will be located at one or the other end of the interlanguage developmental continuum according to individual motivation, aptitude, exposure, practice opportunities etc. Since within an educational system catering for all segments of society, there is no way of knowing which *learning model* individual learners will adopt, a *teaching model* must at present be based on the native speaker's norms. Very little research has been done in the area of what *learner models* constitute appropriate *communication models* for particular types of interaction. Further research is needed in the area of what has been called error gravity (Johansson, 1975; James, 1974) to determine which learner models function as the most effective communication models. Such research will have to go beyond the investigation simply of grammatical and phonological variables, and examine the communicative effect of violation of speech-act rules, language-function rules and code-marking rules. Hence the need for research into the ethnograph of second and foreign language communication. Until a great deal more research is done in this area, the degree to which *teaching models* can be identified with *learning models* remains a question of speculation and opinion (cf. George, 1972, where *teaching models and learning models* are not sufficiently separated).

Where English has indigenized, communication models for English have been institutionalized for different types of interaction in the community. Basilectal, mesolectal and acrolectal speech varieties can be recognized for different types of interaction. The goal of English teaching in such settings is not to improve proficiency or to eradicate errors, but to develop fluency in the different lectal norms of the community according to rules for their sociolinguistic appropriateness. The school and the classroom are only one source of input to the learning process in such contexts, and may be seen as a primary factor in establishing the acrolectal functions of English. English language teaching has here the goal of lectal addition and expansion.

5 WHAT VARIETIES OF ENGLISH SHOULD WE TEACH?

In the Singapore context, it is neither feasible nor desirable to teach a variety of English that is indistinguishable from "Standard British English". When we consider *writing* in English, we can and should set such a standard. However, for reasons that we have mentioned in the preceding sections (the desire to express one's national identity and the need to recognize the fact that English has indigenized), in matters of pronunciation, stress, rhythm and intonation, the acrolect would serve as an adequate teaching model.

The attitude of the English language teacher is important in the Singapore context. He or she should be aware of the great amount of "lectal switching" that goes on all the time. He will not therefore condemn expressions like "Stop shaking legs and get to back work la" as substandard but consider its appropriateness in terms of the formality of the situation (it would be appropriate in an informal but not a formal situation), the participants involved in the communication (it would be appropriate for a Singaporean to talk to another Singaporean like that but not to a foreigner), and the media (it would be appropriate in speech under certain conditions but never in writing).

Thus, it is important to distinguish between formal instruction in English and its use by English-speaking members of the society. In formal instruction in school, teachers should certainly aim to teach the acrolect and expect their students to add the acrolectal features to their already acquired basilectal features. Upgrading the teachers' English would then be seen as basically one of lectal expansion (perhaps from the mesolect to the acrolect) but not of making it look more like British English.

6 CONCLUSION

Within the field of second language learning, descriptive and explanatory models need to be developed to enable researchers and educationists to better account for the dynamics of language use and language evolution, particularly in multilingual societies where English has taken on significant internal functions.

In this paper we have considered some of the dimensions that need to be accounted for in descriptions of second and foreign language proficiency, and illustrated with the example of language use in Singapore, how terms such as *native language*, *mother tongue*, and *second language* may not have clear-cut meanings in such situations. The indigenization of English in Singapore and many other newly independent nations has led to the emergence of new varieties of English, with distinctive and unique norms of lexicon, syntax and phonology. The complex interplay of social and linguistic factors that must be referred to in accounting for such linguistic phenomena constitutes a new and exciting area of linguistic study.

4 Unity and Diversity in L2 Teaching: English in Non-Native Settings from a Canadian Perspective

H. H. Stern

INTRODUCTION: SEPARATIST AND UNIFYING TRENDS IN LANGUAGE TEACHING

Coming from a country in which separatist and unifying political forces tussle with each other, I would like to begin by making some observations on separatist and unifying trends of thought in language teaching.

In the history of language teaching, different languages have evolved their own traditions, institutions, associations, journals and so on without much reference to each other. Thus, ESL/EFL teachers often go their way without much contact with teachers of, say, French, German, or Russian. In Germany, the separate professional affiliations are emphasized when an English, German, French or Russian teacher describes himself as an Anglist, Germanist, Romanist, or Slavist. In Britain or Canada, language teacher-training courses are usually separately directed to teachers of French, German, Spanish, and sometimes ESL. These compartmentalizations of language teaching are nourished, no doubt unwittingly, by national institutions established to foster national languages and cultures, such as USIA and the British Council, which cultivate English; the Alliance française, which is concerned with French, or the Goethe Institute, which sustains German studies. All these estimable institutions are geared in cultural interests, methods, and language concerns to a nationally determined single-language tradition.

Moreover, there are reviews addressed only to single-language interests, such as *English Language Teaching Forum, English Language Teaching Journal, TESOL Quarterly*, or *Le Français dans le Monde*.

Against this language-specific pedagogy, there has always been a trend to recognize and develop commonalties of language teaching and learning. Some of the great scholars of the turn of the century, such as Sweet (1899) and Jespersen (1904), took a view of second language teaching which transcended particular languages. As Catford (1964) pointed out long ago (1951) in a paper on teaching English as a foreign or secondary language or L2, as I believe he called it for the first time, "the teaching of English as L2 is not a fundamentally different problem from the teaching of any other secondary language . . . the tendency to isolate every foreign language for special treatment has been a hindrance to the spread of information concerning foreign language study" (p. 138).

The creation of modern language associations in Britain, the USA, Canada, and more recently the American Council on the Teaching of Foreign Languages (ACTFL), and their equivalents in other countries, as well as, on the international scene, the Fédération Internationale des Professeurs des Langues Vivantes (FIPLV), suggests the same unifying trend. One of the salutary effects of the development of linguistics, psycholinguistics, and sociolinguistics has been to strengthen the common bases in the underlying disciplines which apply equally to all language teaching.

Treating all language teaching alike may be the result of recognizing underlying commonalties. But it may also be an indication of failing to make necessary distinctions. Hence, when we are faced with a relatively new set of concepts, "English for international and intranational purposes (EIIP) ", we are bound to ask whether EIIP is a necessary and productive differentiation or, alternatively, whether it introduces distinctions which are not needed or are already covered by existing concepts. I would therefore like in this paper to look at EIIP in the light of these unifying and diversifying trends of thought.

I A CANADIAN PERSPECTIVE

I am approaching this question from a Canadian perspective. In Canada, language issues play a crucial role in national and regional politics; and—this is interesting to note from the point of view of EIIP—it is hardly possible to adopt a single-language position, for two world languages, English and French, play a part in this situation. Canada is often described as a bilingual country, because it has two "founding groups", a large English-speaking majority and a strong French-speaking minority. In one of the provinces, as the ten regions that make up the Canadian confederation are called, Quebec, Francophones

constitute the majority and Anglophones a minority. There are also sizeable French minorities in other provinces, for example, in Ontario, Manitoba, Alberta, British Columbia, New Brunswick, and Nova Scotia.[1]
. One of the major issues has been the difficulty for the French-speaking minority to maintain itself linguistically, culturally, and economically as an equal, on an otherwise largely English-speaking sub-continent. The sense of loss, deprivation, and injustice engendered by this discrepancy has led since the sixties to a resolute attempt to resolve these difficulties by a deliberate policy of bilingualism and bicultu-ralism, first spelled out in a remarkable six-volume report, composed by a Royal Commission which studied this issue for a number of years.[2] Numerous interesting legislative and administrative measures resulted from it. These have included, since 1969, the passing of the Official Languages Act by which both English and French are declared the official languages of Canada at the federal level; the setting up of a very large language training programme for civil servants in French and English as second languages;[3] the creation of the office of a language ombudsman, the Commissioner of Official Languages,[4] as well as schemes of federal subsidies for French and English minorities, and for teaching English as a second language and French as a second language in schools.[5]

In spite of these measures, the demand for the establishment of Quebec as an independent French-speaking state has increased, particularly since the election of a separatist *Parti Québecois* govern-ment in the province of Quebec in 1976. The French–English language issue continues to be an important factor in Canadian sociopolitical developments.

It would, however, be misleading to represent the Canadian language situation as a purely English–French issue. Canada—like the USA— has its native Indian and Inuit populations and large groups of immigrants, most of whom have their own linguistic and ethnic traditions. This third group of languages and cultures makes up a third of its population. Canada has adopted as a national policy the maintenance and development of indigenous languages and cultures and of languages and cultures of immigrant ethnic minorities. The federal government and the provincial governments, to varying degrees, encourage and support multicultural activities, ethnic associations, and language programmes in Portuguese, Chinese, Ukrainian, German, Italian, Hebrew, Estonian, and other languages. The ethnic minorities are often critical of the public support they receive because, in comparison with the attention paid to the French–English issue, they feel it is half-hearted.[6]

A consequence of the presence of large groups of people whose native language is neither English nor French is the importance of training in

English or French as second languages. Such programmes are offered (1) to adult immigrants through adult education and to child immigrants within the school system; (2) to native Indians and Inuits as part of schooling; and (3) in French as a second language to Anglophones and English as a second language to Francophones. These programmes vary in quality and quantity from sporadic and poor improvisations to well planned and imaginative schemes. For example, among good schemes, immigrants, under a Canadian manpower programme, receive free tuition in English as a second language for six hours per day for six months with a cost-of-living allowance so that an immigrant is given a genuine opportunity to acclimatize himself and to learn the language. There are other day and evening classes, including special classes for parents with pre-school children and special classes for people with particular trades, enabling them to take qualifying industrial trade examinations. Among innovations at school level, large-scale immersion programmes in French as a second language for young Anglophone children are particularly noteworthy.[7]

In these different situations, EIIP or some equivalent concept, as envisaged in the present discussions, does not occur. However, the terms "first language" and "second language" are widely used. English is learned as a second language by Francophones or ethnic minorities. French is learned as a second language by Anglophones or ethnic minorities. The term "foreign" language is never used in relation to these two official languages or in relation to the ethnic languages. In many instances, the dividing line between first and second language has been blurred. The term "native speaker" is not unambiguous. Some members of Francophone minorities outside Quebec have a limited command of French as an L1.[8] Equally, some members of different ethnic groups have a problem in maintaining their ethnic language. Here, too, first or native language may range from limited comprehension of family talk via a semi-literate spoken command to full literacy in the ethnic language. Even where ethnic languages are maintained, there is a linguistic and cultural shift—similar to the shift described for Norwegians in North America by Haugen (1953). Language shift, language loss, the problem of language maintenance or redevelopment become issues for a variety of groups or individuals. Many Canadians, therefore, face questions of a bilingual and sometimes bicultural existence in which French and English are involved, or in some other cases, for example, English and Ukrainian; English and Italian; French and and Italian; or sometimes trilingualism in, say, English, French and Hebrew.

In these varied language situations, which have been publicly discussed for decades, a few universities and centres have played a role in undertaking linguistic, psycholinguistic, and sociolinguistic research and providing some form of advanced training. Among these, mention should be made of the International Centre for Research on Bilingualism at Laval University which came into prominence under its first director, William Mackey; and the Language Research Group at McGill University in Montreal which has made a variety of highly significant studies on language learning and bilingualism under W. Lambert. As an individual, working also at McGill, the neurologist Wilder Penfield did much to bring the question of bilingualism before the public eye. Another group at the University of Western Ontario under R. Gardner, a former student of Lambert's, is prominent for its work on language attitudes.

Lastly, the Modern Language Centre at the Ontario Institute for Studies in Education in Toronto, founded in 1968, studies second language teaching and learning, bilingual education, and educational linguistics in the context of an institute which is concerned with educational research and development and graduate instruction in educational theory.[9]

Although the Modern Language Centre research and development has been mainly in French as a second language, the Centre regards all second language learning as its province. Some of its Ph.D. students have been concerned in their research with other languages and language situations outside Canada, including English teacher education in Thailand, the teaching of Pilipino in the Philippines, and the teaching of Spanish to Jamaican Creole speakers in the West Indies.[10] One recent study on the learning of English in India (Seshadri, 1978) and another current study in progress on the learning of English as an international language in Ivory Coast and French as an international language in Nigeria have direct bearing on the discussions on English for cross-cultural communication.

Thus, we never find ourselves in a single-language situation; and I do not regret it. The experience and conviction that I can therefore contribute to these discussions is that of someone who believes that any language teaching situation, such as the teaching of English as an international and intranational language, can be better understood and treated more effectively, if it can be related to second-language teaching theory in general.

Accordingly, I would like to propose a three-level approach to it: a general or universal level where we find those aspects, concepts, principles, and so on which are common to all second language teaching. A second level refers to certain generic types of language situations. It is here that, I think, it is appropriate to make distinctions such as "second", "foreign", "international", and "intranational". At the third level, we come to concrete, specific aspects of teaching English to a given group of learners in a particular context.

By making this kind of analysis, it seems to me possible to come to terms with some of the questions and uncertainties that the notion of

EIIP has provoked and arrive at some suggestions for research and development.

II A THREE-LEVEL APPROACH

Level 1: Universals

If we want to avoid the splitting up of language teaching into different language-specific disciplines and sub-disciplines, it is important to recognize universals or common elements. EIIP shares with all other forms of second language teaching the common basic disciplines and research in linguistics, psycholinguistics, sociolinguistics, applied linguistics, and educational theory. For example, whatever theory of first and second language learning we arrive at is equally relevant to all forms of language teaching. The relationship of linguistic research and theory to application in language teaching is the same for EIIP as for other language teaching situations. EIIP—like any other L2 situation—sets out from a basic distinction in which one language is primary or native and another, in this case English, is secondary and non-native, and somehow deliberately taught and learned.[11] All such language teaching shares curriculum concepts, definition of objectives, choice of teaching and learning strategies, syllabus design, materials development, and test construction.

   That this wider perspective can be useful to EIIP as well as to second language teaching in general can be illustrated by two examples.

Culture in L2 Teaching
The first relates to culture teaching. EIIP is said to be different from TESL/TEFL in that cultural references to the UK or the USA or other English-speaking countries are not necessary, or may even be inappropriate. This argument may be specific to English in non-native settings but the issue of whether language teaching should be related to a single culture, a variety of cultures, or whether under certain circumstances it can be culturally neutral, is a general issue of language pedagogy. In recent work in the Modern Language Centre, there has been a clear tendency to conclude that all second language teaching has inevitably a cultural reference; that a second language course can be culturally related to many different settings, but that the setting selected should be one in which the L2 is likely to come into use (e.g. G. Richards, 1976). Thus, courses in French as a second language in some of the Canadian provinces, e.g. Ontario or Manitoba, should not ignore the fact that there are Francophone communities within their own province; they should certainly also have a strong Quebec orientation. The absence of teaching materials dealing directly with life and culture in

Canada or the French fact as an issue for all Canadians is strongly felt by Canadian teachers of French as a second language and has provided a strong impetus for one of our curriculum development projects.

In the same vein, it appears entirely justified that when English is taught for international or intranational purposes one would expect the course to be based on cultural references which are more directly relevant than cultural references to Britain and the USA. In one of the studies in progress at present, already referred to, a member of our team is investigating to what extent the teaching of English as an international language in the Ivory Coast and the teaching of French as an international language in Nigeria is in fact adjusted to their role as international languages within the West African Economic Community. Cultural reference in that case does not mean, of course, simply replacing in the textbooks, say, London by Lagos and Paris by Abidjan. It is a question of basing the entire second-language curriculum on a cultural and pragmatic analysis of the use of the second language in given settings. Such an analysis has bearing on topics and themes in textbooks; on the choice of texts; on the voices in recordings; and on contacts, visits, and exchanges as part of the educational programme.

In other words, the relationship of language to culture in second-language teaching can be conceived in terms that are relevant to language pedagogy in general, but the solution that is applied to a particular instance of teaching ESL must be related to the circumstances and needs of the particular situation. The sociolinguistic and ethnographic analyses, proposed in papers by Richards and Kachru,[12] are equally relevant to other situations of language learning and use.

Interlanguage, Goals, and Norms
For a second example of a universal issue, I refer to the model proposed by Lester (1976) in which English as an international or auxiliary language in non-native settings is related to the interlanguage hypothesis. Along with other theoreticians on L2 learning, Lester visualizes the progress of the learner of English in this situation as a continuum, rising diagonally from zero competence, where the second language is not known at all, to an ideal end point of full or native-like competence.[13] On this interlanguage continuum, he recognizes two way-stations or bands close to, but below, the upper end of the continuum. The higher way-station would be that level of interlanguage which is not completely native-like but adequate for international communication. The lower way-station would be that level of interlanguage which is deemed to be adequate for communication within a certain region, e.g. West Africa or India. This somewhat lower-level regional English, e.g. West African or Indian English, is, in his analysis, the area of English for intranational purposes.

In this interpretation, Lester applies concepts which are not restricted to ESL. One is the concept of interlanguage stages, plateaux, and fossilizations, first described by Selinker (1972), which learners of any language experience. The other is the principle of establishing goals and norms for different levels of proficiency. All language teaching is of necessity goal-directed and, however vaguely, must attempt to determine a language norm or norms by which to guide it. The European efforts to establish a basic or threshold level of English or its equivalent, *niveau-seuil*, in French, illustrate differentiation of goals as a current approach to goal definition in language pedagogy (e.g. van Ek, 1976; Coste et al., 1977). Another example is a Canadian proposal (Ontario, 1977) in the province of Ontario, to distinguish in the learning of French as a second language three goal levels—basic, middle and top. Instead of demanding of all learners a hypothetical native-like perfection as a general goal, school systems under this scheme are invited to offer as goals either an elementary level, a working knowledge level, or an optimum level of L2 proficiency, and to design different programmes with different time allocations and activities which would lead to these different levels. Naturally, each of these levels can also be looked at as progressive stages or, in the terms of the educational theorist Benjamin Bloom, as mastery levels which a learner can reach and then use as a platform from which to advance to the next stage (Block, 1971).

Lester's model is also related to another general principle in present-day second-language teaching, i.e. to be less rigid about language norms and to be more open to varieties within a single language. The question of what norm to use for French has been a problem in the teaching of French as a second language in Canada. In line with what Quirk, et al. (1972) have called a "supra-national" standard English which comprises "what is common to all", a Canadian group of French textbook writers speak of "International French".[14] In a current study, a member of our team is examining the question of norm, or norms, in relation to second-language teaching and specifically applies the results of this examination to the teaching of French as a second language in Canada, counteracting the conventional or traditional snobbery about Parisian French as the only valid norm; instead, she is putting forward the claim that intelligibility and comprehension among Canadians and flexibility to varieties of usage is more important. Another study examines the acceptability of interlanguage French to different groups of French native speakers.

In Lester's theory of interlanguage, applied to English in non-native settings, then, a number of general issues are fused. One is the question of the stages through which learners normally advance in learning English as a second language. The second is the choice of different goals for different learners or classes of learners; and the third is the norm or norms which should guide the learning of English for international or intranational purposes. It is ingenious to bring these different aspects together in a single model; but such a model carries with it the danger of mixing up the three issues which should not be confused. Let us briefly, therefore, consider the question of language norm for EIIP.

In discussions on norms in relation to second language teaching, quite contradictory trends have tended to emerge. On the one hand, it is recommended to acknowledge and tolerate dialectal, sociolectal, and interlanguage variations. On the other, there is the demand for an international universally acceptable nuclear or core English or international French. I do not think that these differences are irreconcilable. We simply have to accept variations of use and even variations of norms as inevitable. At the same time, the establishment of a minimal common English or French, acceptable across the world, would indeed be helpful to the teaching of English or French as second languages. In other words, the tolerance of variation is not unlimited. The question is how to establish its limits.

Much of the thinking on EIIP, reflected in many papers besides the one by Lester (1976), has focused on this single issue. It is indeed crucial, but I can see a danger in that it monopolizes our attention and leads to a neglect of other equally important questions.

One direction to resolve it lies no doubt in the proposal made by Quirk[15] to develop a linguistically up-to-date nuclear English as a minimum international norm. Another direction might be to re-examine objectively and critically the history of international and auxiliary languages, including Basic English and *français fondamental*, and possibly Esperanto and other artificial auxiliary languages. I believe such a broad approach might provide illuminating insights and would avoid EIIP running into the same difficulties that have led to the ultimate failure of the earlier efforts.

The fact that EIIP has many issues in common with other language teaching situations does not invalidate the concept of EIIP. But it offers an opportunity and acts as a reminder. It is an opportunity for ESL, learned and used internationally and intranationally, to benefit from general language teaching theory and to contribute to such a theory. But it is also a reminder not to treat as specific to EIIP problems that have already been treated elsewhere or are under investigation in other language teaching situations.

Level 2: Generic Distinctions

Let us now examine the concepts "intranational" and "international" as generic distinctions among different types of non-native language teaching and learning. The main generic distinction usually made up to now has been that between "second" and "foreign" language learning.[16] Is "intranational" and "international" intended to take the place of the earlier pair? Or is it an added pair, so that altogether four major types of language teaching are to be distinguished: "second", "foreign", "international", and "intranational"?

In spite of the confusion that has surrounded the terminology "second" in contrast to "foreign", there is consensus that an important distinction is to be made between a non-native language learned and used *within* one country to which the term "second language" has been applied, and a non-native language learned and used with reference to a speech community *outside* the national or territorial boundaries to which the term "foreign language" is commonly given. A second language usually has official status or a recognized function within a country which a foreign language has not.

These two different situations frequently have important consequences to which attention has been drawn by a number jof theorists, (e.g. Marckwardt, 1963; Hartmann and Stork, 1972; Quirk et al., 1972; Christophersen, 1973; Harrison et al., 1975; Paulston, 1974). First of all, the purposes of second-language learning are often different from foreign-language learning. Since the second language is frequently the official language or one of two or more recognized languages, it is needed "for full participation in the political and economic life of the nation" (Paulston, 1974:12–13); or it may be the language needed for education (Marckwardt, 1963). Foreign-language learning, on the other hand, is usually undertaken with a variety of different purposes in mind, e.g. travel abroad, communication with native speakers, reading of foreign literature, or reading of foreign scientific and technical works. A second language, because it is used within the country, is usually learned with much more environmental support than a foreign language whose speech community may be thousands of miles away. A foreign language usually requires formal instruction. A second language may often be "picked up" within the environment. However, none of the consequences that have been indicated as characteristic of foreign versus second-language learning are inherent in the conceptual distinction between a non-native language with status within a country, a second language, or a non-native language spoken by a speech community outside territorial boundaries, a foreign language.

The new pair of concepts, advocated by the East–West Culture Learning Institute, differentiates intranational and international from second or foreign languages. The concepts referred to by this distinction have not been previously unknown; for example, Stewart's typology of languages in multilingual societies (1968) includes among ten language functions *wider communication*, which corresponds to intranational, and *international*, which is roughly equivalent to the same term used here. But the main characteristics of these two concepts have not previously been specifically formulated nor have their implications been fully worked out and particularly applied to the use of English across the world. The East–West Culture Learning Institute, by making this conceptual distinction, is differentiating an important aspect of language teaching and learning. Second or foreign-language learning both imply a specified speech community or communities as a territorial reference or contact group for the language learner. Thus, English in France is a foreign language and is normally learned as such with reference to Britain or the USA. In the same way, French as a foreign language in Britain is learned with reference to France. Likewise, English for Francophones in Canada is learned as a second language with a clear reference group in the Anglophone communities in Canada and the USA; and French as a second language has a reference group in Canadian Francophone communities. Equally, English as a second language for immigrants in the USA has an obvious reference group in the English-speaking society of the United States.

On the other hand, when English is learned and spoken in India, no such territorial and cultural linguistic reference group exists within India. For this situation, e.g. learning and using English for wider communication within India or for educational and commercial uses, English can be referred to as an intranational language. Equally, in Nigeria, English, which has the status of an official language but has no native English reference group within Nigeria, is learned as a means of internal or intranational communication. French in the Ivory Coast has the same intranational function. If English is learned in Ivory Coast schools and French in Nigerian schools, these can be learned, not necessarily as foreign languages with reference to Britain or France respectively, but with reference to inter-communication among West African states. For this role, the East-West Culture Learning Institute has proposed the term *international* language.

These distinctions can be tabulated as follows:

	Presence of a specified linguistic and cultural reference group	Absence of a specified linguistic and cultural reference group
Use of language within country	1. *second language* learning L_{sec}	3. *intranational language* learning L_{intra}
Use of language outside country	2. *foreign language* learning FL	4. *international language* learning L_{inter}

The two questions to be examined are: (a) to what extent the distinction between second/foreign (1 and 2) on one side and intranational/international (3 and 4) on the other, and (b) to what extent the distinction between intranational L2 use *within* a country (3) and international L2 use *across* countries (4), are appropriate. The general assumption of EIIP must be that the absence of a specified L1 speech community as a linguistic and cultural reference group has important consequences for English language use and teaching. What these consequences are is still to be discussed at the level of specifics (see p. 69 below).

The common characteristics of intranational and international language teaching situations and the differences between them can best be discovered by comparative case studies which are suggested by several papers. In the work of the OISE Modern Language Centre, the two pilot investigations in India and in West Africa are examples of enquiries in this direction. It would be valuable also to compare systematically situations which can clearly be described as EIIP with situations in which English appears as ESL or EFL so that the common elements and differences between these four types of language learning can be clearly recognized. As a result of a number of such studies, the special value of EIIP as a distinct set of language teaching situations can be established and the findings of these studies can then usefully be applied to many situations across the world.

I suspect that in many instances of L2 learning, the language learning types, foreign language (FL), second language (L_{sec}), intranational language (L_{intra}) or international language (L_{inter}) are not mutually exclusive categories. One may be dominant but others are likely to be present to a lesser degree. Thus, English in India is typically dominantly (L_{intra}, but this does not mean that an important secondary function could not be that of English as FL with reference to the UK and the USA or without such reference as an international language (L_{inter}). Equally, English in France or Sweden can be learned as FL with reference to the UK and USA, but it can also be learned as (L_{inter}).

To sum up on the four generic L2 distinctions, by laying emphasis on the use of English without territorial reference, the learning and use of English in these circumstances has for the first time been unambiguously distinguished from the concepts "second" or "foreign". Although this distinction was not unfamiliar in the past, it was not always made and certainly it has not always been made clearly enough.

There are other generic differences which could no doubt be made. One is the distinction between general-purpose and specific-purpose language teaching; another, the distinction between language teaching to adults and language teaching to children; and a third might be that between initial, intermediate and advanced language teaching. It is not necessary to provide an exhaustive inventory of all generic distinctions. What I intended to do was to place EIIP at this second level of analysis and to point out that it is here that the most important and characteristic contribution can be made in research and development that will benefit all those who need English for international or intranational communication. The findings at this level could also make use of experiences with other languages, e.g. French, Spanish, Arabic, Swahili, or Mandarin, which have a similar international or intranational role to perform, and, in turn, findings on EIIP can be applied to these other languages.

Level 3: Specifics

It is not sufficient to identify and distinguish universals and generics. EIIP appears in particular regions, territories, systems, and schools. Each of these has its own needs, characteristics, and unique features. These must be identified and brought to bear on specified programmes in particular situations, such as English as an internal medium of communication in the state of Gujarat in India or, even more specifically, English in a particular university in Baroda in the state of Gujarat, or English as an international language in the schools of Abidjan in the Ivory Coast. To what extent can training and research programmes, developed at a distant centre, such as the East–West Culture Learning Institute, be useful to such specific situations? In the first instance, the planner needs instruments enabling him to analyse and interpret given situations of English use and teaching. Specific schemes of analysis for EIIP situations in which English is taught without a territorial reference group do not yet exist; but I believe that a centre such as the East–West Culture Learning Institute might well set itself the task of producing such schemes which could then be applied in the field. As we have seen, experience in field studies and case studies related to these situations is at present being gathered. Moreover, we can draw on typologies and analyses made in other language-planning situations. For example, analyses of language situations have been proposed by Stewart (1968), Ferguson (1966), Lewis (1972), Kloss (1966), or the Brazzaville Symposium (Conseil Scientifique, 1962). There are precedents for analyses of a sociolinguistic kind in a survey of language use and language teaching in East Africa (e.g. Ladefoged et al., 1972; Whiteley, 1974; Bender et al., 1976) and in Harrison, Prator and Tucker's (1975) *English-language policy survey of Jordan*, and in Emmans et al.'s analysis of language learning needs in Britain (1974). Moreover, Carroll (1969) has described background variables that are critical in language teaching. Spolsky et al. (1974) and Mackey (1976) have developed analysis schemes for bilingual education. The categories proposed in schemes of this kind can be adapted to the use and learning of English in non-native settings. Through questionnaires, interviews, and participant observation, the use of English can be assessed. Moreover, English language use in the media (newspapers, radio, TV, and books) can be estimated by means of content analysis.

What information on English language use is to be gathered can be indicated by the following questions: *Intranationally*, to what extent is English used as the language of work (industry, commerce, the professions)? of the courts? of political activity? of literature and the arts? of the media? of education? of the home? of informal education outside the home? *Internationally*, to what extent is English used across countries for personal communication? in correspondence? for visits and tourism? in political interaction? for conferences? on the telephone? in journalism? in industry, trade, and commerce? in joint regional organizations? With which countries, by whom, and how frequently is English used? Intranationally and internationally, further distinction must be made between use of English *now* and the prediction of the estimated or needed use of English *in the future*.

The answers to these questions will help in determining learning needs and objectives, and in defining language norms and standards of acceptability. On this basis, it is then possible to make some broad decisions which have implications for curriculum, learning materials, and teacher education. For example, the factual information on actual or potential uses of English has a bearing on the choice of a phonological model or models, on lexical or grammatical selection, and on semantic or discourse features to be included in a syllabus. It is further likely to influence the choice of topics, themes, and cultural references, as well as learners' contact experiences in the planning of a teaching programme.

Achievement in English can be measured by such tests as the international IEA tests.[17] Admittedly, this group of tests was designed for situations in which English is taught as FL; nevertheless, they can provisionally provide measures of achievement even in other non-native situations, pending the preparation of more appropriate tests.

It is undoubtedly necessary to gain further experience in the systematic description, analysis, and interpretation of English language needs and uses in a given population, and to review the teaching and learning of English in these settings, followed by evaluations of the extent to which English language training is adequate or in need of modification in line with the special demands of English for intranational and international communication.

On the basis of such comprehensive studies, an English language teaching–learning plan can be drawn up. Such plans will again have common features with other similar plans for English as a foreign or second language. But in certain respects, each plan will respond to the interpretation of a particular English language situation in a specified country at a particular point in time. A planning study of this kind, having mapped out the English language teaching needs within this system, would lead to curriculum development; that is, it would find or prepare learning materials and suggest teacher pre-service and in-service education, designed in relation to the specific situation in question.

In order to meet these demands for curriculum development, it is important that all kinds of resources, pedagogical as well as linguistic, sociolinguistic, and cultural ones, are made accessible, and it is in this respect that a centre, such as the East–West Culture Learning Institute, in cooperation with field centres in different parts of the world, can be immensely useful as a clearinghouse and as a place where the basic research is stimulated, where instruments are developed, curriculum packages of a sufficiently flexible kind prepared, and plans for teacher education developed. All such activities are the more satisfactory the more they pull together first-level common elements and respond to the second-level circumstances of the teaching of English for intranational and international communication. At the same time, however, they must be adaptable at the level of specifics to the particular setting with its individual characteristics within which English is to be taught and learned for intranational or international purposes.

CONCLUSION: RESEARCH AND DEVELOPMENT SUGGESTIONS

In this paper, I have attempted to forestall any tendency to separate EIIP from other forms of English language teaching or indeed from other forms of language teaching in general. At the same time, I have tried to recognize the characteristic emphasis that is implied in the teaching of English in situations where it has no specific reference to an Anglophone territory and where it is used for communication within one country or, internationally, across countries among speakers of other languages.

These two goals can be reconciled if we recognize (1) that English in these varied contexts has much in common with all language teaching, (2) that it has certain generic characteristics which distinguish it from other forms of second language teaching, and (3) that it must respond— in common with all other forms of language teaching—to the unique features of a particular situation.

If this analysis is right, the international planning of English teaching for intranational and international uses has a threefold task:

1. to identify the aspects of the general theory of language teaching which are applicable to these situations;

2. by means of field studies, to analyse those needs of teaching English as an international or intranational language which are common to these situations and different from EFL/ESL situations, and to develop resources in order to meet these needs in diverse situations across the world; and

3. to develop instruments and techniques in order to analyse specific EIIP situations and, in cooperation with local and regional field centres, to develop curricula and training programmes suitable for them.

The following projects arise from these considerations:

1. The question of an *international English norm* or *Core or Nuclear English* deserves highest priority. Since this would be a major project of considerable proportions, it might be preceded by (a) a feasibility study which would establish the scope of Core English and (b) an historical study and critical assessment of other recent efforts of a similar nature, such as Basic English and *français fondamental*.

2. A publication or a number of different levels of publications should be considered which would give practical guidance to EIIP planners on *the crucial variety-norm issue.*

3. With English in non-native settings in mind, *a review of recent and current studies on language pedagogy and related disciplines* should be made and the relevance of such studies for English in these settings should be assessed.

4. A number of *case studies of EIIP situations* should be made and followed up by suggestions for experiments in programme development, teacher training, and evaluation related to these situations. Such case studies should include investigations on the linguistic and cultural implications of the use of English in typical non-native situations.

5. In connection with (4), *instruments* (e.g. questionnaires, interview schedules, tests) *should be developed* for the analysis and evaluation of EIIP-type situations.

6. Arising from (4) and (5), examples of *curriculum guides, learning materials and teacher education aids should be prepared*, specifically geared to the needs of teaching English for international and intranational purposes.

NOTES TO CHAPTER 4

1. (Canada consists of ten provinces, the Yukon and the Northwest Territories. According to the 1971 census, Quebec has a population of 4,867,000 Francophones and 482,000 Anglophones; Ontario has close to 6,000,000 Anglophones and 500,000 Francophones. New Brunswick has 410,000 Anglophones and 215,000 Francophones. Provinces with minorities from 30,000 to 60,000 Francophones are: Nova Scotia, Manitoba, Saskatchewan, Alberta and British Columbia. It has been estimated that nearly $1\frac{1}{2}$ million persons of Francophone origin live outside Quebec. For a recent study on Francophone minorities, see Churchill (1976).

2. The Royal Commission on Bilingualism and Biculturalism was initiated in 1963. The last volume of its report appeared in 1970.

3. A thorough, critical review of the entire public service language training programme was made in 1975–6. See Bibeau (1976).

4. Frequently witty and entertaining reports written by the Commissioner of Official Languages have appeared annually since 1971.
5. For details of these, see Canada (1977).
6. For a recent and detailed investigation on ethnic minorities in Canada, see O'Bryan et al. (1976). According to the 1971 census, 26.7 per cent of the population are of non-English and non-French ethnic origin. Some of the educational and linguistic issues of ethnic communities in Canada are discussed in an issue of the Yearbook of the Canadian Society for the Study of Education (Swain, 1976).
7. French immersion, now no longer experimental, is offered as an alternative programme, particularly in Montreal, in parts of Ontario and, to a lesser extent, elsewhere. The development of French immersion has been very fully documented. See, for example, Lambert and Tucker (1972), a special issue of the *Canadian modern language review* (Harley, 1976), Swain and Barik (1978).
8. As examples of studies on French in contact situations outside Quebec, see, for example, Mougeon et al. (1978).
9. The main languages under investigation in the Modern Language Centre are French and English as second languages but the Centre is also interested in other languages. One aspect of the work of this Centre consists of graduate studies for language teachers at the Master's and Doctoral level in educational linguistics. Another is research; the main areas are: (1) long-term studies on French/English bilingual education (e.g. Swain and Barik, op. cit.; Harley, op. cit.; Stern et al., 1976); (2) inquiries on second language teaching and learning (e.g., Naiman et al., 1978; Bialystok and Frohlich, 1977); (3) second language curriculum research and development (e.g., Stern, 1976); (4) studies on theoretical aspects of second language teaching (e.g., Stern, 1974; Stern, Wesche and Harley, 1978).
10. Doctoral theses by Brudhiprabha (1975), Natividad (1975), and Lewis (1974).
11. In keeping with widespread practice, I use the term "second language" for all non-native language teaching.
12. See papers by Richards and Tay, and Kachru in this volume.
13. For a similar view of L2 learning, see Stern (1975).
14. The concept of "International French" was popularized through an influential series of French as a second language course material originally devised in 1966 (and since revised) by G. and F. Rondeau, J. P. Vinay, and P. and M. Léon, under the title *Le français international* (Montréal, Centre Educatif et Culturel).
15. See Quirk paper on *Nuclear English* in this volume.
16. In the pair "second" versus "foreign", the meaning of "second" is, of course, more specific than in the use of "second" suggested in note 11, above.
17. For descriptions of these tests, see Lewis and Massad (1975).

5 Teaching English for International and Intranational Purposes: Philippine Context*

Aurora L. Samonte

English is used in many countries today either as a first language or as an alternative means for cross-cultural communication. In the Philippines our main concern is the latter use among non-native speakers of the language. What are the possible situations in which English may be used instead of the native language? I can think of the following: (1) international situations where nationals of different countries may use English at international conferences or conventions, or in international travel and correspondence; and (2) intranational situations where nationals of the same country use English instead of their mother tongue when speaking or writing to one another.

In the case of the Philippines, English may be used by Filipinos
(1) in situations, formal or informal, whether in the Philippines or abroad, between and among the following Filipinos who are literate in English, or at least able to use it for communication purposes: (a) those who have the same native language, and (b) those whose native languages differ;
(2) in communication situations in the Philippines between Filipinos and foreigners in the country, such as (a) foreign residents, and (b) foreign transients;
(3) at international conferences, with foreigners of different native language backgrounds and with varying degrees of control of English;
(4) in international travel; and
(5) in correspondence, local or foreign. The problem of communication varies in these situations.

* This is an abridged version of the original paper presented at the Conference on English as an International/Auxiliary Language, East–West Center, Honolulu, Hawaii, April 1978.

In situation 1, that is, among Filipinos themselves, communication is possible even with a minimum of oral control of the English language since both listener and speaker are usually familiar with the characteristic vernacularized local varieties of Filipino English, which show marks of the influences of the native languages. Since there are similarities in the local Philippine culture and in the patterning of some of the native languages, and through frequent exposure to these varieties of Filipino English, the Filipino listener is usually able to guess and understand the context of the message much of the time.

In situation 2 (between Filipinos and foreigners in the Philippines) communication is less easy until the foreigner's familiarity with the local culture and idiosyncrasies of the local variety of Filipino English, and his receptiveness and desire to understand, force him to make an effort and enable him to guess what the Filipino is saying. The Filipino, on the other hand, finds it more difficult to understand the foreigner's English, especially if the latter speaks at the speed and degree of clarity of speech that he uses with his countrymen, which to the Filipino is too fast or is what he sometimes calls "slang" (that is, idiomatic, nasalized, and possibly liberally sprinkled with slang expressions), and culture-bound.

In situation 3 (at international conferences), the problem of communication is complicated by the number of adjustments that the Filipino listener has to make to the foreigners' spoken versions of English, depending on the latter's oral control of the language and the Filipino's degree of understanding of spoken English. The problem, however, is not as great as one would suppose since familiarity with the subject matter of the conference and the availability of the written text usually greatly aid understanding. When the conferee's ears get attuned to the various "foreign-English" versions, communication becomes easier.

In situation 4 (travel in foreign countries), the problem is similar to that in situations 2 (between Filipinos and foreigners) and 3 (at international conferences), except that the Filipino generally has to deal with a much more complex group—local people engaged in the tourism business, other tourists who happen to be travelling or sightseeing with him but who come from other foreign countries, and possibly other local citizens with whom he may get in contact. People in tourism, however, especially hotel staff, generally have sufficient command of English to communicate with foreigners. Communication is mostly oral; whatever reading and writing there is, is minimal, usually just reading and filling in hotel information cards, and understanding business and street signs, unless the traveller is interested and has the time for the local newspaper in English.

In situation 5 (correspondence), the problem is reduced to that of reading and writing English in conventional, commonly understood forms. But even here there are still problems since national habits of writing the local language (such as spelling, capitalization, punctuation, indicating time or money) may creep into written English. Local vocabulary and culture tend to affect communication too. For local correspondence in the Philippines, the problem is simpler since there are some similarities in capitalization and punctuation between English and Pilipino, the national language. The problem is in spelling since English and Pilipino letters and sounds are not identical, and Pilipino is largely phonemically spelled. Students often inadvertently slide from one language to another and may spell English words as they would spell similar Tagalog words.

In all the situations where oral English is involved, it is obvious that responsibility for success in communication does not rest with the speaker alone. The listener has as great a responsibility to make an effort to catch the sounds and mentally make the necessary adjustments or substitutions to make what he has heard intelligible to him. The context is usually a great help in understanding, as is familiarity with the culture and the patterning of the first language. For instance, /ʃə sop iz tu hat/ should not be too difficult to understand coming from one at the dining table. It would be a different matter if the situation were one in which both /sop/ and /sup/ would be meaningful, as when the maid is asked to get some /sop/ (or /sup/, depending on which is needed) and give it to the man of the house. Then trouble really starts. This responsibility of the listener has implications for teacher education, curriculum makers, and language teachers. Listening must be recognized as a skill to be developed and included in the curriculum and taught in the classroom. It is one skill that is often neglected.

It may be seen from these situations that the resolution of the problem of teaching English for international and intranational purposes is not easy if the goal is to cater for the particular needs of the users of the language in the given situations.

Among the problems that could come up for discussion may be the following:

1. What degree of competence in English will be acceptable in each situation? On the oral level? On the written level? What are the implications for the national educational system?

2. What can be done to help reduce the problems of communication in each situation?

3. Is the problem entirely an educational one?

4. Is the problem purely a national one?

The answers to these questions are bound to raise other relevant problems. There are, for example, the following problems:

1. what speech model or models to use in each country;

2. what conventions of writing are internationally acceptable and are to be taught the world over, if that is at all desirable and possible;

3. what instructional materials and strategies would be more effective

and economical in terms of national goals;

4. what resources are needed and are available; and

5. what the implications are for teacher education.

Later I shall comment on some of these problems.

So far I have assumed that English will continue to be taught as in the present environment, which, briefly, is as follows:

1. In the new bilingual programme, English, like Pilipino, is taught as a subject in the elementary and secondary schools. English is used as medium of instruction in the English subjects and in mathematics and science. (It used to be the medium of instruction in all subjects throughout the educational system.) Pilipino is the medium of instruction in the Pilipino language subjects and all other subjects in the curriculum. The vernacular is used as an auxiliary medium of instruction only in the first two grades.

2. English is the main language of government and commerce and of civil service examinations, with Pilipino as an alternative language. In the provinces the vernacular forms a third language of trade.

3. There are quite a number of publications in English of nationwide circulation. There are some also in Pilipino. Those in the various vernaculars are of local circulation. It is interesting to note here the appearance of a hybrid of Tagalog[1] and English, which is referred to by some writers as Taglish if there is more Tagalog than English or as Engalog if it is mainly English with some Tagalog. Even in respectable English newspapers one finds nowadays advertisements in English with portions expressed in Tagalog. Occasionally a magazine article may appear, written in this hybrid language sometimes lightly called "mix-mix", which is really an evidence of code switching and code mixing.

4. Radio and TV broadcasts are mainly in English with Tagalog coming perhaps a close second, or possibly sometimes first at certain times. These are heard practically throughout the islands.

5. At government and social functions, English, Tagalog, and the local vernacular may be heard, with English having the edge sometimes.

6. English is one of the official languages.

There is thus a nationwide English-speech community brought about by government prescription, educational implementation, and the cooperation of media and the public. The use of English is not confined to the classroom. The language is used either as the main language or as an alternative language of communication of government and society.

Should nationalism and regionalism prevail to effect a change in the present set-up so that, say, the environmental situation is reversed in favour of the national language and a regional language, the problem of retaining the use of English will loom larger because opportunities for its use may be reduced further. Then the problem of teaching English as a functional language of communication will probably become more serious than it is now.

Let me now comment on some of the problems I mentioned earlier:

1. What degree of competence in English should be aimed at? In the Philippines, if our concern were only about Filipinos speaking English among ourselves, we could, at a minimum level, be satisfied with a heavily accented Filipino English with peculiarly Filipino un-English expressions reflecting the pressure of Philippine idioms and culture, yet commonly understood among Filipinos.

But this is not the only situation in which English is used in the Philippines. Especially now that tourism has become an industry in the country and Metro Manila is becoming a convention centre, there are more occasions for a greater number of Filipinos to communicate with foreigners. For this purpose the level of expectation of English competence should necessarily be higher. But it is not possible, for instructional purposes, to segregate those who will speak only with Filipinos from those who will speak with foreigners.

The expected level of control of the language at the minimum level therefore would have to be that which would enable both Filipinos and foreigners to communicate with the least probability of misunderstanding. What that would be—that is, how much control of English is internationally understandable—should be the subject for further research.

2. What can be done additionally to help reduce problems of communication? Some suggestions could be these:

(a) Complications of Filipino "un-English" expressions and how to say the same ideas in idiomatic English could be undertaken.

(b) Similarly, the following data may continue to be gathered: (1) sound substitutions made by Filipinos in speaking English; (2) the stress and intonation patterns they tend to superimpose on English words, and (3) the English segmentals and suprasegmentals for these substitutions.

(c) All this material in (a) and (b) above may be made available to curriculum makers and teachers as source materials for teaching. Possibly it may be printed in a consolidated succinct form and distributed for easy reference at convention, tour, and travel centres for use by interested parties as an aid to better understanding.

(d) Tape recordings of the speech of Filipinos (highly educated, literate, and semi-literate in English) and similar recordings of the speech of foreigners that Filipinos are likely to meet in the Philippines, at conventions, and possibly in their travels abroad could be listened to by students and other interested parties. It would be useful to have the written texts of the recordings available along with the recordings.

(e) Radio broadcasts, TV programmes, and movies in English will be helpful in attuning the ears to the different varieties of English that will be involved.

3. Is the problem entirely an educational problem? Philippine

experience has shown that the schools did not do it alone. Government, public, and media have all helped create and support the English speech community in the country. A country's economy too is a potent factor in the success of its language teaching programme for without the necessary financial support no programme will succeed. Politics is often a deciding factor. Whatever the nation's leaders decree becomes reality. The enthusiasm and expertise of implementors of these decrees can also spell the difference between the success or failure of the programme. The history of language planning in the Philippines attests to this. Without the enthusiastic support of the Spanish friars, who were to teach Spanish to the Filipinos, the language was not taught as widely as desired by the Spanish crown that prescribed it.

4. Is the problem purely a national one? Teaching English for cross-cultural communication looks like a problem that goes beyond national boundaries. In today's shrunken world, with jetting convention delegates and tourists constantly on the move, not to mention national and regional involvement in international politics, as long as English continues as an international language of communication in politics, government, commerce, and society, the problem will not be a purely national one.

5. What speech model or models should be used? An attempt to answer this question in the Philippine situation was made as early as 20 years ago. This little "experiment" was tried on groups of teachers and college students on a number of occasions: Phonemic transcriptions of passages in English representing (a) British English (represented by New England English), (b) General American, (c) American English as spoken in the South, and (d) English spoken by Ilocanos, Pampanguenos, and Visayans in the Philippines were presented to the groups for them to read and decide which variety of English they would want their own children or relatives to learn in school. Invariably the answer was General American. The reason? It the was the variety closest to the English of educated Filipinos and the variety they were familiar with and that they best understood because of greater exposure to it. Owing to the many years of Philippine relations with America and her people through government and commerce, more Filipinos have had longer exposure to American speech and publications than to, say, British or Australian. That was before tourism came into the Philippine scene. Although the Filipino variety of American English has to some extent served some Filipinos well at international conventions, one wonders if the current situation will change the Filipinos' choice of model. The "experiment" could be tried again.

6. What conventions of writing are internationally acceptable? These will have to be catalogued and agreed upon, I suppose.

7. What instructional materials and strategies would be more effective and economical in terms of national goals? These will probably

emerge after experimentation. We have tried the conventional ways. Each theory has stimulated research which has contributed much that is still useful information as to what to do and what not to do. Still we know things are not working out as we want them to and we wonder. Puzzlement makes one search for possible explanations and solutions elsewhere.

8. What resources are needed and/or are available? Again, these need to be surveyed and catalogued.

9. What are the implications for teacher education?
I have two main observations here:

(a) That teachers should be developed who understand the nature of English and how it operates; teachers who are aware of the historical development of current trends in language teaching/learning and language planning concepts as well as methodologies and strategies; teachers who not only know principles and theories but can actually look at an instructional problem, diagnose it, and attempt to solve it to the extent of devising their own instructional materials and strategies instead of relying on what are available but which may not be entirely satisfactory for the purpose they are to serve. How this is done is the headache of teacher education, but it is essential that the teachers are so equipped.

(b) That for English to remain in a country for international and, as in the Philippines, intranational use, it must continue to perform the four functions mentioned by Kachru[2] and maintain the features described by Strevens.[3]

According to Strevens the features that differentiate local forms of English may fall under the following categories:

1. Status and use of the local form of English (LFE) in the community;

2. Whether English is a vehicle for public education, science and technology, media, entertainment, and literature;

3. Attitudes of the local intellectual and educational community; and

4. Sociocultural affinity and aversions.

Kachru mentioned four functions of English which result in the nativization of English:

1. Instrumental—it is used in schools;

2. Regulative—it is used in courts and administration;

3. Interpersonal—it is a link language; and

4. Imaginative/Innovative—it is used in creative literature. Checked against these two lists, English in the Philippines is seen to have all features and to perform all functions. It also has all the levels in the continuum of acrolect, mesolect, and basilect. If it has all these, and if Filipino English is recognized as a form of international language used internationally and intranationally, then we probably have got some kind of a hold on the slippery concept of English as an international and

intranational language (EIIL): English is used for international and international purposes together with the native language(s) as a part of the way of life. It is a language, owing to its international utility and prestige and through language contact, which has spawned a great number of local forms or varieties (like Filipino English), each local form (which is really just a label for the group of local varieties—that is, local LFEs—identified with a country or nation) having its own LFEs (like Ilocano English, Visayan English, Tagalog English—all varieties of the variety Filipino English). It has all the features of LFE mentioned by Strevens and all the four functions listed by Kachru.

Let me now briefly summarize some of the things that I have tried to say about English in the Philippines:

1. That language is for communication and that the teaching of EIIL focuses on the goal of making English function as a language of communication for international and intranational purposes. Any means that will help achieve this goal may be used.

2. That by setting our goals at communicating with both foreigners and nationals, expectations should be higher than just for nationals.

3. That language is not an inert thing, but a living one assimilated by a human being with intelligence, emotions, attitudes, interests, motivations—something of a very complex nature that is difficult to parcel and feed piecemeal to a learner.

4. That greater attention should be given to the responsibility of the listener in doing his part to make communication possible and not leave it all to the speaker to make himself understood. There should be more research on the listening process, on what the listener does or can do to understand what he hears. Offhand I would say that some relevant information on the culture and language patterns of a linguistic group, especially as they contrast with those of native speakers of English, would be useful. This information need not be released in scholarly form. Interesting anecdotes, jokes, dialogues illustrating the humorous or embarrassing situations that arise from contrasts in languages in contact go a long way in helping one remember and make the necessary mental adjustments to be able to understand spoken English.

5. That teacher education has the responsibility of developing in the prospective teacher not a vessel of information and a blind follower but one aware of relevant developments, able to formulate clear and reasonable teaching goals and to evaluate and select materials and strategies that will help achieve these goals in his students.

6. That the language programme is not the responsibility of the national educational system alone.

7. That government, commerce, media, and the public are important contributing factors.

8. That in dealing with English as an international language, we are

really dealing with varieties of English used internationally as well as intranationally.

NOTES TO CHAPTER 5

1. Tagalog is what Pilipino is in reality.
2. See Kachru in this volume.
3. See Strevens in this volume.

6 Will EIIL Succeed where ESL and EFL Fail?

M. L. Boonlua Debyasuvarn

This paper is an attempt to give a glimpse of the language situation in Thai society and the school system, and also to make some suggestions for the improvement of learning and teaching English so that it can be used more effectively as a means of international communication.

The English language enjoys high prestige in Thai society. It has been used as a means of international communication for more than a century. King Mongkut, who reigned from 1851 to 1868, was a great scholar, interested in astronomy, religion and history. He communicated in English with several men of importance in his time among whom was the Governor of Singapore.[1] He also wrote to President Buchanan of the United States suggesting that elephants should be reared and used as beasts of burden in that country.[2] King Chulalongkorn (1868–1910), his eldest son and successor, who is regarded as one of the most resourceful monarchs, who changed Siam into a modern state, also spoke and read English. Unlike his father there is no evidence of his English writings. After compulsory education was introduced in the reign of King Chulalongkorn's successor, King Rama VI (1910–25), the English language was made a required subject in all government secondary schools.[3] The first university, Chulalongkorn University, which King Rama VI established as a monument to his father in 1917 used English as a medium of instruction for science subjects from the time of its inception down to only a few decades ago.

For the process of modernizing, or Westernizing the country, it has been necessary to select a number of intelligent young men to send to Europe, and later to the United States of America, to study science and technology. Since English is taught in school it is obvious that the highest proportion are sent to English-speaking countries. The ability to communicate in English became and remains the mark of a modern educated person as opposed to one who receives the traditional, or synonymously old-fashioned, education.

From the time of its first organization along Western lines, under King Chulalongkorn, the school system of Thailand has seen a number of changes. After World War II, in the area of English instruction the country has received several groups of advisers. However, many confusing suggestions have been given to educators and teachers which frustrate them and hamper the improvement of learning and teaching. At the moment it must be said that Thai educational leaders are still lacking in sophistication in the field of learning and teaching language.

Although several methods have been advocated, the real central issue has not been tackled seriously—that of the qualification of teachers. There are far too many teachers with inadequate knowledge of English teaching the subject in the school system. There are far too few well-qualified trainers of teachers. Proposals have been made to the Ministry of Education to introduce measures that will enable teachers of English to get specialized training, but not much has been effected.

A new school system came into use in 1978, consisting of six elementary grades and six secondary grades, whereas the old system consisted of four junior elementary, and three senior grades. Under the old system, English was required from the fifth grade upwards. Under the new system English is not taught in the sixth grades of the elementary level which all Thai children have to attend under a new Act of Compulsory Education. In the secondary school, i.e. from the seventh grade upwards, one foreign language can be elected. The new system will, however, affect only the first grade of the elementary, and the first grade of the secondary level. It will take six years for the new system to take effect in all the schools of the nation.

From the promulgated national curriculum, I do not see that the teaching of English is going to be much influenced by the new national system. A brave English curriculum committee has proposed the preparation of teaching materials for individualized learning. With the highest degree of optimism, I cannot visualize from where the qualified material preparers will materialize. Of course, it is always better to hope than to give up before trying.

Before suggesting what might be done, we might perhaps clear up some of the points of confusion, keeping in mind that a new standpoint or a new approach may help in improving the learning of English. We have heard the terms Teaching English as a Second Language, and Teaching English as a Foreign Language, or TESL and TEFL. It seems to me that around the 1950s, the first term was much used in the United States and the second one outside. In terms of methodology, it was not quite clear what the difference was between the two until the English Project of SEAMEO (Southeast Asia Ministers of Education Organization) was established in 1968. The Governing Board of the Project decided that the first term, TESL, applied to countries which used English as a second language. That is to say English was used for official correspondence and as a medium of instruction in secondary schools and at colleges and universities. The other term, TEFL, applied to countries which taught English in school as a foreign language, and outside school there was not much opportunity of using English except in special circumstances. The TESL countries are those like the Philippines, Malaysia and Singapore. The TEFL countries are those like Thailand and Indonesia. This, of course, is a case of oversimplification but it is sufficient for the discussion which is to follow.

It should be fairly clear that where there is little opportunity for using the language, the motivation on the part of learners would not be very high. Where there are opportunities for using it and where social and economic advancement depends on it, the learners would be more highly motivated. It would follow that the aims and purposes of the curriculum need to be different between the two groups—TESL learners and TEFL learners. This naturally would affect the preparation of materials and the system of evaluation. It is generally accepted that motivation plays the most important role in the learning process, and where language is concerned, the hours of exposure also have great importance. It is also believed that intensive learning brings about the best results. It should be clear, then, that the TEFL countries which cling to the practice of distributing English instruction over six or eight years with a few hours each week, would not obtain much satisfaction from their English programmes. What else is there to be discussed, especially when we remember again with some pain the fact that there are not sufficient numbers of qualified teachers?[4]

Should we give up teaching English, or any foreign language altogether, seeing the hopelessness of the situation? We remember the small percentage of successful learners who seem to become proficient after a few years at school no matter what sort of programmes are offered and what methods of teaching are employed. There has been no systematic research on how this small percentage of students learn. Only personal observations and experience show that they can absorb everything taught in every subject. Almost every learning item they have been through, is grasped and retained. This, I believe, is the answer to the question why about 10 per cent of the students from the Thai school system can use English fairly effectively.[5]

Whatever methods are used, I believe this 10 per cent of students will become proficient to the extent that they can communicate satisfactorily for the purpose they have but I think we ought to think of the next 15 per cent. Those students, if well taught, will gain a more satisfactory result than they have done in the past. And it is for these 15 per cent that different methods have been tried and should be tried again.

Does the oral approach help this 15 per cent? School Broadcasting was introduced in 1958. There are now about 7000 participating schools. Every year some kind of survey is made. Twice, once in 1962, and again in 1972, researches were carried out to evaluate the project. From the reports no real conclusion can be made. Schools not in the project and participating schools, selected and used for research purposes, seem to achieve more or less the same result. In all skills, the participating schools do not seem to show superiority. In my opinion, the tests used involve the reading skill more than any other skill. School Broadcasting was introduced to improve the listening skill, with the hope that by listening to native speakers who acted as "radio teachers" (the term used in School Broadcasting) pupils would improve their own pronunciation. The team of evaluators suggest in their reports that no real conclusion can be drawn because of insufficient supervision in the participating schools resulting in irregularity of participation; that is, some schools listen when it is convenient and often skip some lessons when it is inconvenient. Anyway there is an interesting point in the reports. The higher the academic qualification of the teachers, the more appreciative they seem of School Broadcasting as an aid to teaching.[6]

Now let us suppose that we take the suggestion made in "ESOL—EIAL: a position paper on the teaching–learning of English as an international auxiliary language" (Smith, 1976b). We shall change our attitude and not make too much of imitating the native speakers. A crucial question at once follows—how far can we deviate? In 1950, I was approached by a Thai naval officer who asked me to help improve his spoken English. He had official business in which he had to deal with a Filipino counterpart. The latter complained that communication was very difficult between a Thai English speaker and a Tagalog English speaker. They both agreed that they would improve their spoken English by making it nearer to the native speech. The question again—how near? In 1951, I was in Manila for a short time. An American teacher of Oral English in a teachers' college persuaded me to visit her class and speak for a few minutes. She explained at the end of the session that she wanted to convince her students that they could understand a foreign speaker without waiting a few months to get used to his or her way of speaking. Her students had been arguing with her that she had been unnecessarily strict with them. If she would wait a few months more she would become accustomed to their speech and would not bother them about improving.

Now we come to the grammatical aspect. Shall we aim at this type of communication? The following oral performance was heard at a seminar for foreign business executives in Thailand:

Auditors are call(ed) vultures. Depot director tell another one "vulture come". Then one day we have an auditor. He is friend he is teacher. He show depot director how to work. They say this auditor is our teacher, our friend, they take him to lunch . . .

The Department of Modern Languages, Faculty of Arts, Chulalongkorn University, collected common errors in composition made by students in Thailand. Among them are the following:

You are obvious that you have a fever.
He finally was suicide.
Use an antiseptic to protect germs . . .
Owing to you are sick you should see a doctor.
He was bitten and became hydrophobia.[7]

The errors have been classified and exercises prepared for the students to help them; but mistakes of the above types, grammatical and idiomatic, are still made by Thai students and will be made again. They are due to the character of the Thai language in which the only (perhaps) grammatical form is the order of words in the sentence. There are no plural forms for nouns, tense forms for verbs, and the like. Very few words belong to any particular part of speech. A word is used as a "noun" in one context, and as an "adjective" in the next. We can see it is very difficult to decide how far pupils should be allowed to deviate from the form used by native speakers and how near they are to be asked to remain.

Also, I am almost certain that the prestigious status of English in Thai society will threaten the new attitude in some degree. Parents who have been successful under the old tradition naturally have become important and influential members of society. This group of people has been against reform of every kind, because educational problems seldom affect them or their children who, naturally again, inherit their intelligence and capacities.

At the moment some doubts have been expressed concerning the position of English as an international medium of communication. At the Conference of ASEAN Writers at Kuala Lumpur, 3–5 December 1977, hope was expressed that participants at the next conference might be able to communicate in a language belonging to the region instead of in English. This might come about but not in the near future. In my opinion, English will remain in its place as a means of communication among Asian nations for a few decades yet. It follows that we will have English to reckon with in our educational systems for some time to come. In Thailand, as already mentioned, English will not be a required subject in school. But the majority will elect English because of the need to learn science and technology. Handbooks from Japanese manufacturing companies are written in English; so are those from continental European countries. Although Japanese and German have become more and more popular among secondary school students, it will take some time for these languages to replace English. In some Asian countries, it seems that English will remain the medium of instruction in schools and colleges for perhaps, at least, one generation.[8]

But granted that we have our way cleared sufficiently to have our new concept of English as an international and intranational language (EIIL) accepted in the school systems at large, which means we will not work for near-native performance, especially in speech, and the Filipino

88 ENGLISH FOR CROSS-CULTURAL COMMUNICATION

students will not have any more cause to complain against their speech instructor, how from here are we to proceed? What grammatical structures are to be ignored? Which sound deviations are to be overlooked? How do we set up our English programmes at various institutions? How, above all, to avoid so-called educators going to the extreme as has happened in the past? How do we make it understood that judiciousness is expected of educators, in the language field or elsewhere? I have sat at a few conferences where long sessions were sacrificed to discussions on whether the learner's language should be used in a foreign language class, and if it was to be used, how much, and in what ways, when surely a good teacher will use any device or technique that helps his students learn. It must also be realized that few teachers and even educational leaders are able to differentiate among approach, method, and technique. This applies to academicians and technicians in other areas besides that of language teaching.

Before we take up the crucial but elusive problem of intelligibility with the accompanying puzzle of kinds and degrees of deviation, I should like to get teacher preparation out of the way. We probably are all familiar with the arguments over the amount of time given to professional subjects as against that given academic subjects and so on. In regard to teachers of English, at least in Thailand, it has become a common question among trainers of teachers whether a trainee needs to learn English literature. When that question is put to me, my response is that usually it depends on what is meant by the term. Do all teachers of English in Thailand have to read Shakespeare's plays? I am all for anybody reading Shakespeare if he can enjoy it. A few years ago I spent half a morning listening to the argument back and forth. I still don't understand why English literature should mean Shakespeare, or Ian Fleming or any particular author. But if somebody takes a degree in English from a certain university English Department, or from any college (that is, he has spent 12 years learning English), and he has not read a few good short stories, a few novels, a few poems, he must have spent some very sad years. As a Thai, I should like a university-educated person of the same nationality as myself to be familiar with Western literature in some form. Thai mentality has grown and developed through the centuries taking advantage in some way of the ideas and process of thinking of other people with whom we have come into contact.

What does not seem to come up at conferences and seminars on teacher education is how many other kinds of English should teachers be familiar with? Can teachers read scientific English? Is their science education background conducive to such an activity? Are teachers able to differentiate between the social sciences and the natural sciences, and the way the two groups of disciplines are treated by writers? Are books being written for non-native teachers to help them move towards the reading of the two branches of science to serve their needs? At the other end are the trades and vocations. How are teachers to prepare students for the kind of English that they must know to meet their purposes in life—to become hotel boys, or tourist guides, or scientists, if they themselves, the teachers, do not learn about these occupations and know how those engaged in them communicate? Specialization has been mentioned but how far is specialization to go?

There is also another angle. As has been the case in Thailand most teachers of English come from the Humanities, but most of the students they teach are science students. Until a few years ago, it was most difficult to convince teachers of English that science students were not just rebellious or malicious but their needs were simply not met in the English classes. Each time I walk past a science students' class and hear drills on tag questions, I always wonder if the habit a friend of mine has would not suffice. He has only one tag-question: "isn't it?" There is now a programme, at one university in Bangkok, which attempts to train teachers of English for science students, in which the trainees have to acquire some knowledge of science, and are taught to produce materials for the science students they are supposed to teach when they complete their training. The programme serves only a very small number of prospective instructors at the university level, however.

We can now go on perhaps to the planning of programmes of English for students of different levels and for different purposes, and preparing teachers for each type of programme. Programme planning is getting to be better understood by a small number of professional English-language teachers in Thailand. But they will have many obstacles to overcome. International communication through English takes place at many levels, from between tourists and hotel boys, to between high-ranking officials of different countries. I once sat in a place where I could hear every word of a conversation between one quite important Thai official and a specialist consultant who was a native speaker of English. On every occasion when the Thai official should have said "we would like to" he said "we will". The specialist consultant came out of the room beaming and told me that all his proposals had been accepted. I was not in a position to discourage him and left the knot to be disentangled, or more entangled, depending on the luck of the official and the consultant. The fact must be faced that a Thai needs a great amount of time to learn English because of the great differences between the two languages, even when we ignore the cultural backgrounds leading to different habits of communication. To discuss vital problems, a senior official must be highly competent in English or use a competent interpreter. At this level, a person exposed to English instruction as offered in the Thai educational system does not have much chance. A Thai speaker to be able to communicate in high-level English, both in speaking and writing, needs a solid base at the beginning, and long and intensive exposure later, which I am afraid he can obtain only by spending some years in an English-speaking country. He must also expose himself relentlessly to English. There is a saying in Thai that a musician cannot neglect music up to seven days. A Thai speaker, to communicate in high-level English, cannot perhaps stop using it in some way or other, for even one day.

For easy reference, I shall pick out three programmes of English instruction in the Thai educational system and discuss the chances of improvement and the obstacles to overcome. The first is the easiest, and I will call it English for Doctors. This programme should not be difficult to design. Medical students in Thailand are supposed to use English textbooks. There is general agreement that they must know enough English in the secondary schools to be able to continue in their pre-medical course leading to the reading of English texts in the Medical School. So far the objectives are clear enough, and since very seldom now do Thai medical students get foreign instructors or even lecturers, there is little concern about spoken English. Students may learn English perhaps like a dead language, and may qualify as Thai doctors. The best ones go on to advanced studies abroad, of course, but these can very well manage whatever English curriculum is offered, whichever methods of teaching are used; they learn in spite of anything, so to speak. But then nowadays doctors of all nations meet at conferences and interchange experiences and ideas. What sort of pronunciation are they to have, how far from the native, or how near? In written discourse they seem to be able to communicate with little difficulty as I have seen in a paper, to be presented at a certain international conference, the sentence "In Bangkok, there are two nervous hospitals". Although I was rather alarmed at the statement, the man who presented the paper was elected a high-ranking officer of the international organization that sponsored the conference. Therefore, the medical English programme, as I see it, presents the least problems, and yet quite a number of questions remain to be answered.

Another programme that may be discussed is quite at the opposite end. This is a programme for a specific occupation not involving academic training, for example, a programme for hotel service personnel. The room maid needs very little reading and writing; she communicates mostly verbally, and the subject is confined to a small number of needs of the guests. She must be able to understand all kinds of accents, however, and so she must be rather intelligent so that she may guess what the guests want mainly from her experience and her knowledge of human nature.

Her colleagues in hotel service, namely, the room-service people, must have a better listening comprehension than the room maid. Orders for drinks and meals are given almost always by telephone. If the order is given within what is on the menu, there is less difficulty. But if a guest makes special requests because he is sick or because he has children or old people travelling with him, the room-service people can get into some trouble. However, hotel service English programmes can concentrate on spoken English with a limited vocabulary, and neglect reading and writing.

Now we come to the most complex programme of all—the English programme for the liberal arts students. The concept of liberal education is rather hazy in Thailand. The university faculties (schools or colleges) whose charge is to provide it, seem undecided whether they are simply to produce educated persons, or to prepare their students for some career, and English has a doubtful role. Because of its long-standing prestige, it is expected that all Bachelors of Arts be proficient in English. But what kind of English? Should students be taught the kind of English that will make them good secretaries or good government officials? If so, what are they supposed to know? Are they supposed to know English literature? of what period? which and how many forms of writing? Sometimes English programmes are criticized as being not intellectual enough, and other times as being impractical. Personally I believe in making liberal education really "liberal". Why can't we make the English programme flexible enough to meet students' needs? Their reading ability, of course, should be fairly high, their critical sense well developed. Being able to read English is an irrefutable asset. As to their writing ability, why can't we leave it to their choice. If they want to become secretaries, they should learn to write letters and notes relevant to their jobs. If they want to go in for creative writing, they can be encouraged to write stories, descriptions, narrations and so on.

However, the practice of accepting liberal arts students as teachers is still prevalent. Here confusion starts afresh. But why not allow a short course of a year, or half a year, to prepare them for teaching jobs? The problem can be solved, but there seems no will among those in authority to tackle the problem.

This means, like everything prestigious, in Thailand at least, a great deal of interest is shown towards English as a school and university subject, but no real attention is being given it.

Will, therefore, the new EIIL attitude advocated, be able to call for real attention. It is prudent to expect that there will at first be an uproar. There will be all kinds of interpretation as has happened to every new idea, every new approach—the direct method, the linguistic approach, intensive English and so forth. Some will be pleased with the idea of not paying too much attention to students' pronunciation. Some will become indignant and proclaim that the people with the new attitude are ready to upset the whole system of education, and are making for mediocrity. But sooner or later they will settle down to the crucial problem of intelligibility. And this is the most vital issue.

Intelligibility must be viewed in terms of both spoken and of written communication. Everybody has heard of the "threshold of compre-hension". The Filipino students who complained against their speech instructor were asking her to widen her threshold. As we become accustomed to a way of speech we can easily communicate with those who use it however far they deviate from what we consider desirable. Indeed we even pick up the habits of those we communicate with. But communication and comprehension of this kind can take place only between two groups of people or among three or four, say, in a multilingual society. It cannot take place internationally. We have to find a core or centre, and we have, I am afraid, to use the native language habits as our starting point.

While there are no results from research we must, I suppose, rely on our common sense. As a point of departure, for spoken communication we probably have to use our knowledge of the phonemes and of the phonology of the English language.

We are compelled to realize, then, that for verbal communication, we have at least two aspects to consider—the sounds and the grammatical points. At the moment, I cannot state which grammatical points are indispensable, and which may be ignored for any particular level of communication. But this need not be of great concern, for, in speaking, communication can be effected by other means besides language proper such as gestures, pointing to objects and so on.

In written communication, we have mostly the grammatical aspect to reckon with. But there certainly will be degrees of clarity and comprehensible idioms to consider. The metaphors and similes, found in certain local varieties, mostly picturesque and vigorous, may not be understood by users of another local variety. Who, then, should judge which constructions and which expressions are acceptable? I am afraid we will have to fall back on research and I am inclined to include native speakers among judges of intelligibility, as we need a core upon which we can lean. As a non-researcher I imagine a host of tactics for the strategy of research, but I don't believe a researcher needs my advice. In the meantime we have to rely on our common sense, of which experienced and devoted language teachers have a plentiful supply. My concern is that the English language will break up into as many varieties as there are foreign users. I do not agree that language teachers in various parts of the world should allow this to take place. Until we have something really better, we should try to keep English a language by which a West African can communicate with a Southeast Asian; a Pacific islander with a Baltic European. Otherwise we are only going to have what had happened some time ago—the Indo-Aryan language breaking up into innumerable branches, and the same with Chinese. Ancient India managed to preserve Sanskrit, and the medieval Europeans Latin. The ancient Chinese developed an ingenious system of writing. We with all our modern technology should do better. We should be able to preserve and also develop English so that it can serve as an international, and also intranational medium of communication in writing and also in speaking.

But let us remember that there is a great deal of work to be done. We must remember that it means hard work trying to change the attitude of educational leaders and teachers who cling to old concepts and beliefs mainly through lack of real understanding, and not, I believe, through malice. And there is always the critical issue of time exposure to the language to be learned. And above all else, if the repetition is not too tedious, there is the all-embracing problem of the training of teachers and the placing of personnel in administrative positions that could stimulate, or hamper, the learning and teaching process.

NOTES TO CHAPTER 6

1. Grishold, A. B. *King Mongkut of Siam*, New York, The Asia Society, 1961.
2. Moffat Abbot Low. *Mongkut, King of Siam*, New York, Cornell University Press, 1961: 91–5.
3. Sayamanond, Rong. 'A Historical Study of the Teaching of Foreign Languages in Thailand', (in English) *Bulletin of the Faculty of Arts, Chulalongkorn University*, 4 (January 1967).
4. Debyasuvarn, Boonlua, M. L. Report (to the Ministry of Education) of the National Coordinating Committee, 13 May 1975, printed in *PASAA*, V (November 1975).
5. National Council of Education, *Reports on Results of Entrance Examinations 2512–2518* (Bangkok, 1976).
6. Center of Educational Technology, *An Evaluative Research on School-Broadcasting*, Report of the Working Group, Center of Educational Technology, Ministry of Education, B. E. 2515 (1972). Division of Educational Information. *Report on School-Broadcasting*. Division of Educational Information, Ministry of Education, B. E. 2505 (1963).
7. Department of Modern Languages, *Grammar Notes: Errors in Composition Made by Students in Thailand*, Department of Modern Languages, Faculty of Arts, Chulalongkorn University, B. E. 2495 (1952).
8. Sibayan, Bonifacio P. 'Language and Identity', paper presented at the SEAMEO Regional Language Centre, Twelfth Regional Seminar, 18–22 April 1977, on Language Education in Multilingual Societies: Its Challenges and Potentials.

7 English in Malaysia

Irene F. H. Wong

1 BACKGROUND

Malaysia is a country with three main ethnic groups (Malays, Chinese, and Indians), each with its own language and dialects. English was first introduced to the country through the trading operations of the British East India Company and spread through religious and educational activities from the early nineteenth century on. Until the country achieved her independence from British rule in 1957, the greatest social and economic advantages came with the learning of English, so that the most ambitious and far-sighted of each race sent their children to English-medium schools for a Western-type education. This has resulted in a fairly large section of the population knowing English, although with varying degrees of proficiency. At the top are those who look upon English as their primary language and who use it with near-native-speaker proficiency. Lower down the scale are those not so fluent in the language but who nevertheless have an adequate command of it for basic communication purposes. All in all though, the standard of English in Malaysia has in the past been among the highest for any EFL country, with the standards of correctness being those of educated native-speaker British English.

One may claim that it is only in the last fifteen years or so that Malaysian English has begun to come into its own as yet another dialect of English, different from any other recognized dialect of English, peculiar to its own region, and yet intelligible on the whole to English-speakers everywhere. Through political independence and growing political maturity, Malaysians have come to realize that no longer is it necessary or desirable to aim at a foreign standard of English for themselves. Moreover, with the withdrawal of the majority of the British from the country, no longer is it even possible to model Malaysian speech on native-speaker British English. This has been recognized at the official level, as can be seen, for instance, in the following statement of aims found in the *Teachers' Handbook for the Post-1970 Primary School English Syllabus*, issued by the Ministry of Education in 1971:

Malaysians are learning English increasingly as a language of international communication. The aim should therefore continue to be to teach children to speak in such a way that they will be understood not only by fellow-Malaysians, but also by speakers of English from other parts of the world . . .

It should however be noted that our aim of "international intelligibility" does not imply that our pupils should necessarily speak exactly like Englishmen: there would not be sufficient time to achieve this, nor is it necessary. What is aimed at is that they should be able to speak with acceptable rhythm and stress, and to produce the sounds of English sufficiently well for a listener to be able to distinguish between similar words, e.g. pan—pen.

(p. 3)

The position of English in the country has also changed. The medium of instruction in all the schools (with the exception of private schools meant for non-nationals) and most tertiary institutions is now the national language, which is Malay (or Bahasa Malaysia as it is called), while English is taught only as a second language. English is thus passing through a transitional stage in the country at the moment; there is still a relatively large section of the adult population who feel most at home in English, while younger ones are coming up for whom English will be but an auxiliary language. Moreover, in the context of the country as a whole, the use of, and exposure to, English is progressively reduced as Bahasa Malaysia correspondingly widens its sphere of use. This changing situation has inevitably affected English as it is used in Malaysia at the moment, and will undoubtedly affect it even more in the future as the percentage of near-native speakers of English dwindles to the point where they will cease to have any influence at all on the use of the language in the country. It will only be in the future, therefore, that the truly distinctive characteristics of English in Malaysia will become more visible.

2 VARIETIES OF MALAYSIAN ENGLISH

Randolph Quirk (1968) has said:

it seems quite natural in most societies for people to recognise two distinct degrees of community: the immediate, local, and familiar community on the one hand; and on the other, a wider and less familiar community to which one also belongs and beyond which begins the foreign world proper. Linguistically, these two degrees are marked by a local dialect and a speech-form which is

not specifically regional and which may have an additional
prestige.
(p. 91)

This concept of local dialect and wider speech-form, or of high and low
varieties (Ferguson, 1959), is more relevant to a description of
Malaysian English than the concept of formal and informal registers or
that of written and spoken English. The local dialect is meant to be used
mainly in speech and limited to conversation on everyday matters only
with familiars who are also Malaysians, who can then be expected to
share the same dialect. With non-Malaysians, it should be the wider
speech-form which is used on all occasions, even in speech and informal
situations. The use of the local dialect often serves to establish a rapport
between speaker and hearer while the wider speech-form would tend to
distance the two. The wider speech-form is normally used with
Malaysians on a more formal level, whether in speech or in writing, and
is usually learnt through formal instruction whereas the local dialect is
picked up informally. The wider speech-form thus has a much wider
sphere of use than the local dialect.

Most English-speaking Malaysians are in command of both these
varieties of Malaysian English. As Tongue (1974) observes:

> Anyone who has been only a short time in these countries (i.e.
> Singapore and Malaysia) will have had the remarkable experience
> of listening to a speaker who has been conversing in near-native
> discourse suddenly switch to very formal ESM i.e. the English of
> Singapore and Malaysia when he speaks to someone familiar only
> with the sub-standard form referred to as the local dialect in this
> paper, or chats on the telephone with an intimate friend. This is a
> dramatic incident—everything seems to change, including gram-
> mar, vocabulary, voice quality, pace of utterance, and even
> gestures. The sub-standard forms, it is interesting to note, are also
> picked up by foreigners who have been in the region for some
> time and used as "intimacy signals" when conversing with their
> local friends.
> (p. 11)

For the wider speech-form, which is the more prestigious form,
Malaysians aim to model their language on an internationally pres-
tigious dialect of English like standard British or American English.
For the near-native speaker of English, the wider speech-form would be
virtually indistinguishable from any other dialect of well-educated
English, at least in its written form. The grammar, sentence structure,
paragraphing, etc., would be common to all well-educated varieties of
English. So would the vocabulary, barring a few localized borrowings

from the contact languages in Malaysia. Any differences there might be would come in on the spoken level, with minor pronunciation variations, but none that would interfere with international intelligibility. For the local dialect, however, Malaysians imitate no one but themselves. The divergence from standard British or American English is therefore much greater than for the wider speech-form.

2.1 The Wider Speech-Form

On the level of vocabulary, even for the near-native speaker of English there is the inevitable departure from other varieties of well-educated English due to the different life-style of this multicultural and multilingual country. Hence, there are loans from contact languages like Hindi (e.g. "dhobi" meaning "washerman, laundry"), Portuguese (e.g. "peon" meaning "office attendant"), Arabic (e.g. "syce" meaning "driver"), Tamil (e.g. "tamby" meaning "errand boy"), Chinese (e.g. "towkay" meaning "proprietor"), and Malay (e.g. "jaga" meaning "guard", "ulu" meaning "in the upper reaches of a river" in Malay but used to mean "in the wilds, out-of-the-way" in English). With Bahasa Malaysia now being the national language of the country, it is inevitable that many Malay words have been brought into Malaysian English: e.g. "bomoh" meaning "to fast", "Menteri Besar" meaning "Chief Minister", and "orang Asli" referring to the aboriginal peoples of Malaysia.

Apart from such loans, there are also words reflecting the colonial background of Malaysians. Thus, the term "shillings" is frequently used to refer to coins, although the local currency is in dollars and cents and was so even in the days of colonization, and to go "outstation" means to leave the place where one lives or is stationed, in order to visit other locations within the country, either on duty or on holiday.

Then there are other words which, although English in origin, may be used in ways unfamiliar to native speakers of English. Many foods are described as being either "heaty" or "cooling", reflecting concepts belonging to some Asian cultures. "Heaty" foods or drinks make the body hot, like brandy, beef, chilli and coffee, while those that are "cooling" have the opposite effect, like beer, certain vegetables and fruits. The terms "auntie" and "uncle" are used not only to express these particular family relationships but also as marks of respect in addressing those either superior or equal to the speaker on the social scale. Thus, salespeople would use these terms to address their customers, servants would use these terms to address their employers (whereas in the past they used an equivalent of "boss" for this purpose), and individuals who do not know each other well enough to use their first names would use the terms to address each other. Children throughout Malaysia are taught to address most adults (with the exception of those considered very low on the social scale) as either "auntie" or "uncle" as marks of respect to them.

As far as the average educated Malaysian is concerned though, as distinct from the élite of the English-speaking population in the country, there are frequent instances of word-usage which are considered deviant from the point of view of the educated native speaker of English, but which nevertheless are gradually being propagated through sheer force of use and numbers. An example of this is the use of the word "alphabet" to refer to "letter of the alphabet", thereby giving rise to the familiar plural form "alphabets", when "letters of the alphabet" are referred to. Other examples are the frequent confusion between the words "take/bring/send/fetch", "come/go", and "borrow/lend". "Follow" is often used in the sense of "accompany" and "chop" is used for "stamp" or "seal". These, and other such examples, are commonly found in the English used by average educated Malaysians, who are generally oblivious of the fact that such usage is considered deviant as far as standard British English is concerned.

On the level of pronunciation, the most striking instances of deviation from standard British English, as far as the wider speech-form is concerned, are in the matter of word-stress. While for the élite of the English-speaking population the standard British pattern of stress is in general adhered to, the average, and thus much more frequent, pronunciations of words such as those given below would place the primary stress differently, as indicated by underlining.

comment (noun)	faculty	competent	character
forfeit (noun)	bargain	colleague	carpenter
content (noun)	purchase	vehicle	literature
market	expert	context	inculcate
association	consider	realize	development
contributor	economic	committee	fascination
alternative	specific	illustrate	co-ordinator
presentation	familiar	technique	opportunity
individual	official	remedial	competition
determine	academic	significant	adolescence
issue	frivolous	assets	differ

While in the past educators might have attempted to bring these pronunciations in to line with those of standard British English, such attempts have faded out now as many educators themselves use these same Malaysian pronunciations in their own wider speech-form. Moreover, the average educated Malaysian pronunciations of these words are internationally intelligible on the whole, although it must be admitted that instances of misunderstanding are not always avoided.

On the level of structure or grammar, the wider-speech-form variety of Malaysian English attempts to come as close to standard British English as the speaker is capable of. While there still exists a relatively small section of the English-speaking population whose wider speech-form may be indistinguishable from standard British English as far as structure or grammar is concerned, more and more deviations from that norm are being noted, indicative of the trend Malaysian English is now taking, following its role as auxiliary language of the nation. However, these deviations from standard British English on the level of grammar are still considered as aberrations at the moment, especially by English language educators, while many of those deviations on the level of vocabulary and pronunciation are not. In other words, while it is recognized by most Malaysians that certain vocabulary and pronunciation differences are allowed between Malaysian English and standard British English, the general feeling is that there ought to be none as far as grammar is concerned. However, in spite of this, deviations on the level of grammar continue to flourish, and are now quite prevalent in average educated Malaysian English. Only a few of the more common grammatical deviations will be mentioned for purposes of illustration.

The problems that the average educated Malaysian has with the complex tense system of English are to be expected. Firstly, the selection of the correct tense, among the many tenses available in English, causes a lot of confusion in the minds of Malaysians used to the simple tense systems of their vernaculars. When does one choose the present perfect tense as opposed to the simple past tense or the past perfect tense? Or when does one choose the continuous tense as opposed to the simple tense? Even after the appropriate tense has been decided on, there is the difficulty of finding the correct forms with which to express it, for many of the more common verbs in English are irregular and must be learnt as such. Moreover, there is the problem of the "dummy auxiliary" "do/does/did" which, when it occurs, carries the tense of the verb phrase so that the main verb remains uninflected. Added to these problems is the fact that many of the modal auxiliaries in English express syntactic, but not temporal, tense so that it is easy enough to sympathize with the average Malaysian's dilemma in the choice between "will" and "would" and between "can" and "could" in expressions such as "He will/would try again" and "He can/could do it himself".

Another major area of difficulty for Malaysians is prepositional usage. Firstly, there are the prepositions used in idiomatic phrases and in phrasal verbs such as "to run up (a bill)" or "to hand in (an assignment)". Very often, Malaysians will use a different preposition from that used in standard British English, as in the expressions "with a view of", "superior than", "arrive to". In addition, there are instances of redundant prepositions, as in the examples "stressed on", "emphasized on", "continued on", "mentioned about", "discussed about", "demanded for", "requested for", "comprising of" and "combat against"

The uncountable nouns are often regularized as countable nouns and treated as such in average Malaysian usage. Thus, the following plurals are commonly found: "jewelleries", "mails", "sceneries", "informations", "equipments", "underwears", "machineries", "clothings", and so on. When such uncountable nouns are used in the singular, it is common enough to find expressions such as "an evidence", "an advice", and "a chalk". Moreover, Malaysians now generally use the determiners "many/much" and "few/less" quite indiscriminately with following nouns, whether these be countable or uncountable, giving rise to expressions such as "less problems" and "much books".

2.2 The Local Dialect

The local dialect is a much "barer" and more simplified variety of English than the wider speech-form. This can be seen, for example, in the vocabulary, which is quite limited and devoid of the richness of synonyms and near-synonyms to be expected of the wider speech-form. As a consequence of this, a number of words have to serve a variety of functions. Thus these words are given extensions of meaning not normally found in standard British English. One notable example is the use of the verbs "open" and "close". Malaysians "open" and "close" lights, fans, taps, radios, and TVs, while they also "open" (but do not "close") shoes and clothes, meaning, to take off these articles of clothing. Another example is the use of the verb "cut". It can be used to mean "overtake", as in the sentence "His car cut mine"; it can mean "to beat someone (in a competition)", as in the sentence "He cut me by only one mark"; and it can also be used in the sense of "reduce, deduct", as in the sentence "He cut me five dollars". Yet another example is the noun "friend", which is used to function as a verb too, as in the sentence commonly heard among school children, "He won't friend me".

On the level of pronunciation, this simplification process of the local dialect can be observed in the treatment of the consonant clusters of standard British English. This simplification usually takes one of two forms, either by omitting one or more of the consonants in the cluster (e.g. "depth" becomes "dep", "guests" becomes "gues", "risks" becomes "ris", "desks" becomes "des") or by inserting a vowel into the consonant cluster, thus breaking it up into two syllables (e.g. "film" becomes "filem" and "little" becomes "lettel"). The "th" sound is often replaced by "t" when it is voiceless (e.g. "thread" becomes "tread", "three" becomes "tree", "think" becomes "tink", "thought" becomes "taught") and by "d" when it is voiced (e.g. "this" becomes "dis", "though" becomes "dough", and "that" becomes "dat").

On the whole, the characteristic Malaysian "accent" tends to be exaggerated in the local dialect as this is the variety of English which most Malaysians feel belongs to them and forms a part of their identity. Hence they are not bound by any anxieties over external standards of correctness. Moreover, it is common enough to find the English of the local dialect interspersed with words and phrases from vernaculars like Cantonese and Malay, not only in those contexts where English lacks a word for a native idea or concept, but also in those contexts where an English word is perfectly accessible, appropriate and suitable. Such a juxtaposition of two entirely different languages undoubtedly has an effect on the pronunciation of both the languages involved.

The "barer" form of the local dialect can be seen also in the grammar, which is essentially a more simplified and reduced version of the wider speech-form, the process of simplification being that of maintaining what is essential for communication purposes and dropping nearly everything else. The simplifications to be found vary greatly with the speaker and the context. A few members of the English-speaking population may disdain to use too many simplifications in their local dialect whereas at the other end of the scale, those with only a rudimentary knowledge of English are forced to use the maximum number of simplifications possible. The local dialect of the average Malaysian, however, often dispenses with grammatical features like subject–verb agreement, the use of the copula, grammatical and "empty" subjects and objects like "it", and many of the inflections of the various parts of speech. The complex tense system of standard British English is largely ignored, and tense is left to be communicated either by the context alone or through the use of "time" words and phrases like "last night", "yesterday", "Friday" and so on. One common question tag, "isn't it?", suffices for all types of structures, regardless of the subject and verb used in the main sentence, e.g. "Just flowers, isn't it?" "She was quite young, isn't it?"; and "You're not doing anything now, isn't it?". Another common and simple way of inviting affirmation (or negation) in the local dialect is to attach the phrase "or not?" to a preceding utterance, e.g. "Can or not?"; "Coming or not?"; and "Watch TV last night or not?".

Still on the level of grammar, the local dialect, perhaps surprisingly enough, retains most of the complex personal pronoun system of standard British English, with the interesting exception of the possessive forms "mine", "yours", "his", "ours", and "theirs", which are generally replaced by "my one", "your one", "his one", "her one", "our one" and "their one" respectively; e.g. "my one is better than your one". This use of "one" is also found with the demonstrative pronouns "this" and "that", which occur in the local dialect as "this one" and "that one" respectively.

What is most characteristic of the local dialect, however, is the use of what Tongue has called "fillers" (p. 83), a term used to indicate those items of language which communicate no particular denotative meaning but which are used to indicate emotive, affective attitudes of the speaker, or sometimes simply to "fill" a pause or a moment of hesitation or reflection in the stream of speech. The most well-known of these fillers is "lah". To quote from Tongue: "The range of meanings it possesses is prodigious; depending upon the way it is pronounced, it can function as an intensifying particle, as a marker of informal style, as a signal of intimacy, for persuading, deriding, wheedling, rejecting and a host of other purposes." (pp. 114–15). Other common fillers are "ah", "what", "one" and "man". It might appear strange that a dialect which is in general characterized by simplification and reduction should also be so impregnated with fillers which do not contribute to essential communication at all. It could be hypothesized here that it is precisely because of the reduction found in the local dialect that fillers have to be resorted to, in order to make up for some of the deficiencies, as it were, but this can be no more than just a suggestion until further research is carried out into this very interesting aspect of Malaysian English. Some examples of the use of these fillers in the local dialect are given below:

> Can't remember his name *man*.
> Too late to save money *lah*.
> I can do it *what*.
> He can sing *one*.
> You like it *ah*?
> What for want to disturb *man*?
> Why not you come *ah*?
> He go there first *one*.
> Come on *lah*, let's go.
> You very clever *what*.

2.3 Trends in Malaysian English

As was asserted earlier in this paper, Malaysia is passing through a transitional stage as far as the position of English in the country is concerned. At the moment there are still sufficient numbers of the English-speaking population who tolerate no deviation from standard British English in their wider speech-form, least of all on the level of grammar. All the rules for "correct", prestigious English are adhered to closely, whether these are essential to basic communication or not. As is to be expected, more is demanded of writing than of speech in the matter of adherence to the rules of standard English grammar. However, as has been pointed out in this paper, many instances of what might have been considered aberrations in the use of English in the past are now laying strong claim to recognition as the norm in the present-day role of English in Malaysia, as these instances of deviation from standard British English increase in frequency in the language of professionals like university and college educators, lawyers, journalists, etc. Though they still attempt to use "correct" English, yet inadequate knowledge of what this "correct" English consists of and inadequate exposure to this type of English result in the many basic deviations which are met with every day, even in the educated use of the language. As such, there is quite a lot of tolerance for "aberrations" in the language, even in the wider speech-form, as far as the majority of English-speaking Malaysians are concerned. "Aberrations" are usually tolerated and overlooked as long as they do not interfere too greatly with communication purposes. This greater tolerance has come about in recent years as more and more English-speaking Malaysians are themselves less and less sure about just what the "correct" forms should be, and because more and more of these "aberrations" are being found in the language of those who can be considered to set the standard for English in the country. It is only in the English language classroom that such "aberrations", especially in grammar, are subject to correction, but much of this loses its effectiveness as more often than not the teachers themselves are no models for the "correct" English contained in the textbook or required by the syllabus.

This greater tolerance is tending to lead to a wider speech-form which is distinct from educated native-speaker English (be it British or American), phonologically, grammatically and lexically, a wider speech-form which incorporates a number of the features of the local dialect into it. This comes about as the wider speech-form is more and more localized and nativized, freed, as it were, from the constraints of standard British English within the country. At the present, indications of this can be observed in the spoken mode as many Malaysians seem to feel quite free to incorporate features of the local dialect into their wider speech-form, for all purposes in speech, formal or informal, with Malaysians or non-Malaysians. This incursion of the local dialect into the spheres of use normally belonging to the wider speech-form can be seen as the result of the fact that native-speaker-type English is beginning to feel more and more like a foreign language to the average educated Malaysian, whereas the local dialect is considered to be indigenous to the country. There will probably still be a speech continuum even in the future, ranging from a pidginized variety of English at the very bottom to near-native-speaker proficiency at the top. However, while there may possibly still be an élite at or near the top of the speech continuum, the average use of English will be somewhat short of this target, though just how far short it will be must be left to be observed and described as the distinctive character of Malaysian English becomes more visible in the future.

3 "UTILITARIAN" ENGLISH IN MALAYSIA

The preceding section has shown that several factors in Malaysia have affected and are continuing to affect the role and character of English as it is used in the country. While the factors mentioned so far have come about naturally, as it were, as a result of the context of English in the country, deliberate education policy in the schools actively encourages this trend as it now focuses on the utilitarian aspects of English, neglecting its stylistic and aesthetic features. This emphasis is due to the realization that, with Bahasa Malaysia taking over from English as the primary language of the country, there would not be sufficient time nor opportunity (nor would it be necessary) to teach English "in its entirety", as was attempted in the past. Indicative of this change in the role of English in the country is the new English Language syllabus recently introduced by the Ministry of Education for use in Forms 4 and 5 of Malaysian schools (that is, the 10th and 11th years of formal education, which begins at age six). It is called the Communicational Syllabus.

The syllabus specifies a number of language *products*, and suggests strategies for realizing these products. While specifying the product, it does not lay down the maximum or minimum level to be reached. For all practical purposes, the minimum level is simply where the communicational *intent* is successfully conveyed, irrespective of the linguistic finesse. The maximum level is, of course, native-speaker ability. The focus of attention is on whether the student manages to communicate, how effectively he does so, and how he can improve on the communication skills that he has (p. 4). The essence of the new syllabus, therefore, is communication, not correct grammar, syntax or style.

It is therefore now declared Government policy to treat and view English as a utilitarian language; a tool to be used instead of an object to be admired. However, no teacher is asked to teach his utilitarian English, for there is no description or grammar or textbook available for it. Moreover, the English language syllabus in use up to the Form 3 level is structural, teaching the finer points of English grammar like correct subject—verb agreement, the whole range of English tenses, and the correct use of determiners. Hence teachers are asked to do no more than allow this utilitarian-type English to be used by those students who can do no better, and accept their utterances which, even though they may not conform to the standards of native-speaker English, nevertheless achieve their basic instrumental function of communication.

4 PEDAGOGICAL IMPLICATIONS

The foregoing account leads to the question of whether or not a utilitarian-type English should be that variety of English taught in the schools, rather than educated native-speaker English. If it is, then many problems arise. Firstly, such a utilitarian-type English has yet to be devised or discovered or described. Thus there are practically no materials available for the language teacher to use; there are no texts and no descriptive grammars of this type of functional English. However, if, somehow, it was agreed upon that this utilitarian-type English should be that variety of English taught in the schools, then the necessary grammars and textbooks would probably be forthcoming. But the problem then remains of what to do with the few who will need to know native-speaker-type English, even in the future. It would not be pedagogically sound to have them unlearn many of the rules of their utilitarian English in order to re-learn the rules of native-speaker English. The ideal, of course, is for them to expand their grammars to accommodate the fuller forms of native-speaker English, but it would be extremely difficult to discover a utilitarian English which is at the same time amenable to expansion in the course of further learning, if necessary.

The other alternative, which appears to be that found in Malaysia at the moment, is still to adopt native-speaker-type English as that variety to be taught in formal instruction. The materials are available for this, and this will also cater for those who will, for some reason or other, either want to, or need to, know native-speaker-type English. The usual objection to this is that this alternative would involve too much wastage of valuable time and resources, in teaching the finer aspects of English which few will absorb and actually use, in the situations in which they normally find themselves. If we teach a utilitarian-type English (rather than merely allowing it to occur), so the argument goes, then will we not be able to make more effective use of the time available to us? Anyway, the proponents of utilitarian English might say, the efforts at teaching native-speaker English all these years have not proved too successful at all.

Arguments can be levelled against the choice of either a utilitarian-type of English or native-speaker English as the variety of English to be taught in the country. However, it would appear that more can be said against actively propagating (instead of merely allowing and accepting) utilitarian English as the target of language instruction instead of adopting native-speaker standards even while realizing that many will fall short of these standards, and naturally so. As a teaching goal, therefore, the aim should probably continue to be educated native-speaker English as far as possible (remembering the auxiliary role of English in the country). However, educators everywhere should be ready to be more tolerant of structures and utterances which do not measure up to native-speaker standards but which still manage to communicate nevertheless. This goal of native-speaker English as the target does not necessarily conflict with the account already given in the earlier sections of this paper of the factors which are affecting the role and character of English in Malaysia. Teachers and all others involved with English instruction in the country should be led to realize that, with perhaps most of the students learning English, there will inevitably be a gap between the target language and what is actually learnt, due to the factors affecting the role and character of English in the country. However, this would at least allow some students to go beyond mere utilitarian English, if they have the capability for this, and there will be a need for a small group of élite English speakers in the country, even in the future, to form the nucleus of English language education in Malaysia.

Moreover, this strategy would also expose the majority of students to native-speaker-type English which, though it might appear in the productive competence of only a handful of students, yet should lodge more readily in their respective competence of English. This would mean that while the majority of English users in the country might not be able to produce native-speaker-type English in their speech and writing, they should at least be able to comprehend it when they encounter it, in their reading and listening. The adoption of native-speaker English as the target of English language instruction in Malaysia will therefore provide the necessary link between average educated Malaysian English and native-speaker English. While these two varieties of the language will not be entirely identical, yet mutual intelligibility on the whole would be ensured if the speakers of a more utilitarian-type English will also be able to understand native-speaker English (through having been exposed to it) and the users of native-speaker English will be able to understand utilitarian-type English (without needing formal instruction in and previous exposure to it). This latter type of comprehension is probably more dependent on language filtering processes which seem to be inbuilt in everybody, as witness, for example, the ability of adults to communicate with children who are still in the process of learning the language. However, when the two parties involved are not adult and child but adult and adult, one who uses native-speaker English and the other a utilitarian-type English, then understanding between the two, and especially that by the native-speaker of the utilitarian-type of English, is dependent more on correct attitudes of willingness to understand and acceptance of variations. It has often been remarked that a person who chooses not to understand will never understand, while one who tries to understand will usually do so. How these "correct attitudes" are to be taught or learnt is not too clear at the moment.

5 CONCLUSION

It would not be incorrect to describe English as belonging now to the entire English-speaking world, and not only to those people who use it as their native language. The realization of this fact should serve to point out to native speakers of English that there are other varieties of English besides theirs which are used in the world today, and that no longer can everyone in the English-speaking world be expected or required to use standard British or American English. The English-speaking world can no longer be regarded as monolithic. The existence of regional standards and non-native varieties in English must be recognized and accepted by English users everywhere. Thus, English courses everywhere, in native-speaker as well as in non-native-speaker environments, should expose students to varieties of English other than standard British or American English or the regional standard of English as found in each particular country, for purposes of comprehension, though not of production. With greater tolerance and acceptance of the diversity of peoples and cultures and their own varieties of English, we can go a long way toward mutual intelligibility. At the same time, non-native speakers of English should never be made to feel ashamed of their own variety of the language, no matter how deviant it may be from native-speaker English.

8 Asian Student Attitudes towards English

Willard D. Shaw

At this point in world history, English is the pre-eminent language of wider communication. In addition to over 275 million native speakers there are millions more who speak it as a second or foreign language. It is used as a library language, as a medium of science, technology, and international trade, and as a contact language between nations and parts of nations. It is also seen as a vestige of British colonialism and as an arm of American cultural imperialism. English is all of these things and more.

Although it is taught in almost all Asian school systems, there is little information available on the attitudes of Asian students towards English. In order to gain some insights into the needs and feelings of these students and the position of English in Asia today, I conducted a survey among final year Bachelor degree students in three locations: (1) Singapore, Republic of Singapore; (2) Hyderabad, India; (3) Bangkok, Thailand. The students in each group were from the fields of English literature and teaching, engineering, and business/commerce. Over 825 students from twelve universities and colleges participated in the study. There were 170 students from Singapore, 342 from India, and 313 from Thailand.

The English language has a prominent role in the educational systems of all three countries. In Singapore it is one of the four official languages. Singapore is pursuing a bilingual policy that requires the learning of English plus one of the other three official languages. India is still continuing a thirty-year-old debate on the status of English with a large segment of the population favouring the termination of its present position as an associate official language and the establishment of Hindi as the sole official language. This debate is primarily between the northern Hindi-speaking states and the southern Dravidian-language-speaking states that favour the retention of English. Hyderabad lies geographically between the radicals of both extremes. In Thailand, English is a compulsory subject from grade five.

Data were collected by means of a closed format questionnaire that directly asked students for their personal feelings about aspects of their need for English. An English language version was given to the students in Hyderabad and Singapore. The Thais were given a translation of the same questionnaire done in Thai by the Central Institute of English in Bangkok. The sampling was done by the researcher who visited each of the countries in early 1978. The information collected dealt with five main topics:

1. The language background of the students.
2. Their reasons for studying English.
3. The pattern of their present and future use of English.
4. The English language skills they wish to develop.
5. Their opinions regarding the English language, target varieties, and the future of English as a world language.

The following discussion will take up each of these topics in this same sequence. Throughout this discussion of the data, I will refer to the three groups by nationality. This is merely for convenience sake and does not mean that I am proposing that these data describe the attitudes of entire nations. They do, however, give an accurate description of the views of the target groups in the cities surveyed.

I   WHO WE ARE

The respondents were final year Bachelor degree students averaging in age from a low of 20.4 years in India to a high of 22.1 in Thailand. Despite variations in the place of English in their curriculum, they all averaged around 14 years of English study. 64 per cent of the Singaporeans and 67 per cent of the Indians reported attending English-medium high schools. 98 per cent of the Singaporeans and 94 per cent of the Indians said they were attending an English-medium college or university. The Thai group presented a much different picture. Less than 2 per cent reported attending an English-medium high school and only 5 per cent said that the main language of their college was English. Most of this 5 per cent came from the group of English majors who receive instruction in English. There are no English-medium colleges in Thailand.

Responses to questions concerning their personal English language backgrounds revealed almost the same pattern of differences. Half of the Singaporeans and 38 per cent of the Indians claimed that English was one of the languages used at home when they were children. Only 2.9 per cent of the Thais made the same claim. 18 per cent of the Singaporeans and 6.5 per cent of the Indians claimed that English was the first language they learned to speak. Some may have interpreted the question to mean the first language they learned in a school setting. However, 40 Singaporeans (23.5 per cent) maintained that English was used at home at least 50 per cent of the time when they were children. Eleven of these people (3.6 per cent) said it was used at least 90 per cent of the time. 46 Indians (6.7 per cent) felt it was used at least half of the time while 2.1 per cent estimated that it had been used more than 90 per cent of the time. When asked to name the language they now know the best, 59 per cent of the Singaporeans and over 46 per cent of the Indians designated English. These percentages seem high; however, the statistics do seem generally to reflect the situation in those countries. Many students do have an excellent command of English and for a large number of them it may be their best language for a number of purposes.

The situation was much different among the Thais. Less than 3 per cent reported that English was used in the home when they were children. The same amount felt that English was their best language while only one person out of 313 said that English was the first language he learned.

Although there were vast differences in the amount of exposure to English between the official-language countries and the foreign-language one, there was very strong agreement among all three groups on one aspect of their background: the presence or lack of parental encouragement for the study of English. 77 per cent of the Singaporeans, 70 per cent of the Indians, and 68 per cent of the Thais said that they had received such encouragement. Not a single respondent out of 825 said that he had been discouraged.

II WHY WE STUDY ENGLISH

To discover the motivating forces behind their study of English, the students were presented with a list of twenty-five possible reasons for studying another language and were asked to rate each one on a scale of one to five from "definitely my reason" to "definitely not my reason" thus indicating the extent to which it was one of their personal reasons for studying English. For the sake of brevity I will only discuss those reasons rated in the top and bottom quarter by each group. Both the Singaporeans and Indians listed the same five reasons among their six most popular ones. Those five reasons are given below along with the percentages of respondents in each group that favoured or rejected that reason as one of their own. Since there was a neutral choice, the two figures do not add up to one hundred per cent.

    (a) I studied English because I will need it for my work.
        Singaporeans: 95/4   Indians: 94/3   Thais: 86/7
    (b) I studied English so I could talk to native speakers of English for business/educational reasons.
        Singaporeans: 78/15   Indians: 74/16   Thais: 92/5

(c) I studied English so I could talk to other foreigners for business/educational reasons.

Singaporeans: 75/18   Indians: 66/21   Thais: 87/6

(d) I studied English because it is required in our system.

Singaporeans: 90/9   Indians: 80/13   Thais: 63/30

(e) I studied English because I believe that a knowledge of another language will make me a better person.

Singaporeans: 71/19   Indians: 71/15   Thais: 33/54

The Singaporeans (90/7) rounded out their top six by claiming that they had studied English in order to get a good job in their country. The final reason for the Indians (81/15) was the desire to use English as a link language in order to "talk with people in my own country whose language is unknown to me".

The Thais also gave high marks to the use of English with native and non-native speakers for business/educational reasons and for general work purposes. Their other three top choices were:

(f) I studied English so I could talk to native speakers about general things.

Singaporeans: 70/23   Indians: 62/24   Thais: 88/7

(g) I studied English so I could talk to other foreigners about general things.

Singaporeans: 70/19   Indians: 60/24   Thais: 86/8

(h) I studied English so I could study in a foreign country.

Singaporeans: 54/35   Indians: 45/40   Thais: 79/14

Just as interesting as the most popular reasons for studying English are the reasons which were ranked at the bottom of the list of twenty-five. Four reasons were placed in the bottom six by all three groups. They were:

(i) I Studied English because I like the countries in which English is spoken.

Singaporeans: 14/76   Indians: 33/52   Thais: 15/68

(j) I studied English because I like the people who are native speakers of English.

Singaporeans: 8/75   Indians: 30/56   Thais: 15/74

(k) I studied English because I plan to travel to non-English-speaking countries someday for my work.

Singaporeans: 11/69   Indians: 16/63   Thais: 18/69

(l) I studied English because it will help me to think and behave as native speakers do.

Singaporeans: 14/63   Indians: 29/59   Thais: 10/81

What is most striking about the rankings of the reasons is that many of the top rated reasons are the ones generally associated with the instrumental type of motivation while most of the reasons rejected by sometimes overwhelming majorities in each country epitomize the kind of integrative motivation that has been stressed as being crucial for second language achievement. In looking at the latter group of reasons, however, it is important to note that these students are not stating how they feel about the English-speaking countries and peoples. They may or may not actually like them. What they are saying is that an affinity for them was not a reason for their study of English. They are also emphatically saying that they are not learning English so that they can change themselves and become more like native speakers. There is a chance that they might also be projecting a view that English does not always have to be considered in reference to the native-speaking countries. Perhaps they see English as a bona fide international or international language which is not inseparably connected to any particular countries.

At the very least I think that these data should reopen the question of the reality and applicability of the whole instrumental/integrative dichotomy. If, as many believe, India and Singapore maintain a generally high standard of achievement in the learning of English, can this success have been the result of instrumental motivation alone? If an integrative motive is still deemed necessary, must it always be in terms of a native-speaking group or can it be interpreted to also mean a desire to become a member of a local English-speaking élite? Or does the point become a moot one when the vast majority come to use English for many of the same purposes as their mother tongue, as in Singapore? Once a country has an active policy of teaching everyone that language in order to make it the major language of the country, are these questions about motivation for learning English as nonsensical as if they were directed to an American child? It appears that this whole area is open for intensive discussion especially in reference to situations like those in India and Singapore.

III THE PEOPLE WITH WHOM WE USE ENGLISH

The Present

Now that we know the general reasons why these students study English the next step is to find out the types of people with whom they use it. In order to get a general picture of the English language environment for each group, the questionnaire presented them with a list of people and asked them to report on the frequency with which they speak English with these people in an average period of two months. Once again the same division occurred between the foreign-language and official-language situations. In every case the Thais reported speaking English less often than their counterparts in the other countries. The responses of the Indians and Singaporeans were very similar as can be seen in Table 8.1.

Table 8.1. The frequency of use of English in an average span of two months

	Many Times Daily 1		At Least Once/Day 2		At Least Once/Week 3		Very Rarely 4		Never 5
Fellow Countrymen:									
Family Members				S	I				T
Friends			SI				T		
Students			SI				T		
English Teachers	I		S			T			
Other Teachers			I	S					T
Govt Officials				I	S			T	
Businessmen					SI				T
Link Language[1]				I	S				T
Foreigners:									
Native Speakers				S		I	T		
Non-native Speakers					S	I		T	

[1] Fellow countrymen whose language you don't know.

Thailand

In general the Thais very rarely speak English. Their highest frequency of use was with English teachers but even this was very low. It therefore seems that English plays a very small part in their daily life and is not essential for their functioning. Because the question had a time frame of two months a low frequency may also indicate a lack of contact rather than the use of some other language in that context. This is probably the major cause for the small amount of use with foreigners.

India

English plays a much more important part in the life of an Indian student. It was the medium of instruction for 94 per cent of them, hence the high frequency of use with teachers and fellow students. They also reported the highest frequency of use of English as a link language. Unlike the Thais, use with foreigners is not as high as with fellow countrymen.

Singapore
The overall average for the use of English reported by Singaporeans was slightly more than the Indians, but the difference was not statistically significant. They did use English with family members much more than any other group. Given Singapore's multi-ethnic composition, it is surprising that the figures for the use of English as a link language are not higher than reported here. Their greater use of English with foreigners is probably due to the greater opportunities for meeting foreigners in this small but tourist-rich state.

The Future

All of the students were required to learn English at some point in their academic careers. In order to see if they would continue to use this knowledge once they had graduated and taken a job, the respondents were asked to anticipate the future and estimate how often they expected to use English with a similar list of people. In terms of overall use, all groups reported significant increases in its frequency of use. No decreases were noted although for some categories no significant increases were predicted.

Table 8.2. The use of English in the future

	Many Times Daily 1	At Least Once/Day 2	At Least Once/Week 3	Very Rarely 4	Never 5
Fellow Countrymen:					
Family Members		S	I		T
Friends	SI			T	
Fellow Workers	S	I	T		
Supervisors	SI			T	
Teachers		I S		T	
Govt Officials		IS		T	
Businessmen		S	I	T	
Link Languages¹		IS		T	
Foreigners:					
Native Speakers		S I	T		
Non-native Speakers		S	IT		

¹ Fellow countrymen whose language you don't know.

The pattern of increases was very much the same for Indians and Singaporeans. Both foresaw dramatic increases in the use of English with government officials, businessmen, and with fellow countrymen as a link language. They also envisaged a greater amount of use with family members, friends, and supervisors. The Thais also predicted a general increase in their use of English but the frequencies foreseen were still not very high. The greatest increase among local groups was with businessmen.

The most dramatic increases for all three nationalities were seen as coming in relationships with native speakers. Singaporeans and Indians predicted they would be using English around once a day with native speakers. The Thais saw themselves using it about once a week. Very significant increases were also shown for contacts with other non-native speakers. These great increases are probably attributable to corresponding increases in the amount of contact with foreigners.

It is apparent from the figures given above that there are major differences between the amount of English used in India and Singapore, on the one hand, and Thailand on the other. In the two countries where English has the status of an official language and where it is often used as a medium of instruction, we see many similarities in the pattern of English use. Students use English in and out of class and with their family and friends as well as their teachers and classmates. Their use of English with these people is much more than with foreigners. The English language occupies a legitimate place in their society and helps a person to function in that society.

The situation in Thailand is quite different. Except for their English teachers, Thai students presently speak English more often with foreigners than with fellow countrymen. In looking towards the future they envisage no significant increases in its use with family members and friends. The big increase will come in its use with foreigners. This dichotomy between the intranational and international use of English was most clearly outlined in a final question on the use of English. The students were asked to rank four groups of people in order of importance vis-à-vis the use of English. The statement is given below along with the rankings assigned by each nationality.

It is important for me to speak English so that I can talk to:

	Singaporeans	Indians	Thais
(a) my fellow countrymen in specific social or business situations	1	1	3
(b) fellow countrymen who do not know my first language	2	2	4
(c) native English speakers	3	3	1
(d) non-native speakers from other countries	4	4	2

The results of these rankings clearly emphasize and summarize all of the more detailed statistics that came before. The official-language situations are marked by the dominance of English for intranational purposes over international ones. Even though English is crucial for the international sphere, it is seen by the students as being even more important to them for its domestic uses. For Thailand the situation is the opposite. The importance of English lies in its usefulness for international communication, especially with native speakers.

IV WHAT WE WANT TO LEARN

Before examining the types of English skills that the students feel are most important, it would be appropriate to find out what they think of their present abilities after almost fourteen years of study. The students were asked to rank the four skills in order of their own command of those skills. The overwhelming choice of all three groups for their best skills was reading. Every group also identified speaking as its worst skill. Table 8.3 shows the order in which the skills were ranked as well as the percentage of respondents labelling that skill as their best or worst.

Table 8.3. The rankings of the four skills

Singapore			India			Thailand		
Skill	% Best	% Worst	Skill	% Best	% Worst	Skill	% Best	% Worst
1. Reading	75	10	1. Reading	73	9	1. Reading	81	8
2. Listening	55	17	2. Listening	50	30	2. Writing	39	31
3. Writing	36	45	3. Writing	38	38	3. Listening	39	42
4. Speaking	33	47	4. Speaking	25	59	4. Speaking	30	62

When asked to name the one skill that they wanted to be their best, all three groups picked speaking. 88 per cent of the Thais and over 71 per cent of the Indians and Singaporeans mentioned speaking. If these statistics are a true reflection of reality, there is a great difference between what the students want and what they are getting from their English classes.

In order to get more specific responses from the students, they were asked to rate a number of detailed skills in terms of their importance to them. The Indians and Singaporeans gave positive ratings to all fifteen of the skills while the Thais only ranked ten as being important All three groups ranked the same three skills at the top of their lists although the ordering of each group was different. These three skills are listed below along with the percentages of respondents judging them eitheir important or unimportant.

(a) Being able to write papers, reports, and business letters in English.
   Singaporeans: 97/2   Indians: 89/2   Thais: 76/4
(b) Being able to read textbooks, reports, articles, etc. in English.
   Singaporeans: 97/3   Indians: 95/2   Thais: 87/1
(c) Being able to talk with native speakers of English in work situations.
   Singaporeans: 95/1   Indians: 83/5   Thais: 89/1

Just as we saw in their earlier rankings of the reasons, the three groups show the greatest preference for the utilitarian uses of English. The work situation is always rated more important than its contrasting social situation. Listening to the radio and television is more important than watching English films. Reading texts is more important than reading English literature and writing business letters is valued more than the ability to write personal letters. There is a continual emphasis on the instrumental uses of English over the integrative ones.

V WHAT WE FEEL ABOUT ENGLISH

We now have some idea of why these students learn English and the types of skills that they wish to cultivate. We also have a good idea of their present use of English and the people with whom they are planning to use it in future. Now we will examine how they feel about the language itself. We shall look at their attitudes towards English and their estimates of what the future holds for the language. We shall also see what variety of English they wish to learn and what variety they think now holds sway in their country.

Much has been made of the love–hate relationship between the citizens of former British colonies and the English language. English is appreciated for its usefulness in a modern world, but it is deprecated as the language of imperialism. But if these students are to be believed, the present relationship is characterized more by love than by hate as we can see by their responses to the following statements:

(a) Of all the foreign languages I could study, I like English the best.

	% Agree	% Disagree	% Neutral
Singapore	57.8	4.8	37.4
India	74.1	8.6	17.3
Thailand	63.5	12.2	24.3

(b) I don't really like English, but I speak it because it is useful.

	% Agree	% Disagree	% Neutral
Singapore	17.3	64.3	18.4
India	17.3	68.1	14.6
Thailand	13.1	68.7	18.2

(c) If English were NOT taught in our schools, I would NOT try to learn it.

	% Agree	% Disagree	% Neutral
Singapore	11.2	70.3	18.5
India	22.4	59.8	17.8
Thailand	8.0	78.6	13.4

These results show that English is not an imposed burden to the majority of students. This majority says that they would make an extra effort to learn English even if it were not a required subject and most of them seem to have an attraction for the language that goes beyond its immediate usefulness. Unlike their forefathers, they don't seem to feel that English is a distasteful necessity that they would rather do without if possible. This is not to say that they would continue to study English if it were as useless as Latin, but that English has lost much of its colouring as a colonial legacy. Perhaps they are looking at it in terms of the future and not the past.

In considering the future role of English in the world, most of the students are sanguine about its prospects. 50 per cent of the Thais, 64 per cent of the Singaporeans, and 74 per cent of the Indians feel that English will continue to be used as a world language even if the United States and Great Britain lose their social, economic, and political power. Apparently they believe that English has attained a position in the world that is much more solid than the base upon which it was built. English is moving away from the status of a national and colonial language to that of a true world language. There may already be more non-native speakers of English than native speakers. As the ratio widens, English increasingly becomes a language belonging to those who use it and not just to those who claim it as their mother tongue.

This growth in the numbers of non-native speakers is bound to continue if these students are an indication of what lies ahead. Tremendous majorities in the Thai (87 per cent), Indian (89 per cent), and Singaporean (94 per cent) groups maintain that they will make sure that their children learn English well. It is obvious that they feel a knowledge of English will be beneficial for their children. In fact a large majority in each group felt that "most of the people in the world will know English in the distant future". 70 per cent of the Indians, 76 per cent of the Thais, and 78 per cent of the Singaporeans felt this way. Such a great expansion in the use of English will not be through conquest, as before, but through increased trade and contact between nations and the world's need for a lingua franca for this developing international marketplace and society. Another difference in this period of expansion will be that many of the proponents will be non-native speakers. At present there are Egyptians in Kuwait and Indians in Yemen working as

English language programme advisors. English no longer belongs to its originators. It has become the property of the world.

If the rest of the world is to participate in this establishment of English as the premier world language, many difficult questions will have to be answered. One of the most important will revolve around the variety of English that is to be taught. In order to get the opinions of the 825 respondents, they were given a list of five varieties of English and asked to choose the one that was spoken by educated speakers in their country. The five choices were: (1) British English; (2) American English; (3) Australian English; (4) unique to my country; and (5) like educated non-native speakers from other countries. The percentages of students choosing each variety are presented in Table 8.4.

Table 8.4. Variety of English presently spoken by educated speakers

	Singaporeans %	Indians %	Thais %
1. British	40.5	27.4	6.5
2. American	6.0	3.2	28.1
3. Australian	0.6	0.0	0.0
4. Unique	42.3	50.6	40.3
5. Others	10.6	18.8	25.1

The Singaporeans were almost evenly divided between describing the English used by their educated speakers as akin to British English or a variety unique to Singapore. Half of the Indians felt that a form of Indian English was prevalent while more than a quarter of them felt that British English was closer to the norm. The Thais were quite divided in their efforts to describe the present situation. The strong responses for British English in Singapore and India and for American English in Thailand no doubt reflect the historical relationships of those countries. The number of people voting for the nebulous category of a variety "like educated non-native speakers from other countries" is very interesting. It may simply have been the safest choice for those who had no idea of how to categorize the present situation, but could it also be that many felt that it represented a form of international English that transcended national borders?

If this is what these students feel about the English language situation in their country at the present time, what do they feel should happen in the future? They were asked to complete the sentence, "I think that we should learn to speak English . . ." with one of the following choices: (1) like the British; (2) like the Americans; (3) like the Australians; (4) in our own way; and (5) like educated non-native speakers from other countries. Table 8.5 gives their responses.

Table 8.5. The variety that we should learn to speak

	Singaporeans %	Indians %	Thais %
1. British	38.3	28.5	49.1
2. American	14.4	12.0	31.6
3. Australian	0.6	0.3	0.3
4. Own Way	38.9	47.4	3.5
5. Others	7.8	11.8	15.5

The Singaporeans are equally divided between accepting a British standard or a unique one of their own making. A plurality of Indians is definitely in favour of propagating their local variety. The Thais are solidly behind the propagation of a native-speaker norm with British English receiving the greatest amount of support. It is in this comparison of native-speaker versus non-native-speaker standards that we can see some possible trends in the choice of a target variety. Table 8.6 compares the totals of the figures given for these two types of standards in the descriptions given by the students of the present English language situation as they see it, and their estimate of how they would like to see the situation develop.

Table 8.6. Comparison of percentages choosing native and non-native standards

	Present			Future		
	Sing.	Indians	Thais	Sing.	Indians	Thais
Native	47.0	30.6	34.5	53.3	40.9	80.9
Non-native	53.0	69.4	65.5	46.7	59.1	19.1

A purely statistical interpretation of the figures in Table 8.6 would have to point out the possibility of a trend away from the status quo and towards a native-speaker standard. The most extreme case is Thailand where only 35 per cent describe educated Thai English as similar to a native variety while over 80 per cent agreed that such a variety should be the desired model. Concurrently there are fewer people aiming for a non-native variety than there are claiming that a non-native variety is now the norm. Looking at the figures in this light one must conclude that the present situation is not satisfactory to some people and that these people would welcome the adoption of a native-speaker model.

However, to look at these figures in terms of the shifting of percentage points is to miss the outstanding message that these statistics convey. For hundreds of years the native-speaker standard has ruled supreme as the only conceivable goal for a foreign language learner. Yet in 1978 we see 59 per cent of these Indian students and almost 48 per cent of the

Singaporeans naming non-native varieties as the ultimate goal for language learning. One must consider that these figures are indicative of a trend towards the acceptance of local models of English and that this trend is much more of a possibility than any sort of movement towards a native standard since the latter formerly had the unquestioning support of almost everyone. This support is still very strong in countries like Thailand but has been sharply eroding in nations like India and Singapore where English is used for intranational as well as international purposes. It is a possibility that those figures may symbolize a veritable revolution in opinion.

VI CONCLUSIONS

It is often said that statistics can be made to prove whatever you want to prove. Much of the actual data was presented in this paper so that the readers could draw their own conclusions. My interpretation of it leads me to make the following general observations.

1. Given the dichotomy in the type of answers given by the Indian and Singaporean students on the one hand and the Thai students on the other, it is obvious that there is great value in using the international/intranational distinction in order to describe various English language situations. Although almost all countries would be using English for international purposes, the number of nations using it within their own culture would be much smaller. The degree of its use for both purposes would probably also show great fluctuations.

2. The reasons for studying English and the skills desired are overwhelmingly the ones normally labelled instrumental. The generally high level of English ability observed in the intranational countries seems to throw doubt on the hypothesis that integrative motivation is essential for achievement in second acquisition. At least the whole aspect of integrative motivation should be re-examined in terms of a desire among learners to join an indigenous group of English language speakers or a vague international one rather than a group of foreign native speakers.

3. The future growth of the use of English seems to be a certainty if these students maintain the same opinions in the years ahead. They now plan to use it more often themselves and they plan to have their children learn it too. They also foresee an expansion in its use throughout the world. Its status as a world language is growing.

4. A major factor aiding this growth will be the decolonization and indigenization of English. It is now seen less as a symbol of imperialism and more as a viable candidate for the world's most important international language. It is also becoming viewed as a local language by those using it for intranational purposes. There is an increasing

acceptance of these educated forms as varieties to be supported as much if not more than native varieties. This movement will have important repercussions on the way English is taught in the non-native-speaking countries. It also raises the question of its effect upon the mutual intelligibility of these varieties.

5. As the number of non-native speakers grows and as they increasingly come to accept English as one of their own languages and not a tool borrowed from someone else, the future of English will become less and less controlled by the native-speaker arbiter in areas outside his homeland. It is often said that the British gave the English language to the world. Perhaps the time has come when the world has finally decided to fully accept the gift.

9 Questions in the Negotiation for Understanding

Ruth Crymes and William Potter

INTRODUCTION

Though people speak of exchanging thoughts and ideas, it is in fact impossible to do so. People engaged in discourse exchange utterances, with accompaniments such as sighs, laughter, grimaces, and gestures, which are apprehended by listeners to some indeterminate degree within the context of some fit between life experiences.

The question that we address is: Granted that the chief strategy that people use to cope with the ambiguities of communication is by *assuming* understanding, are there also strategies for *pursuing* understanding? We ask this question about participants in a particular kind of discourse—a discussion with an externally imposed focus—and we look at one particular kind of understanding—the participants' understanding of their fellow participants' ideas about the topics under discussion.

We are looking for uses of language which manifest such strategies; that is, we are looking for language—in this case English—in the pursuit-of-understanding function. We ask if the language used for the pursuit of understanding correlates in any principled way with identifiable features in the discourse or in the situation or in both, and if so, if it does so in the same or different ways for native and non-native English speakers. With English increasingly used as an international language, it seems to us important to explore how non-native as well as native speakers shape its use in discourse.

This paper will present some tentative findings on native and non-native-speaker use of questions in the pursuit of understanding. We will argue that the specific ways that the questions are used in the pursuit of understanding correlate primarily with the questioner's role in the discourse. We are thus working in the area of discourse analysis in the sense that we are trying to find relationships between language form and language function and to identify elements in the situation which influence the form/function relationship. We would call our investigation a sociolinguistic one and place it within the framework laid out by Hymes (1962).

SUBJECTS AND DATA COLLECTION

Our twelve subjects were three groups of ESL specialists: four non-native English speakers (NN = non-native speakers) who had known each other about six months, one each from Burma, Fiji, Korea, and Thailand, in mid-career, three participating in an East–West Center professional development programme and one a doctoral student in linguistics; four native-speaker faculty members from the University of Hawaii ESL Department in mid-career (NM = native speakers in mid-career) well known to each other and comparable in professional status with the four non-native speakers; and four native-speaker graduate teaching assistants at the beginning of their careers (NB = native speakers at beginning of career) doing MA level studies in the University of Hawaii ESL Department, three of whom had known each other for about nine months, the fourth being a newcomer one month preceding the discussion. The NMs were three men and one woman; the NBs and NNs each were two men and two women. The NBs teach English language skills to non-native speakers; the NMs and NNs are engaged in teacher training, administration, and curriculum development. The NNs had, in addition to their six-month stay in Hawaii, all spent other time studying abroad, two in the mainland United States and two in England. All four had excellent command of English.

We asked each of these three groups to meet as a working committee. We assigned them a task which required discussion of set topics with the goal of reaching a consensus on each topic. The data that we analysed were tapes of these discussions.

The discussions were staged. We told our subjects that we were interested in comparing the ideas of international (in this case, Asian and Pacific) and American ESL specialists on selected pedagogical practices. To stimulate discussion, we borrowed a type of values clarification exercise (Simon, Howe, and Kirschenbaum, 1972: 252–4) and gave it ESL content. It was a questionnaire listing five statements about what an ESL teacher should do (e.g. Teachers should expect students to read aloud with good pronunciation). There were four possible responses to each statement: Strongly Agree (SA); Agree Somewhat (AS); Disagree Somewhat (DS); and Strongly Disagree (SD). Such a questionnaire is of course deliberately designed to forestall "no opinion" responses. See Appendix 9.1 for a copy of the questionnaire.

Our procedure was to set up a one-hour meeting with each of the three groups at which one of us was present to give instructions and to take care of the taping. We withdrew from the interaction after giving the instructions. The instructions were for each person to respond independently and privately to each of the statements, to compare answers with each other, to mark for discussion those on which there was no consensus, to spend about five minutes thinking about their own responses to the statements so marked, and then to discuss the statements and attempt to reach a consensus, changing the wording of the original statements as appropriate to reflect their consensus. We suggested a maximum time limit of five minutes for the discussion of each statement. We told the participants not to spend any time in writing out their final positions. We said that we would do that, getting our information from the tape.

Our analysis is based on the discussions of all five statements, as there was no initial consensus on any of them by any of the three groups. The NNs spent 28 minutes about equally divided among the five statements. The NMs spent only 12 minutes and spent most of that on the first and fifth statements. The NBs spent 26 minutes, also with disproportionate time on the first and fifth statements.

METHOD

We first transcribed the data following the system of Sacks, Schegloff, and Jefferson (1974), and in our subsequent study of the data we worked back and forth between the transcripts and the tapes. Intonation and tone of voice were crucial to our understanding of what was being said. Also, one of us had been present at each discussion, and so we had some memory of our understanding of what had gone on at the time.

From examining the data we concluded that there were two obvious strategies for pursuing understanding: one was for speakers to use statements to summarize their perceptions of what another had said and the other was for speakers to ask questions of one another. We decided to examine questions, since their variation in form gave us a linguistic point of departure. We think that analysis of the statements would require a discourse point of departure, and our analysis of the discourse structure of these discussions is at present extremely sketchy and intuitive.

We identified questions both on the basis of their having question form, using our own linguistic and communicative competence to fill in ellipses and interpret malformations, and on the basis of finding an answer. We marked for study only those questions which in our judgment related to the substance of the topic under discussion. We did not concern ourselves with rhetorical questions or questions about how the discussion was or should be proceeding. We then classified each question on the basis of its function, its place in the discourse and the role of the questioner. From there we proceeded to look for form/ function correlations and for relationships between those correlations and discourse position and questioner role.

FINDINGS AND DISCUSSION

We found 30 substantive questions, 12 in the NM data, 10 in the NB data, and 8 in the NN data. On the basis of their use in the interaction, we identified 4 question functions:

1. *Open* questions, seeking information.
2. *Leading* questions, helping another formulate or clarify his or her own ideas, helping the group reach a consensus, or seeking confirmation of another's ideas.
3. *Challenges*, indicating disagreement with another's expressed ideas, and, if carefully attended to, serving to provide information about the beliefs of the questioner.
4. *Softened assertions*, stating one's belief or understanding and at the same time seeking confirmation of it from the others.

We distinguished two questioner roles, that of *discussant* and that of *middleman*. Another role, that of traffic controller, was not directly relevant to our investigation. All participants in the discussions were by definition discussants. All discussions had at least one person who assumed the role of middleman. The middleman oversaw substantive matters; the traffic controller, procedural matters. The middleman spoke not in the engaged voice of the discussant but in the detached voice of the intermediary.

We concluded that only participants in the role of middleman asked leading questions. Indeed our definition of middleman has come to be that he or she is the person who is asking a leading question—though the middleman does other things, too, like summarizing the ideas of others, which lie outside the scope of this investigation. The other three kinds of questions were asked by participants in their role as discussant.

We identified, in a very rough and intuitive way, three parts to the discussion of each of the five topics: the beginning, which we have called the *presentation*, the middle, the *exploration*, and the end, the *accommodation*.[1] We think that these may be exchanges in terms of Sinclair and Coulthard (1975), but we are not sure. We found only one question in our data the analysis of which depended on locating it in the discourse. We will return to this point below.

In Appendix 9.2 are excerpts from the tapescripts of all three group discussions containing a sampling of the thirty questions and our classification of them in terms of form, function, role of questioner, and position in discourse. The beginning of each group's discussion is included, and we have tried to provide enough of each discussion to suggest the flavour of it.

In looking at form/function correlations, we found some WH questions that were open, some polar VS questions that were leading, some polar elliptical (SV?) questions that were challenges, and one (of two) affirmative tags with *right* that was a softened assertion (see left column below). But we also found WH questions that were leading, polar VS questions that were challenges, and one polar SV question that was a softened assertion (see right column below).[2]

WH, open (W$_1$NM)

►G. Well if you two had them read aloud, in the first place, what would you expect?

C. Oh I'd try for uh, well I don't know if I would uh, I would have em read aloud.

W. °Yeh, but uh, you wouldn't expect them to, =

C. °Yeh.

W. = °read aloud.

Polar VS, leading (P$_5$NM)

►G. (Well) would you put it in their way? Would you put, new vocabulary in their *way* so they'd *have* to learn? (2 sec.)

W. No. I wouldn't.

WH, leading (W$_2$NM)

Q. I think grammatical explanations will help our students learn a foreign ⌈language.⌉

→ O.   ⌊What⌋ level of instruction do you have in mind when you say that?

Q. U:h.

O. Like at the begin, beginner's level or intermediate level?

Q. Intermediate level.

O. I see.

Polar VS, challenge (P$_4$NMB)

M. Uh, I don't know. I don't really agree with this *building* block theory, yaknow, that you start, after you have this then you put this on top and that on top I think it's much, more a, scatalogical, process which is going on lots of directions and you *learn* what you need. (3 sec.)

→ T. Do you think something that unfocused there's really learning taking place?

M. Mmhmn. Sure. ⌈Look at uh the =

B.   ⌊   ) natural language]

M. = number of peo]ple who learn languages wi ⌈th*out* going to =

B.   ⌊Without, sure, yeh]

M. = school] you know,

Polar SV(?) (*elliptical*),
challenge (P₁NM)

G. Yeh, well I I uh dis-
agree somewhat because
uh if they're reading
aloud there must have
been a purpose for it
in the first place. And,
uh I'm not sure that I
would have them read
aloud much but if
they're doing it [C.
Laughs] there must be
a reason.

→W. But with good pronun-
ciation? (Does ⌈n't)]
[Laughs]   ⌊
G.   ⌊Yeh,
that,] that could be a
reason.

*Affirmative tag, softened as-
sertion* (P₇NM)

W. . . . I'm, en- envisioning the idea of- the
ideal classroom, where
students interact and
learn English, and
whatever they needs
they have, they'll learn,
that vocabulary right?
[Laughs]
C. Wrong.
[All laugh]

Polar SV, softened assertion (P₂NB)

B. And I'm willing to ch, switch it to
"strongly agree," too. [Female
laughter]
M. Because I can't see any uh,
Vocabulary it seems to be like
yk- now one of the *ma:jor* [B.
Mmhmn.] *problems*, you know,
and I can't see any reason *not* to.
B. In other words these restricted
books in the beginning where they
have- a *limited* vocabulary like if
you have a beginning class, [M.
Mmhmn.] uh, the're several series
that have very limited
⌈ vocabularies.]
T. ⌊ Seven hundred wor ⌈ds,]
twelve =   ⌊
(N.)   ⌊Guided
vocabulary.]
T. = hundred] words,
B. Yeh.
M. Hnh.
→ B. And that ch you- think that right
from the beginning there should
be a beefing up of the
vocabulary?
M. Attention drawn *to* it. Uh I don't
think you have to use controlled
materials.
B. Yeh, OK.

In seeking an explanation for this lack of form/function fit, we noted first that it is in the nature of a polar question that it can contain all the constituents of an assertion and of a WH question that it cannot. We would like to propose that the questions which we have examined represent a cline from softened assertion to no-assertion questions (see Figure 9.1).

FIGURE 9.1 Cline from softened assertion to no-assertion

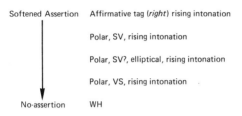

When we line up question forms along this cline and note the functions that we have identified for each, we get the display in Figure 9.2, where we also indicate the number of each kind of question asked by each group.[3]

FIGURE 9.2. Form/function correlations.

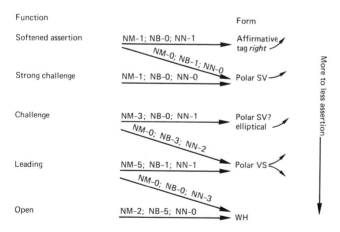

In Figure 9.2 the horizontal arrows indicate the expected correlations and hence might be considered unmarked. Downward arrows indicate the unexpected, or marked, correlations. The marked correlations show a systematic downshifting of the function from the expected form to the form which is down one step on the cline, which is one step less assertive.

The downshifting of Leading to WH and Challenge to Polar VS appears to result from the desire of the questioner to be less assertive. But the downshifting of Softened Assertion to Polar SV does not fit that characterization (see P_2NB above). It was at this point that we looked to the position of the question in the discourse for a clue. P_2NB occurs in the accommodation period. A challenge could occur in this period, but if it does, it either goes unanswered or else exploration is reopened. Neither happens here. So P_2NB is not a challenge. But it does make sense to view it as a softened assertion. Further, the questioner is assuming the role of middleman, the only example we found in the data of a middleman asking other than a leading question. Hence position seems the crucial determinant of function. This is the only evidence that we found in the data of the relevance of position to function.

We can make the following observations about the form/function correlations displayed in Figure 9.2.

1. Of the 30 questions asked by all 3 groups in 66 minutes (12 by NMs, 10 by NBs and 8 by NNs), 11 were challenges, 10 were leading, 6 were open, and 3 were softened assertions.

2. Only the NNs and the NBs used *downshifting*. 5 of the 8 NN questions were downshifted and 4 of the 10 NB questions were downshifted.

3. The NBs used the most *open questions* (half their total—5 out of 10) and the fewest leading questions (1 out of 10). They used 1 softened assertion and 3 challenges, all 4 of these downshifted.

4. The NNs used the most *leading questions* (half their total—4 out of 8). They used 3 challenges, all downshifted, and 1 softened assertion.

5. All three groups used proportionately the same number of *challenges* (about one-third of the total) but only the NBs and the NNs downshifted them. The only strong challenge was used by the NMs.

6. Each group used one *softened assertion*. Only the NBs downshifted.

To try to account for these different ways of exploiting the available resources in language, we need to look at the roles of the questioners more closely. We summarize these in Figure 9.3, also showing there the number of questions asked by each participant and the function of each.

To the information in Figure 9.3 about the roles of discussant and middleman we need to add information about the role of traffic controller, which we mentioned earlier as being only indirectly related to our investigation. The traffic controller, it will be recalled, manages procedural matters. In all three groups the person that self-selected himself or herself to speak first assumed the role of traffic controller by so doing. For the NMs it was C, who retained that role throughout with

FIGURE 9.3. Questioner roles and question functions

	Subject	No. of questions and functions		Role of questioner and no. of questions asked	
NM	C	Leading	1	Middleman	1
		Challenge	1	Discussant	1
	W	Challenge	1	Discussant	2
		Sof. Asser.	1		
	R	Challenge	3	Discussant	3
	G	Leading	4	Middleman	4
		Open	1	Discussant	1
NB	M	Open	1	Discussant	1
	T	Challenge	1	Discussant	1
	N	Challenge	1	Discussant	3
		Open	2		
	B	Leading	1	Middleman	2
		Sof. Asser.	1		
		Challenge	1	Discussant	3
		Open	2		
NN	L	Challenge	2	Discussant	2
	O	Leading	4	Middleman	4
		Sof. Asser.	1	Discussant	2
		Challenge	1		
	Q	No questions			
	F	No questions			

minimal assistance from the others. For the NBs B was the first traffic controller but later the role was shared about equally by all four members of the group. For the NNs O was the first and only traffic controller.

Taking into account both the distribution of the traffic controller role as narrated above and the middleman role as displayed in Figure 9.3, we make the following observations:

1. With the NMs and NBs the two managerial roles of middleman and traffic controller were assumed by different people; with the NNs they were assumed by the same person.

2. The NBs assumed the middleman role the least. Though our display does not reveal it, the tapescript shows that the NBs often worked communally to put utterances together.

3. All four of the NMs and all four of the NBs asked questions. But only two of the four NNs did so. The sole middleman/traffic controller was one of these two. Further, this person asked six of the eight questions.

CONCLUSIONS

The main conclusion that we have come to in this investigation is that the participants in these focused discussions did not make very extensive use of questions to pursue understanding. In 66 minutes only 30 questions were asked for that purpose. Challenges (eleven) and leading questions (ten) each accounted for one-third of this total. As we have already suggested in our characterization of the question functions, challenges can throw light on the beliefs of the questioner, since they can be viewed as concealed assertions. Leading questions are sometimes simply probes for known answers, though they may at times also help the respondent formulate and clarify his or her own beliefs. Of the seven open questions, two were answered evasively (W_1NM and W_2NM), and one was restated as a yes/no question before it was answered (W_4NB). The evasive answers turned out to be clues that there was a mismatch between the ways the questioners and respondents were interpreting the statement under discussion. The ones that were answered directly shed light on the perceptions of the respondents.

With so few subjects and such limited data we cannot tell if the differences between the groups lie only in the individuals who happened to comprise them or if those individuals typify at least to some degree their age group, their professional group, their cultural group— meaning by cultural group American contrasted with non-Western, predominantly Asian—or other groups of which they might be members. We presume that the differences derive from both sources, but we do not know how to sort them out.

There *are* differences. We have already pointed out that the NNs had one person in control of both procedural and substantive aspects of the discussion. Only this person and one other asked substantive questions, the former asking six and the latter two. The NNs' discussion was the most firmly managed of the three.

The NBs' discussion was the least managed. Among the NBs the person who asked the most questions (five as compared to one, one, and three for the other three) was also the initial traffic controller and performed minimally as middleman. But for the most part the four members of the group shared managerial responsibilities and worked communally to reach agreements. Half of their ten questions were open, and their three challenges were downshifted. There seems to have been a clear effort on everyone's part not to "take over", either procedurally or substantively.

The NMs struck a midpoint between the NNs and NBs. They had one person who was the primary traffic controller and another who was primary middleman. The role of middleman was assumed proportionately less often by the NMs than by the NNs. Their challenges were not downshifted, as were those of the NBs and one of their challenges was a strong one.

All three groups used the same language resources but they used them in different ways. We think that in discussion groups made up of both native and non-native speakers of English both could benefit from some understanding of how the other uses the language for the pursuit of understanding.

NOTES TO CHAPTER 9

1. We believe that a focused discussion is a kind of discourse that has at least a beginning and an end. It may also have a middle. During the beginning, *the presentation*, the topic is stated and each participant indicates his or her position and the reasons for it. In effect they all put their cards on the table. We did not count a presentation to be ended until everyone's position was known. The middle, that is, the *exploration*, then proceeds and continues as long as the participants are trying to find out more about the ideas of others or are trying to elaborate their own ideas. Once their minds have met as much as they are going to, they come to the end, the *accommodation*. This may result in a consensus, real or *pro forma*, or in a decision to agree to disagree or just in throwing in the towel. After efforts at accommodation are under way, exploration may be re-introduced and the cycle picked up from there.
2. S = subject; V = verb. In the parentheses, W = WH question; P = polar question; NM = native speaker in mid-career; NB = native speaker at beginning of career; NN = non-native speaker; subscripts = question number in order of occurrence in tapescript.
3. Incorporated into the numbers in Figure 9.2 are three seeming departures from the system presented there. We explained them away as follows: (1) One polar SV question (P_6NM) was not a challenge but a leading question. But it was a repetition of a preceding leading question that *was* polar SV. Hence, the presence of repetition may explain the departure. That is, it may explain the occurrence of SV instead of the expected VS; (2) There were two *how about* questions in the data. *How about* questions are special cases. The explicit question simply focuses on a topic: *How about SOMETHING*: There

is, in addition to the explicit question, an implied question, which may be either a polar or a WH question: *As for SOMETHING, VS?* or *As for SOMETHING, What VS?* We have classified the two *how about* questions in our data (P_2NN and P_2NM) as polar questions because in context they were paraphrasable as polar questions.

APPENDIX 9.1:   QUESTIONNAIRE—PEDAGOGICAL PRACTICES IN ESL

Circle the response which most closely indicates the way you feel about each item.

SA = Strongly Agree
AS = Agree Somewhat
DS = Disagree Somewhat
SD = Strongly Disagree

Teachers should
1. expect students to read aloud   SA   AS   DS   SD
   with good pronunciation.
2. emphasize vocabulary acqui-   SA   AS   DS   SD
   sition from the beginning.
3. make a lot of use of dialogues.   SA   AS   DS   SD
4. give grammatical explanations   SA   AS   DS   SD
   to their students.
5. teach simple structures before   SA   AS   DS   SD
   complex ones.

APPENDIX 9.2: EXCERPTS FROM THE TRANSCRIPTS

Text 1. Native speakers—mid-career (NM)

Topic: "Teachers should have students read aloud with good pronunciation."

C. Number one. I'm uhs, a strong disagreer.

W. I, I strongly disagree, too ( ) expect students to read aloud with [good pronunciation.]

G.   [°Disagree somewhat.]

C.   [W is a] disa just a DSer.

G. Yeh, well I I uh disagree somewhat because uh if they're reading aloud there must have been a purpose for it in the first place. And, uh I'm not sure that I would have them read aloud much but if they're doing it [C. Laughs] there must be a reason.

P₁NM W. But with good pronunciation? (Does [n't] [Laughs])

G.   [Yeh, that,] that could be a reason.

W. Yeh, oh.

G. But uh. I'm not in favour of reading aloud in the the first pl[ace,]

C. [Right,] for starters.

W. Yeh.

C. That's:

G. So that's why I'm, I'm a "disagree somewhat" [R takes es-

P₁NM

Form: Yes/no, elliptical, rising intonation, prefaced with *but*, probably SV order

Position: Presentation

Questioner and Role: W as discussant

Addressed to: G

Answered by: G

Function: Challenge

Note: W accepts G's answer in the sense that she confirms that he did mean what he said.

sentially the same position as G—that though he himself would not have students read aloud he assumes that teachers who do must have some purpose in doing so and that work on pronunciation might be that purpose. W and C make it clear from their responses to G and R's reasons that they don't think good pronunciation has any relevance to reading. But the two sides don't seem to have it clear that W and C are associating the reference to reading aloud with a reference to the reading process and G and R are associating it with oral production.]

W₁NM G. Well if you two had them read aloud, in the first place, what would you expect?

C. Oh I'd try for uh, well I don't know if I would uh, I would have em read aloud.

W. °Yeh, but uh, you wouldn't expect them to, =

C. °Yeh.

W. = °read aloud.

P₂NM R. Never? Can't think any circumstances under which you'd have, people read aloud?

W. Oh, maybe uh, you know "What sentence you got there" f- for [teaching- writing.]

P₃NM R. [How about poetry?]

W. Oh no. I wouldn't uh,

R. Poetry shouldn't be, said aloud? read aloud?

C. [Performed] aloud.

W. [Mm.] The idea of *good* pronunciation is the part, particularly—[Laughs] (you'd say uh), correcting their pronunciation all the time.

W₁NM
Form: WH (*what*)
Position: Exploration
Questioner and Role: G as discussant
Addressed to: W and C
Answered by: W and C—evasively
Function: Open
Note: W and C found the question meaningless. A challenge by R to W follows.

P₂NM
Form: Yes/no, Elliptical, rising intonation Two related questions; both probably have underlying SV word order.
Position: Exploration
Questioner and Role: R as discussant
Addressed to: W
Answered by: W
Function: Challenge
Note: W makes small concession; R continues his challenge.

P₃NM
Form: Implied Yes/no (*how about*)

Position: Exploration
Questioner and Role: R as discussant
Addressed to: W
Answered by: W
Function: Challenge
Note: W's answer leads to further challenge by R.

R. *I didn't say anything about correction. I's just =*
W. Well.

W_2NM

Form: WH (*how*), interrupted = How do you ensure good pronunciation?
Position: Exploration
Questioner and Role: C as discussant
Addressed to: R
Answered by: R, who counters with a rhetorical question, which he answers
Function: Open
Note: Question is rejected by R as invalid G goes on to summarize the source of their disagreement.

W_2NM C. Well, how do you ensure-
R. = expect them to. [All laugh] What's good-
W. (Yeh) expect em to be good anyway.
R. Good to me is understandable.
G. Yeh. Well it seems two things are mixed up. You know, if you're teaching uh pronunciation, you're uh probably not at the point where you're going to have them read aloud anyway. It seems as though the two things are, out of focus. [They conclude by agreeing to "Disagree Somewhat" with the original statement, one of the few instances in all three groups that a consensus was couched in negative form.]

Topic: "Teachers should emphasize vocabulary acquisition from the beginning."

[All have agreed somewhat except W. W is the first to present reasons.]

W. I said "Disagree Somewhat." Uh (2 sec.) Mm. (5 sec.) Well, I don't know, I, hm, I feel that tuh they'll learn, what they need to learn. Now-"from the beginning," I don't know. That's the hard part but, (3 sec.)

P_5NM G. (Well) would you put it in their way? Would you put, new vocabulary in their *way* so they'd *have* to learn? (2 sec.)

W. No. I wouldn't.

P_6NM G. You wouldn't, deliberately (do anything about it)?

W. No, of course I'm, en- envisioning the idea of- the ideal classroom, where the students interact and learn English, and whatever they needs they have, they'll learn, that vocabulary

P_7NM rights? [Laughs]

C. Wrong.

[All laugh]

W. OK. I guess you do have to- I don't know-
  [I think emphas, *emphasize* it,] =

C. [Yeh:: I guess, kills it.]

W. = *emphasize* vocabulary acquisition.

R. R. Mm.

W. (°I wouldn't do it.)

[R then points out that in his personal experience he felt handicapped by not knowing words and so he believes vocabulary should be emphasized. C says that he had interpreted the statement to mean that teachers should help students learn how to acquire words, not just give word lists. W says that she can go along with that.]

P_5NM
Form: Yes/no, inverted, falling intonation
Position: Presentation
Questioner and Role: G as middleman
Addressed to: W
Answered by: W
Function: Leading, to help W formulate her thoughts
Note: W's answer leads to G's repeating the question.

P_6NM
Form: Yes/no, SV word order, falling intonation
Position: Presentation
Questioner and Role: G as middleman
Addressed to: W
Answered by: W
Function: Leading, seeking further

confirmation of W's ideas

Note: This is a repeat in different
words of P_5

P_7NM

Form: Affirmative tag (*Right?*) Rising
intonation

Position: Presentation

Questioner and Role: W as discussant

Addressed to: Group

Answered by: C

Function: Softened assertion

Note: W knows the others probably
won't agree with her.

Text 2. Native speakers—beginning career (NB)

Topic: "Teachers should expect students to read aloud with good
pronunciation."

B. Uh (2 sec) for the- questions first of all how did you interpret
them? For what level? 'K did you lump them all together under one level er, when you were, thinking of these items?

M. No. I didn't. I was thinking (3 sec) ah of various levels, um,
that, generally there's a, can be a purpose, hmn? for any, of
these, that's I really didn't strongly disagree, in the sense, of
excluding anything, cuz I think uh there's something, within
each one that tuh, can fulfill a certain, function.

B. Yeh, but I think it would determine like if you were have talking about a beginning class it would determine (2 sec.) if you were talking about a- a beginning class whether you used dialogues or not, as compared to an advanced or intermediate class.

T. Yeh I think the responses to these would- cuz I was thinking of, OK like- when I've had students like a junior high level, I would tend to, feel more strongly about some of these as being important to that level [M. Mmhmn.] as compared to the ELI students now.

M. Mmhmn.

B. Yeh.

T. So I don't know if the're that many =

B. °That we can make- °That you could-

T. = general statements that we can make.

B. Maybe we can put in, qualifiers.

M. Mmhmn.

B. What did everyone have for one?
   [T strongly disagrees; N and M somewhat disagree. N thinks that there might be a place for some oral reading. B then poses the following question to the group.]

P₁NB   B. But dya think 'st oral reading has a place, even in, [M. Mmhmn.] a reading class?

M. Well I think, like my interpretation was that tuh, to expect students to read aloud with good pronunciation that tuh, I would, use that, specifically, as a pronunciation exercise, *not* as a reading exercise.

B. Uh.

P₁NB
Form: Yes/no, inverted, rising intonation, prefaced with *Dya think*
Position: Presentation
Questioner and Role: B as middleman
Addressed to: N and possibly M

Answered by: M
Function: Leading, to help N and M straighten out their ideas
Note: We know that B thinks their ideas need straightening out from her own position, which is expressed later.

T. Or a [communic]ation exerci[se.]
M. [But I] [I think,] by using uh, you know a text, and uh you know you can kind of get into a uh, some intonation patterns uh, various things that, again, just for this *purpose* of pronunciation.

B. I think reading is entirely different from speaking, and that, I don't see reading being any, use at all er uh oral reading.
[The ensuing exploration of the topic is mainly about situations where pronunciation might be dealt with through reading. In the end they agree on the disassociation of reading and pronunciation but say that there may be aspects of pronunciation that can be handled through reading.]

Topic: "Teachers should emphasize vocabulary acquisition from the beginning."

T. Emphasize vocabulary acquisition from the beginning. Let's see we both: what, what did you,
[N and M say strongly agree and T says agree some-what.]

B. And I'm willing to ch, switch it to "strongly agree," too.
[Female laughter]
Because I can't see any uh, vocabulary it seems to be like yknow one of the *ma:jor* [B. Mmhmn.] *problems*, you know, and I can't see any reason *not* to.

B. In other words these restricted books in the beginning where they have- a *limited* vocabulary like if you have a beginning class, [M. Mmhmn.] uh, the're several series that have very

limited [vocabularies.]
T.   [Seven hundred [wor]ds, twelve =]
(N.)   [Guided vocabulary.]
T. = hundred words.
B. Yeh.
M. Hnh.
P₂NB B. And that ch you- think that right from the beginning there should be beefing up of vocabulary?
M. Attention drawn *to* it. Uh I don't think you have to use controlled materials.
B. Yeh, OK.
[Discussion ends shortly with agreement to strongly agree].

P₂NB
Form: Yes/no, SV word order, rising intonation, prefaced with *you think*
Position: Accommodation
Questioner and Role: B as middleman
Addressed to: Group
Answered by: M
Function: Softened assertion, serving as a summary of B's understanding of the groups position.
Note: M offers a refinement of the summary. Consensus was easy on this topic. There was no exploration of the topic.

Topic: "Teachers should teach simple structures before complex ones."
[The group spends considerable time trying to decide what "simple" and "complex" mean. Examples of "complex" structures are given.]
T. But, but things like passive voice or participials er, that's something that, they would really need, several years of, of

living in an English-speaking community to really become fluent. I think at *that* level, either in speaking or writing (3.5 sec.) so that's not the kind of problem that you really worry that mu]ch about.

M.   Well in a =]

M.   = I think frequency, uh would have a, a, a bearing. We use, certain, complex structures, frequently (2 sec.) and I think uh, those should be, made, available, soon.

W₃NB B. °Like what?

M.   (°I don't think I can think of one.) [Laughter] But uh: relativization. Uh, really, [B. Rel, uh]°in a sense uh. Of course that's pretty much in writing though yaknow? I'm not so sure, we use them that much in speaking.

[Discussion continues about 2 minutes with differing points of view on how much structures should be controlled.]

M.   Uh, I don't know. I don't really agree with this *building* block theory, yaknow, that you start, after you have this then you put this on top and that on top I think it's much, more a, scatological, process which is going on lots of directions and you *learn* what you need. (3 sec.)

P₄NB T. Do you think something that unfocused there's really learning taking place?

M.   Mmhmn. Sure. [Look at uh look at the number of peo]ple =

B.   [( ) natural language]

M.   = who learn languages wi [*thout* going to school] you know,

B.   [Without, sure, yeh.]

(2 sec.)

W₃NB
Form: WH elliptical (*what*)
Position: Exploration
Questioner and Role: B as discussant
Addressed to: M
Answered by: M
Function: Open

P₄NB
Form: Yes/no, inverted, rising
        intonation
Position: Exploration
Questioner and Role: T as discussant
Addressed to: M
Answered by: M
Function: Challenge

M. Well OK, language class. And the number of people who *don't* learn, by going to language class.

T. Mhm. But peo- but motivation factor's tremendously different though. [M. Mhm. Mmhmn.] I mean you could study Japanese here for three years and probably not be able to, to speak it very well at all but if you spent a year in Japan, [M. Mmhmn.] cuz the moti [vation-

M.   [Where you' re]
    bombarded with complex structures right from the start-

W₄NB N. How do you know it's the complex structures, though?

M. Hmn?

N. Being in, uh, the person who learns a language, not in a classroom, uh can we be sure that he's picking up on the complex structures first? Er, maybe *he's* building up from

P₅NB   simpler structures? [B. Yeh.] I mean he hears the simple structures first and then, builds on those. I don't- [M. Mhm.] U:h I don't know. I would- question whether or not- you hear the complex things and, and learn them first.

M. Mmhmn. Well, I, you know, I don't think, there doesn't *seem* to be any pattern to the way people, learn, eh?

N. That's: debatable [I guess.]
                       [But- yeh.]

    [Discussion about how people learn continues. The group finally concludes that they can't reach a consensus because they can't come to any agreement about what is simple to learn and what is hard to learn.]

W₄NB
Form: WH (*how*)
Position: Exploration
Questioner and Role: N as discussant
Addressed to: M
Answered by: M, who requests restatement
Function: Open

P₅NB
Form: Yes/no, inverted, rising intonation
Position: Exploration
Questioner and Role: N as discussant
Addressed to: M
Answered by: M
Function: Challenge
Note: Restatement of preceding question, which was WH in form.

Text 3. Non-native speakers —mid-career (NN)

Topic: "Teachers should expect students to read aloud with good pronunciation."

O. OK then. We'll go down the list then. It's about ( ).

( ). (   )

O. Let's look at item number one. "Teacher should expect students to read aloud with good pronunciation." I have selected DS: "disagree somewhat."

Q. I have selected, "agree somewhat."

L. I have strongly disagreed.

F. Uh we agree, "a- agree somewhat."

O. In the first place you know this "agree somewhat" and "disagree somewhat" I think are s ⌈imilar = ⌉
⌊Similar,⌋ that's right.

Q. = similar. Have the same connotation =

O. = because we're hitting for a mid-point.

L. Yeh.

L. Uh huh. Maybe they ⌈just run together.⌉
⌊You see, "disagree somewhat]" it's⌋

O. going to be fi- be a matter of fifty fifty.

L. ⌈That's right.⌉

F. ⌊Uh, uh,⌋I- I kinda have reservations for this particular thing. I know I, I went through that and uh one of my teachers encouraged me to uh to read aloud you know, and so, few times I've read a whole book, you know, aloud and that helped speech.

L. That's [true but with- with good pronunciation. That's =

O.   [Reading aloud, yes, but with good pronunciation- =]

L. = *another* thing.]

O. = That is the-

F. Uh, uh.

O. Uh, OK. Carry on with your reasons.

F. And uh,

O. That's why you agree somewhat.

F. Yes.

    [The discussion goes on about two minutes; everyone pre-
    sents reasons. O is pushing for a consensus.]

O. Yeh, so the point is, shall we se- settle on AS or shall we
    settle on DS [sighs]. SA and SD are out of the question
    now, =

F. Hm, you see-

O. = to arrive at a consensus.

F. Right [because] the problem the problem is- =

L.   [Right.]

F. = that in your countries you don't stress uh oracy wh-
    whereas we stress [O. Yes.] oracy. And I see this as,

O. So that's why you agree, so you are uh, you have a positive
    attitude towards that, that's what you are saying, whereas we
    have a, a bit of a negative attitude.

L. Right.

F. And I've seen myself in my own society, it was not a bad
    thing.
    (3 sec.)

O. I mean it's *not* harmful.

P₁NN L. It's *not?*
O. Even though it is not uh, ok we all settle, AS. What do you say.
L. No but the thing is [it,] it can be quite a waste of time to- =
( ).   [( )]
O. Yeh?
L. = this reading aloud and then correcting the pronunciation and then the interest of your student will be shifted to the, pronunciation.
[The group finally concludes that reading aloud with good pronunciation was not possible with large groups anyway, and so they give up trying to reach a consensus.]

Topic: "Teachers should emphasize vocabulary acquisition from the beginning."
[All state their positions. L is the first to give her reasons.]
L. The reason I strongly agree to that is because uh probably is my level of instruction as well, [the] students- =
O.   [Yeh.]
L. = are supposed to acquire as much vocabulary as they can-
P₂NN O. How about the phrase "from the beginning?"
L. Hm?
O. The phrase "from the beginning".
Q. "From the beginning".
L. Yes- when I [say-] beginning =
O.   [from the beginning] =

P₁NN
Form: Yes/no, elliptical underlying SV order, rising intonation
Position: Accommodation
Questioner and Role: L as discussant
Addressed to: O (?)
Answered by: Not answered
Function: Challenge
Note: O is concerned with reaching a consensus. L presses her point and re-opens the discussion.

P₂NN
Form: *How about.* Implied polar (What does "from the beginning" mean? Does it mean "from the beginning of your level"?)
Position: Presentation
Questioner and Role: Q as middleman
Addressed to: L
Answered by: First O, then L
Function: Leading
Note: O interrupts L while she is giv-

O. = of your level.
L. = of my level of teaching [of teaching] not from the beginning =

                [oh:::]

Q.
L. = of English teaching.

Topic: "Teachers should give grammatical explanations to their students".

    [All state their positions. L is the first to give her reason.]

O. OK L. Your reasons.
L. I guess my reason is:: because I'm teaching rather *remedial* English and what- what we usually end up doing is uhm trying to help our student unlearn all the bad habits, and one way to do it is try to give them some, some grammatical explanation so that probably,

    [we hope migh-]

P_3NN O. [Well, you see, uh] I want to ask a question which may have nothing to do with the discussion but, do you think it has *helped* your students a lot to have s- =

L. It does, [it does-]
O.   [= to get a better] grasp of [the]
L.   [Yes] especially with certain contrastive analysis of the two languages, for example the [use of ( )]
O.   [But in that] case you're thinking in terms of the level of the students you are [teaching.]
L.   [Right,] right.

---

ing her reason. He gives the answer to the question before she does.

P_3NN
Form: Yes/no, inverted, mid-intonation, interrupted, pre-faced with *do you think*.
Position: Presentation
Questioner and Role: O as middleman
Addressed to: L
Answered by: L
Function: Leading, to help L formulate her position.
Note: L answers affirmatively and goes on to elaborate.

W_1NN
Form: WH = Yes/no "Would you give grammatical explanations at the beginning of teaching?"
Position: Presentation

W₁NN O. What would be your opinion, of giving grammatical
explanations at the, initial stages ⌈of teaching.⌉
⌊No⌋ not at all I

L.   don't ⌈think that.⌉
               ⌊You would⌋ strongly disagree then.

O. No, I would strongly disagree.

L. No, I would strongly disagree.

O. So you're you're speaking in terms of the level of your ⌈L.
Right.⌋ learners. Yeh?

L. I guess all my answers here ⌈because I have decided to =
O.   ⌊Yes, of course ( ) yeh related

to your-⌋

L. = base my answers on-⌋

O. °Q.

Q. I think grammatical explanations will help our students
learn a foreign ⌈language.⌉

W₂NN O.   ⌊What⌋ level of instruction do you have in

mind when you say that?

Q. Intermediate level.

O. I see.

Q. Intermediate level. °Yeh. But I don't want to spend too
much time =

O. No ⌈you wouldn't.⌉

Q.   ⌊= with gr⌋ammatical explanations.

O. No.

Q. That's why I uh agree somewhat.
[The discussion continues for some time. F (Disagree
Somewhat) and O (Agree Somewhat) set forth their po-

Questioner and Role: O as
    middleman
Addressed to: L
Answered by: L
Note: Question is answered "no" like
    a yes/no question.

W₂NN
Form: WH (*what*)
Position: Presentation
Questioner and Role: O as
    middleman
Addressed to: Q
Answered by: Q
Function: Leading, to help Q clarify
    that meaning

sitions at considerable length. No consensus is ever reached. They comment that they think the questionnaire was a deliberate device to evoke different responses.]

10 International Communication and the Concept of Nuclear English

Randolph Quirk

International communication—an indisputable desideratum—does not presuppose, let alone prescribe, a single international language. But it has long been held as virtually axiomatic that this would constitute the ideal basis. For over a century,[1] and especially in the past quarter-century, we have come to believe that this goal is within reach, with English rating a greater world spread than any other language in recorded history. Yet within the past decade, many people have started to wonder: people concerned with international affairs in general as well as members of the profession engaged throughout the world in teaching English.

The doubts have been arising on two grounds:

(a) the degree of variation in the forms of English in use—fears, indeed, of its rapid dissolution; and

(b) the practicability—not least in view of (a)—of teaching the language, especially on a mass scale, to the level required for international usefulness, given the enormous deployment of educational resources that this demands.

The divergence between one man's English and another's is great enough to be striking (though hardly, I think, alarming) within each of the English-speaking countries. The steadfast Anglo-Saxon opposition to academy-style attempts at standardization has harmonized in recent years with an educationist's orthodoxy discouraging interference with a child's most local and intimately felt language. The absurdities of an earlier generation's preoccupation with "correctness" have been abandoned, and in some places the pendulum has swung to a position where quite extreme permissiveness has been actually encouraged. Where this trend has coincided with political movements towards community identity (as with "Black English" in the United States), counter-standard policies have become especially radical without anyone—so it seems to me—having much clear perception of the long-term implications.

Naturally, in this context, the divergence between one *country's* English and another's is seen to be in danger of growing much more seriously wide, with no common educational or communicational policy even theoretically applicable, but rather with nationalism strongly (if haphazardly and even unconsciously) endorsing a linguistic independence to match political and other aspects of independence. The voices of Australia and New Zealand and the Irish Republic (as heard for instance on the national radio) are as limited to purely intranational norms as are those of Britain and the United States. I shall say something later of centripetal influences, not least in the name "English" being applied confidently to all these varieties. But it would be idle to pretend that the name itself is adequate guarantee of linguistic integrity or that the varieties of English used in Britain, America and Australia are more unified than the varieties of "Scandinavian" used in Norway, Sweden and Denmark where each is regarded—and named— as a separate language.[2]

Diversity within English is liable to be much greater, however, and to lead to far more acute problems in those countries (such as India, Nigeria, the Philippines) where English is not a native language but where it nevertheless has widespread use for administrative, commercial and other internal purposes. Here, in contrast to the native English-speaking countries where the language—in whatever variety— is naturally acquired, English has to be formally taught; and here therefore the question of standards is actively and often agonizingly debated. Since the teaching has to be done by teachers who had similarly to be taught the language and who inevitably learnt it to varying degrees of adequacy, change in the acceptable standards of achievement is not surprisingly very rapid. In any case, in a vast country like India, with a long history of English for internal communication, the natural processes of language–culture interaction have produced a large number of phonological, grammatical, lexical and stylistic features that have become thoroughly imbued and arguably inalienable (cf. Kachru, 1976b). Indeed, with an estimated 25 million people making regular use of the language, India is the third largest country in the world with English established as a medium for internal purposes.

It is from this that there springs (by the imperfect analogy with British English, American English, and the like) the concept of recognizing Indian English as a comparable national variety with its own internal determinants of acceptability, however much it may be seen historically as largely derivative from British English (cf. Strevens, 1977: 133, 140). Clearly, the range of English in India (from the pidginized dock-worker to the government clerk, to the judge, to the voice of All-India Radio) is very much greater than the nearest analogy in Britain or America—as well as sharply different in kind. Clifford Prator[3] is prominent among those who have argued that it is fundamentally unsound to encourage the recognition of non-native varieties of English. But so far as the sub-continent is concerned, the insightful researches of such specialized observers as Braj Kachru leave me convinced that it is not a matter of heresy but of accepting plain facts.[4]

Yet the facts are unquestionably daunting. We are confronted in the world by three, largely independent (and largely uncontrolled, if not uncontrollable), potentially limitless types of diversification within English. If we concede, with current educational orthodoxy, that the individual benefits by seeking community identity through repose in his most local variety of language, can we afford to neglect the same individual's needs in a wider role—ultimately as a "citizen of the world"? And what can be done, in this connection, to mitigate the growing despair of the teacher with day-to-day classroom concerns—not least in the English-speaking countries themselves, but of course far more acutely in countries teaching English as a foreign language and (with the present world's demands) on a mass scale?

Teaching any single one of the national varieties (say "standard southern British" English) is a hard enough assignment. With its gargantuan vocabulary, its subtly difficult syntax, and with the recently accentuated emphasis on teaching phonetic accuracy in speech, the language is difficult enough for a specially trained native speaker to teach with small classes of highly motivated pupils. But in the vast majority of classrooms all over the world, the teacher is not a native, his English is far from perfect, his training has been seriously inadequate, his classes are by no means small, and—partly as a result of all these factors—his pupils have by no means an automatically high motivation. Add to this an examining system that is seriously at variance with classroom goals and we clearly have a potentially disastrous situation even before we grapple with the fact that the initial postulate is in doubt. Can the teacher's model be "any single one of the national varieties"? And if so, which? And what guarantees can he (or his education authority) have of the international acceptability of that variety, now, or in fifteen years? Is the colossal allocation of national resources to the teaching of English worthwhile?

Now of course all this is to take a very black look at the black side of things. Such pessimism may be quite unjustified. Developing countries may get richer and be glad to maintain or even increase their contribution of GNP to teaching English. Better provision may be made for teacher training. Better methods of teaching English already in existence may be more widely implemented: and still better methods may yet be devised. We now have better dictionaries and grammars of English than we have ever had, and we are developing techniques for sensitizing learners to national and stylistic varieties of English and for helping them meet a predicted range of communicative needs. We are beginning to think more realistically of the goals in language learning, and especially about whether it is reasonable or even responsible to seek achievement in a foreign language of all the skills we master more or less effortlessly in our native language.

Again, the diversity of English in the world may not in fact be leading to dissolution into several distinct languages. I am among many observers on record as seeing powerful centripetal, unifying forces at work, offsetting the fissiparous tendencies that local needs and nationalist susceptibilities are fostering (cf., for example, Quirk, 1972, 1978). Thanks in no small measure to a traditional spelling system which ignores the passing of the years as it transcends the vagaries of pronunciation, books and newspapers use a virtually identical English whether they originate in Bloomsbury or Baltimore, Canberra or Calcutta.[5] As regards the spoken language, too, we must not ignore the impact of radio, television, film, faster travel, and even the wide access to the same pop songs. These factors are certainly making the different varieties familiar and comprehensible to increasingly large numbers of people, and to an observable degree as between British and American English at least, they seem to be causing productive usage to limit its variation.

But let us stay with the black side—not in any spirit of alarmist masochism but to look prudently for alternative strategies if our worst fears prove to be well-founded. What happens to English in the world (or—in due succession to English—any other language of international currency) if teaching the full language proves too costly, if new techniques of teaching turn out to be disappointing, if the natural process of language diversification effectively shatters the linguistic goal? Do we then abandon hopes for the universality of English? Do we switch to some other language in which there is less inhibition about proclaiming a single world standard? Do we abandon the democratic ideal of teaching English on a mass scale and swing instead to educating an élite small enough to make the teaching effective? Or do we abandon the idea of an international language altogether and contemplate a future of linguistic frontiers manned by faceless simultaneous translators?

It is in this context that some of us have been taking a fresh look at what linguistic theory may be able to provide. Now of course linguistics has been much involved in the turns and twists of language description and language teaching for a couple of generations, and many look upon its contributions with something less than enthusiastic gratitude. Many indeed attribute a large part of current disillusion to the intervention over the years by successive waves of brash "experts", at one and the same time advocating doctrinaire rigour in various fashionable methodologies and squishy permissiveness in goals, norms and standards. But we need not throw away the bath water because we do not think the babies' faces are shining. Part of our trouble is that linguistics and the social sciences in general have remained at the data-gathering, model-building and speculative stage comparable to that of physics in the eighteenth century. In part also, no doubt, the emphasis in the current climate of opinion on environmental and cultural conservation is inhibiting our getting to the manipulating stage—manipulating the medium, that is (e.g. through planned simplification[6]), rather than only the learner. No doubt we have been rightly apprehensive of the danger of filling our green valleys with dark satanic linguistic mills. But it seems to me that the time has come to enquire whether linguistics and its sister disciplines are now mature enough to direct their insights not only to language description as hitherto but also to something more like language design.

For the purposes of this enquiry, let me ask that the following propositions be regarded as axiomatic:

(1) The world needs a single medium for international communication (*needs* is important and implies willingness to pay the price—educational, social, cultural, even financial).

(2) The possibility of a wholly new or artificially constructed "language" has been excluded.[7]

(3) The only viable possibility is either (a) to adopt or (b) to adapt one of the world's natural languages: the starting point must be a linguistic force with existing momentum.

(4) The best current candidate for (3) is English.

Bearing in mind the black picture I have seen fit to paint, however, one further assumption is required, namely that (3a) has been tried with dismal results and prospects. I thus postulate a situation in which we are left with (3b), and I would like to explore some of the questions that would be involved in adapting English (or of course any other language) to constitute a nuclear medium for international use.

To satisfy the relevant need, "Nuclear English" would have to possess certain general properties. It must be:

(a) decidedly easier and faster to learn than any variety of natural, "full" English;

(b) communicatively adequate, and hence a satisfactory end-product of an educational system; and

(c) amenable to extension in the course of further learning, if and as required.

Communicative adequacy is to be understood as providing the learner with the means of expressing, however periphrastically, an indefinitely large number of communicative needs (in principle, all), with the minimum of ambiguity, the limit being imposed by his personal concerns and his intellectual capacity and not by the capacity of the medium. As to (c), extensibility may be thought of in terms of "English for Specific Purposes" modules—which would thus entail the property (independently required in any case) of the lexical and grammatical content being fully explicit, so that the "fit" of additional modules may be exactly predicted. But extensibility should also be seen in terms of less programmed skill-acquisition towards fully natural English in any major national variety, and this in turn entails that, since nothing should have to be "unlearned", the lexical and grammatical properties of Nuclear English must be a subset of the properties of natural English (presumably of the "common core", in the sense of Quirk et al., 1972: 1.15).

Both (b) and (c) are obviously vital in their own right. But they are vital also in anticipating misunderstandings about the nature and role of Nuclear English.

Culture-free as calculus, with no literary, aesthetic, or emotional aspirations, it is correspondingly more free than the "national Englishes" of any suspicion that it smacks of linguistic imperialism or even (since native speakers of English would also have to be trained to use it) that it puts some countries at an advantage over others in international communication. Since it is not (but is merely related to) a natural language, it would not be in competition for educational resources with foreign languages proper but rather with that other fundamental interdisciplinary subject, mathematics. Nor, by the same token, could its teachers be accused of wasting resources (as sometimes happens, distressingly, with foreign languages and literatures) on an élitist disciplinary ornament for the few. The relations of Nuclear English are less with the ivory tower than the public convenience.

Equally, however, (b) and (c) make clear that Nuclear English can carry no such stigma as that frequently perceived (however unjustly) in relation to basilect forms of English or the pidgins of tropical seaports. It is not a matter of offering a second-class language to the masses of the twenty-first century where the élite of the nineteenth and twentieth were privileged to have English in all its storied splendour, metaphysics and all. The emblematic consumers of Nuclear English should not be seen as Indonesian children in a village school room, but as Italian and Japanese company directors engaged in negotiating an agreement.

Reluctantly ignoring issues in the lexicon[8], let me ponder a little on seeking appropriate nuclei in grammar. It might, for example, be decided that the English tag question (so often in the English of Wales and of Southeast Asia replaced by the invariant *isn't it?* or *is it?*) was disproportionately burdensome, with its requirement of reversed polarity, supply of tensed operator and congruent subject:

I'm late, *aren't I?/am I not*?
She used to work here, *didn't she*?
They oughtn't to go there, *ought they*?

For all of the italicized pieces, whose function as a response promotor is arguably worth retaining, we could achieve the same objective with *isn't that right*? or *is that so*?, in full English a perfectly acceptable expression though of course a minority one (except as shortened to *right* in AmE).

Or again, there is arguably no need for non-restrictive relative clauses, many of which are in any case semantically inexplicit:

I chatted with the captain, who was later reprimanded.
I expressed my sympathy to the captain, who had been
    reprimanded.

If these mean, respectively,

I spoke to the captain and *as a result* he was (later) reprimanded.
I expressed my sympathy to the captain *because* he had been
    reprimanded.

it would do no harm to say so and at the same time rid us of structures that could be misunderstood (especially in writing) as restrictive clauses. Nor need we retain in Nuclear English the option to construct noun clauses or restrictive relative clauses with "zero" particle ("He was afraid she was hurt", "The man she loves"), and with non-restrictive clauses gone we could generalize *that* as the single invariant particle for relative and noun clauses.

A further example: we need non-finite constructions with certain verbs like *cause* which will almost certainly (unlike perhaps *condescend* and *assist*) remain in the nuclear lexicon: "He caused the experiment to fail". But we could exclude this construction where it was merely optional for a *that*-clause and hence banish the multiply ambiguous "They expected a doctor to examine John" (the more readily so if, in addition, the lexicon admitted *expect* in only one of the conventional senses).

In none of these instances, it will be noticed, does the "solution" lie in going beyond the rules of ordinary acceptable English. But equally noteworthy: for none has the proposed solution any bearing at all upon frequency of occurrence in ordinary English. If anything (as we shall see below with modal auxiliaries), the most frequent items are those that are most to be excluded from Nuclear English since they are the most polysemous. Rather, the solution must lie in a principled mediation between (a) the grammatical structure of ordinary English and (b) a language-neutral assessment of communicative needs. The order here is vital: the starting point must be (a), not (b). If we adopted the converse, we might for example seek a number system going beyond the existing two terms ("singular" and "plural") to include a third ("dual") in view of the large number of items in human experience that go in two's (eyes, thumbs, feet, parents, etc.). An additional inflection (parent *sg*, parenten *dual*, parents *pl*) would enable us to avoid the ambiguity that is common in sentences like:

The permission of parents is required.

(Does each child need to get permission from both parents or will the permission of only one be sufficient?) Needless to say, such a proposal would infringe one of the basic properties of Nuclear English (that it should contain nothing that had to be "unlearned" by the user who proceeded to any extension beyond it) and would therefore be rejected.

The starting point must therefore remain firmly in the grammar of ordinary English, and the major systems (like countability, transitivity, gender, tense) will be retained along with their ordinary exponents, their use defined explicitly in terms of relevant communicative needs. By "major systems" would be understood those affecting more than one word-class and having reverberations on other systems—as in the case of the count/non-count distinction which is reflected in both the determiner system and in verb inflection.

Much research and experiment will be necessary to find out the extent to which these principles can be translated into a blueprint for prescribing the grammar of Nuclear English. Unquestionably, there will be many problems in identifying for omission those minor systems for which alternative expression can be found within major ones. Thus (in terms of Quirk et al., 1972) "complex transitive" and "di-transitive" structures might reasonably be excised from the transitivity system. We glimpsed a possible treatment of complex transitives in the *expect* example above. Ditransitives are on the face of it even easier to handle—through replacement by the corresponding prepositional alternative:

We offered the girl a drink. ⟶
We offered a drink *to the girl.*

But there is the problem of certain verbs for which there is no prepositional alternative (cf. "He charged her a high rent") and of verbs on the other hand which have alternative prepositional complementation (cf. "serve X to Y" = "serve Y with X"). It is of course likely that verbs with such lexical compression would be replaced by nuclear periphrases ("He caused her to pay a high rent", "He said that it was necessary that she pay . . ."), but to the extent that such verbs are retained in the lexicon on purely lexicological grounds, they present interesting difficulties as to grammatical treatment.

More miscellanea of this kind could be easily supplied, but I shall confine my attention to the problems posed by the modals, an area of notorious difficulty in English and other languages, and liable to cause difficulty in communication even between native speakers. I shall begin with a reminder of the complexities, and in the course of what follows I shall attempt to project what must be conveyed in Nuclear English.

Take one of those doom-laden stellar conjunctions beloved of Arthur Hailey. We're in an electric storm over Indiana on a flight from New York (hereafter designated—quite fictitiously, needless to say—Able Baker 123). In the bad and intermittent radio reception, our pilot hears a ground control voice:

Able Baker 123 may land at O'Hare in five minutes.

Now, it is easy for the philosopher or linguist in his study to see that this is ambiguous. But for the ordinary speaker in discourse, including the ordinary pilot on the flight deck, speech contains no ambiguities: we tune in to the meaning that happens to be uppermost in our expectations. If the pilot thinks he is merely eavesdropping on a message about his aircraft to someone else, he will at once interpret it as:

Able Baker 123 will possibly land at O'Hare in five minutes

—an expression of opinion which he will check against the probabilities suggested by other factors, including his instruments. If on the other hand he takes it to be a message addressed to himself, he will just as instantaneously interpret it as:

Able Baker 123 is permitted to land at O'Hare in five minutes

—a very different matter indeed. Either way, radio conditions may make it difficult to check or correct the interpretation.

If the radioed sentence used *can* and referred to an airfield not on his flight plan (say, Fort Wayne, Indiana), further possibilities occur, again without warning the hearer of their existence:

Able Baker 123 can land at Fort Wayne.

This could still mean "is permitted to land", but it might equally mean "has the capability of landing" (i.e. can adopt the right approach angle or has the appropriate landing speed for Fort Wayne; or Fort Wayne has a sufficiently long runway for a 747, or whatever). Then again, interpreted as a message between two controllers, the sentence could be interpreted as:

It is conceivable that we could divert Able Baker 123 to Fort Wayne.

Introduce a past marking and new ambiguities appear:

Able Baker 123 could have landed at Fort Wayne

(= either "had the capability of landing . . . but didn't"; or "had the possibility . . . but didn't"; or "had permission to land . . . but didn't"; or even "It is possible that 123 did in fact land").

Withdrawing from air travel melodrama, we find analogous ambiguities with other modal expressions:

They ought to be here

can mean "There was a requirement that they be here"; or "I expect that they are here"; or "I expected that they were here, but they're not".

John WILL fail his exams!

can mean "I confidently predict that he will"; or "John persists in failing"; or even "I insist on his failing".

John must stay at home on Wednesdays

can mean "John is obliged to stay at home" or "It seems certain that John stays at home".

John is supposed to be asleep

can mean "There is a requirement on John to be asleep"; or "There is a requirement on us to believe that John is asleep"; or "People suppose that John is asleep".

Not surprisingly, as every EFL teacher knows, errors among foreign learners are legion and apparently ineradicable.[9] Even non-natives in post as university professors of English (let alone professionals in other disciplines, whatever their fluency) make errors like the following; indeed I have taken them from such sources:

You could like to forward the book to me	(for *might*)
For this reason he would not write it	(for *would not be writing*)

The study should be of great value	(for *would*)
The conductor arrived and the concert should start	(for *was due to*)
After many attempts, he could succeed	(for *was able to*)
The students had better write clearly	(for *should*)
He tells me that he must write it last year	(for *had to*)

There are additional difficulties lurking in the relation between assertive and non-assertive modality. Thus, although with some modals the correspondence is straightforward ("he can drive a car", *He can't . . ./If he can . . ./Can he . . . ?*), with others it is not, and quite experienced non-natives are apt to slip into expressions like:

He must not complete his thesis before January
He may not answer every question

where "need not, is permitted not to" happens to be meant in both cases. And among the further difficulties, there are those arising from differences in discourse orientation: the contrasting expectations involved between for example *He may go* (which will probably be deontic but may be epistemic) and *I may go* (which will almost certainly be epistemic but may be deontic). (Cf. Palmer, 1974:100ff.)

The problems inherent in modality have of course long been the subject of discussion. In that pioneer study of linguistic engineering, the *Essay Towards a Real Character* of 1668, John Wilkins distinguished "primary" and "secondary modes", the latter being being concerned in "modal propositions" where "the Matter in discourse . . . is concerned not *simply by itself*, but *gradually in its causes*" (p. 316). These modal propositions he sees as involving either contingency or necessity, each being itself bipartite. So far as contingency is concerned, either the speaker expresses "only the *Possibility*" of something (which is dependent "upon the power of its cause"), or "his own *Liberty* to it" (when there is "a freedom from all Obstacles either within or without"). With *necessity*, says Wilkins, "the speaker expresseth the resolution of his own will" or "*some external obligation*, whether *Natural* or *Moral*". As we could expect from this, when Wilkins comes subsequently to propose his "real characters", he offers distinct symbols for each of these modal values (p. 391).

It seems clear that Nuclear English cannot afford to do less. Whether we need more distinctions is quite another question. It will be noticed that Wilkins anticipates modern philosophers and linguists in his insistence on awareness of the speaker's involvement, but I am doubtful whether we need to follow more recent scholars in recognizing—at any rate explicitly—a three-tier modality in every sentence (designated neustic, tropic, and phrastic in Hare, 1970). But in view of the unfortunate overlaps demonstrable in the ordinary English use of modals, it seems clear that such factors bearing upon propositional content as the speaker's commitment, the factuality, and the constraint upon the agent need to be given formal expression.

Within speaker's commitment, we need further to bear in mind the relevant contrasts arising as between his knowledge, his belief, his desire, and his mere declaration. Factuality involves the range from certainty through probability to possibility and improbability. With constraints upon the agent, it is important to distinguish on the one hand between those that are internal to the agent (whether relating to his ability or to his volition) and those that are external to him (whether compulsion or absolute *necessity* on the one hand, or social or moral *duty* on the other).

These parameters enjoin the recognition of three theoretically quite distinct types of modality. We have *epistemic* modality expressing the degree of speaker's knowledge (e.g. *He may go* = "I think it possible that he will"); *deontic* or "root" modality expressing constraint, whether imposed by the speaker (as in imperatives) or by some other agency (such as the law); and *potential* modality, concerned with the agent's volition or ability. A fourth modality, *alethic* (cf. Lyons, 1977), can be disregarded in ordinary linguistic communication, concerned as it is with purely logical necessity ("Since he is unmarried, he must be a bachelor").

The question now arises as to how these modalities and their partially overlapping concerns with speaker, agent, and external world might best be expressed in Nuclear English. We might consider three possibilities.

(a) We could try to separate off those that are in some sense most "important"[10] and disregard the rest. This seems in effect to be what happens in pidgin languages such as Neo-Melanesian, but among its objectionable aspects would be the failure thereby to meet the requirement that Nuclear English must provide full communicative adequacy.

(b) We could retain the ordinary range of English modals but restrict their use to avoid overlap. Thus *may* might be restricted to epistemic use ("be possible") and excluded from deontic use ("be permitted"). This proposal has several disadvantages. It would tend not to oblige the speaker to analyse the precise intention of his message, and it would be very difficult for the speaker with a partial or good knowledge of "full" English to avoid making "mistakes" and forming just such ambiguous sentences as were illustrated earlier.

(c) We could retain the full range of modalities but restrict their expression to carefully prescribed and maximally explicit paraphrases,[11] banning the use of the normal modal auxiliaries altogether.

This is a sharply radical proposal but it is of course in line with the theory of Nuclear English as envisaged in this paper. In repudiating the claims of "frequency in occurrence", we would achieve the objective of avoiding the ultimately far greater disdavantages of extreme polysemy. In requiring paraphrase, we would be insisting on a speaker's clarifying his own intention in advance, while yet expressing himself without departure from fully acceptable forms of ordinary English. Indeed, paraphrases of the kind "It is possible that this is not true", "It is not possible that this is true" present the means not only of separating modality from proposition but of stipulating such features as the scope of negation, frequently obscured in ordinary language. In all of which, we achieve a mode of expression reflecting distinctions that have been the subject of considerable discussion in the "higher sentence" debate of current linguistics (cf. Ross, 1969; Anderson, 1971; Erdmann, 1977). Indeed, it could even be argued (cf. Lightfoot, 1974) that our proposal would amount to "restoring" predications that have been submerged in the course of linguistic history.

It will be seen that Nuclear English is conceived as having great power but also as exercising drastic constraints. Not only is the language to be learned by the non-native carefully and explicitly restricted: so equally must the language of the native speaker be constrained to a precisely corresponding extent when he is using Nuclear English as an international medium. A tall order? Yes, but surely more than a mere pipe dream if we consider the continuous thought that has been given to these issues from Francis Bacon onwards—and if we take seriously the issue of international needs.

The word *international* was coined nearly 200 years ago by a man whose mortal remains, clothed and seated, are on prominent display at my place of work, University College London. Jeremy Bentham's utilitarianism explicitly and emphatically embraced questions of linguistic engineering. He was impressed by Francis Bacon's observation that learning suffers "distemper" through the fact that words effectively mask and obscure the "weight of matter" that should be at the centre of our attention (*Advancement of Learning*, 1605). Bentham based his concern for the clarification of linguistic expression on the great tradition that extended from Bacon, through Comenius, Mersenne, Wilkins, Leibniz, Berkeley, to Horne Tooke in his own day. Indeed he strove (vainly, as it turned out) to have appointed as the first Professor of English in my College the polyglot John Bowring who has keen on the notion of establishing a universal language.

This "great tradition" was seriously disrupted by the advent of comparative philology in the early nineteenth century, and the subsequent development of phonetics—in part supportive of it, in part directed in the opposite direction: the examination of substance features in living languages. This in turn gave a different emphasis in language teaching (towards speech fluency, measured especially in terms of phonetic accuracy), while the embracing by the universities of these twin branches of inquiry, phonology and comparative philology, as the dominant foci of intellectual excitement, had the effect of pushing philosophical linguistics and universalism back from the footlights. Though never entirely forgotten by academic philosophers, it was only a minority of linguists who persisted with their interest, and those have been largely on the periphery of the academic establishment. One thinks of Ogden, Korzybski, Hayakawa, and the pages of *ETC*, etc.

With the discovery of J. L. Austin—some years after his death—and with a greater catholicity, eclecticism, and perhaps pragmatism in linguistic theory than we have known for nearly half a century, I feel that this is the time for serious re-engagement with the issues that occupied Wilkins and his successors.

NOTES TO CHAPTER 10

1. I am indebted to Gregory Trifonovitch for a Japanese reference of 1859 (Fukuzawa Yukichi) predicting English to be the most useful language in the world of the future.
2. There are of course further internal linguistic complexities in Norway.
3. Cf. 'The British Heresy in TESL' in Fishman et al., 1968:459–76.
4. On the basis of such facts, it is clearly a matter of internal policy for governments (in India, Nigeria, and the many other countries in this position) to decide the variety of indigenized English to be taught in their education systems, weighing the immediate local needs of the many against the wider needs of those who must in addition master a form of English current in international use. It need scarcely be added that this question arises only in countries making use of English for internal purposes. Other "national" varieties of English are of course equally discernible; but while "Japanese English", "German English", "Russian English" may be facts of *performance* linguistics, there is no reason for setting them up as facts of *institutional* linguistics or as models for the learners in the countries concerned.
5. It is worth noting, however, that acrolectal English in such countries as India achieves this universality by looking outward (in contrast to the basilects) for its standards.
6. Simplification of the language, that is. Predicting failure nearly thirty years ago, George Bernard Shaw saw a way out in simplification of the teaching. In pleading for rationalization in the teaching of English as a common world language, he was ready to encourage wholesale pidginization, and thought that teachers effectively sold the pass by setting their sights too high. "All teachers should bear in mind that better is the enemy of good enough, and perfection not possible on any terms. Language . . . should not be taught beyond the point at which the speaker is understood"

(*Atlantic Monthly*, 186, October 1950:62). This presupposes a highly simplistic view of comprehensibility, and in the context of an unrestricted and uncontrolled concept of "English", Shaw's prescription would probably be worse than valueless. In the context of a strictly limited lexicon, however, comprehensibility—phonetic and graphic alike—becomes less of an imponderable, and at any rate many would agree with Shaw that the teacher's goal of getting his students to achieve native-like control of a foreign language is a dangerous chimera. A somewhat analogous point has been strenuously made by Professor Takao Suzuki (*Japan Times*, Tokyo, 24 June 1979), arguing (a) that it is wasteful to teach English as widely as at present in Japan, and (b) that the English taught should be a simplified form ("Englic"), based on non-native usage.

7. Despite the ingenuity and (often) very attractive features that such inventions may display. Cf. the little known Interglossa described in quite fascinating detail in a Pelican book so titled by Lancelot Hogben (Harmondsworth, 1943). Hogben's sketchy handling of modality is of some interest: pp. 126f.

8. But see G. Stein, 'Nuclear English: Reflections on the Structure of its Vocabulary; *Poetica*, 10 (Tokyo, 1979).

9. They must not of course be exaggerated. In the first place, there are grossly overloaded modality systems in other languages beside English, and the same analogies and "metaphors" are very generally involved. Secondly, pragmatic factors (including common sense) often preclude misunderstanding: *May I go?* is unlikely to be epistemic since a person does not ask other people about what in the nature of things he must know better than anyone else. Thirdly, in many instances modal properties effectively merge, however theoretically distinct they may be: *He can leave immediately* cannot normally involve possibility without simultaneously involving permission.

10. In this connection, it would be worth examining the implications of current work by Gordon Wells of Bristol on the order and rate of acquiring modal expression in children and on the types and distribution of modal values expressed in parent–child interaction.

11. In the present programmatic outline, the specific properties of the optimal paraphrases must be ignored. Among the formidable topics for study, however, is the nature of deontic passives like "is obliged", "is permitted" and the question of specifying agency.

11 Discoursal Patterning and the Equalizing of Interpretive Opportunity

Christopher N. Candlin

I want in this paper to explore some relationships between discoursal patterning and learners' interpretive strategies in the process of English language learning, and to focus my attention on communication and discourse in general, and ways of developing the interpretive competence of English language speakers. To do this as English language educators, we can examine the relationships between the products of discourse analysis, the psycholinguistic evidence for interpretive strategy, methodological procedures and classroom activities, and evaluate how well they intermesh, and, in particular, how they can be brought together to promote an equalizing of interpretive opportunity among very varied learners. The levelling, therefore, lies not so much in the object or the product of understanding, rather in the ability and in the process.

I MEANING IN DISCOURSE

Let me begin with a quotation:

> A sentence does not convey meaning the way a truck conveys cargo, complete and packaged. It is more like a blueprint that allows the hearer to reconstruct the meaning from his own knowledge.
> (Winograd, 1974)

Winograd captures much of what I wish to refer to in this section and section III by isolating the twin crucial characteristics of discoursal meaning. Firstly, the distinction to be drawn between signification and value (Widdowson, 1973), or between sense and force (Leech, 1977), and secondly, the creative and dynamic process of interpretation, which

166

in concentrating on what transpires between interlocutors, acts to create meaning. These twin characteristics are related in that values and forces are not stable phenomena but vary and shift according to the nature of the discourse type, the interpersonal relationships involved, and (among other factors) the influence of setting and topic. Winograd's "cargo" is the sense of sentences, his "blueprint" suggests the values and forces the sentences attract and produce in communication, and his notion of "reconstruction" emphasizes the interpretive "work" performed by those engaged in understanding.

The distinction between an abstract sense and a concrete, pragmatic force reflects a more general distinction which has been drawn between language seen as a formal system (competence in the traditional sense) and language seen as a behavioural process; between form and function. In referring to sense we are concerned with what a speaker (or writer) is saying when he makes certain propositions, while with force or value we are concerned with effect, with what is being "done" or "accomplished" when a speaker makes these propositions. As many have pointed out, Austin's distinction between "saying" and "performing" (Austin, 1962) lies at the heart of discourse analysis and emphasizes the distinction to be more generally drawn between semantics and pragmatics.

Unfortunately, this distinction is not at all clear-cut, particularly in terms of how each relates to the other in a given case, and whether we can establish any general rules for such a relation. Linguistic semanticists like Lyons (1968) or Kempson (1975) can be understood for regarding the handling of contextual features as intractable; involving knowledge of the world and hence outside the domain of semantics. For discourse analysis and its application to language learning, however, the relationship is central, since here the chief task is to demonstrate how the uttering of particular words by particular people in particular circumstances can (as with Austin), given certain culturally-specific appropriateness criteria, constitute the performing of certain conventional acts.

In examining how we can begin to recognize, distinguish and evaluate the variable likelihood of this or that force, I should like to illustrate the argument from two recent contributions to the understanding of discourse: firstly, the linguistic (philosophical) pragmatic view taken by Geoffrey Leech in a recent article (Leech, 1977) entitled "Language and Tact", and secondly, the sociolinguistic pragmatic view of Labov and Fanshel (1977) in a book entitled *Therapeutic discourse: psychotherapy as Conversation.*

Leech's arguments for the interrelating of semantics and pragmatics owe much to work of Searle (especially Searle, 1975) and to Grice (1975), as he acknowledges. Leech criticizes Searle's earlier work on speech acts (Searle, 1969) on the grounds that it implies a certainty in allocating illocutionary force which is belied by the variation in speaker/hearer interpretation in actually occurring communication. One cannot always and uniquely maintain that a given utterance has this or that value. Utterances are valued in clines, and appeal to condition such as "authority" as in the case of the cline between *requests* and *commands* in Searle's examples constitutes no valid distinguisher, since, as Leech points out, "authority" is a social variable. Just so, and as we shall see in examining the obstacles to understanding set out at the end of this section, these occasional references to social relativity (indulged in by Searle and by Grice) have to be made consistent and central; they ought not to be adduced now and then, and certainly not in some universalist way. More helpful to Leech (and indeed to discourse analysts concerned with applied linguistics) is Grice's paper on "Logic and conversation" (Grice, 1975) and Searle's related paper on "Indirect speech acts" (Searle, 1975). Grice suggests that under the general label of "The Cooperative Principle" can be grouped a set of conversational maxims which he asserts derive from "general principles of human cooperative behaviour" and in relation to which force can be derived from sense.

Leech's important departure from Grice is to take up the notion that utterances are "placed" by speakers and "taken up" by hearers at varying points along continua between points of value. Thus, *requesting* and *commanding*, for example, are not clear-cut and separate but at either end of a value continuum. To explain this, Leech incidentally postulates a further Gricean maxim, that of Tact. The Tact Maxim is invoked where a strict adherence to the original set of maxims would produce impoliteness and "disturb the social equilibrium". For example, for a diner to utter " Can you pass the salt?" (an example from Searle, 1975) is to break the original Cooperative Principle by being periphrastic and thus offensive to the Maxim of Manner (Avoid obscurity and ambiguity: be brief and orderly) and, as Leech points out, if the hearer manifestly *can* pass the salt, then the utterance offends the Maxim of Quality [Make your contribution one that is true] also. Tact is concerned with the avoidance of conflict and, as such, is firmly anchored in a social world of rights and duties. Following Brown and Levinson (1974) and Brown and Gilman (1960), Leech argues that *tact* is required when the solidarity relation between authoritor and authoritee is inadequate to prevent the power relation from leading to conflict. What the Tact Maxim requires you to do is to assume that you are the authoritee and that your interlocutor is the authoritor, and to adjust your language accordingly. Breaking *tact* has to be regarded as socially perilous, if only to prevent the iterative employment of the language of *tact* outrunning the linguistic resources of the language. For example, as Leech observes, an utterance intended to exhibit *tact* (let us say an imperative plus "please" intending a request) may not ward off conflict (being seen as a directive), and the speaker has then to resort to ever more circumlocutionary utterances in order to repair the dykes. (Leech notes that indirectness of utterance, *in English*, is a *tact* marker). Leech observes that skilled conversationalists will take advantage of an interlocutor's unwillingness to break *tact* as a means of getting them to comply with their otherwise infractory directness—as with the utterance "I want you to give me some money" said by A to B (which itself breaks *tact*). Recent work at Lancaster (Sexton, 1976; McKnight, 1976) into the discourse of schizophrenic patients in a psychiatric ward has other, related, examples of such tactics.

The concept of a value continuum leads Leech to suggest the idea of "pragmatic space" within which three interrelated axes work on each other to suggest to the speaker/hearer the degree of *tact* required in a given case. The axes are those of *power* (authoritor to authoritee), *social distance* (degree of lack of familiarity), and *cost-benefit* (degree of advantage/disadvantage to speaker/hearer). Interlocutors estimate reaction as in this example:

(concerning the status of A vis à vis S) . . .
1. The more power A holds over S
2. The more socially distant A is from S
3. The more costly E (i.e. what is being proposed by A) is to A
then, the more *tact* required.

I have referred to Leech at some length because he suggests a framework in terms of which sense can be related to force in a principled way (taking social relationships into account) and where the interpretive strategies of interlocutors are constantly at work. His stance, however, is that of a semanticist rather than a sociolinguist, and this leads him into social and cultural generalizations which are unhelpful to applied linguists concerned with interethnic and cross-cultural communication. I shall return to these (and other) difficulties in a moment; before doing so, however, I would like to sketch an alternative but related attempt to propose general rules for the interpretation of particular speech acts, from a socio-psycholinguistic standpoint.

In a recent book concerned with formulating rules for the interpretation of psychiatric patient talk (Labov and Fanshel, 1977), the authors insist, like Leech, on the need to take account of sociological concepts of role, rights and duties if particular values are to be assigned to utterances. To do this (building on earlier work by Labov, 1972) they suggest formulations of the following type:

If A addresses to B an *imperative* specifying an action
X at a time T_1 and B believes that A believes that:
1. (a) X should be done for a purpose Y (*need for the action*)
    (b) B would not do X in the absence of the request (*need for the request*)

2. B has the *ability* to do X
3. B has the *obligation* to do X or is *willing* to do it
4. A has the *right* to tell B to do X
then A is heard as making a valid *request for action.*

We can notice the connection with the Conversational Maxims of Grice, and the axes proposed by Leech. However, as Coulthard (1977) notes, such a rule deals with the case where there is a close match between sense and force. To handle indirectness, other rules are, however, possible; Labov and Fanshel suggest, as an example, a general rule "governing challenges to other persons' competence", which they formulate thus:

Rule of Overdue Obligations
If A asserts that B has not performed obligations in his role R, then A is heard as challenging B's competence in R.

This general principle allows for special cases, such as:

Rule of Delayed Requests
If A makes a request for B to perform an action X in role R, based on needs, abilities, obligations and rights which have been valid for some time, then A is heard as challenging B's competence in role R.

or again:

Rule of Repeated Requests
If A makes a request for action X of B, and A repeats the request before B has responded, then A is heard as strongly challenging B's performance.

To give an instance of this sub-rule, in a British English context, we could imagine a service station where A says to the mechanic B: "Can you just give it a short service and then have a look at the engine, I think it's knocking or something", and then, *before B answers*, A says again: ". . ., oh and have a look at the engine, it's not working right", then A utters a strong challenge to the competence of the mechanic B. Rules such as these, I shall be arguing, are not only central to a generative understanding of discourse (specifically the sense–force relation) but constitute a major objective of a language learner's interpretive strategy; in a communicatively oriented syllabus and materials they are as essential goals a the rules of language form.

However important the formulations of Leech and Labov and Fanshel are for applied linguistic concerns, there still remain obstacles to complete acceptance; obstacles which arise in the process of designing learning materials (whether for foreign and second language learners or, indeed, native speakers).

Obstacle 1: Cultural Bias

Leech (like Searle and Grice) operates within a specific cultural and ethnographic frame; the "general principles of human cooperative behaviour" seem Western European, even Anglo-Saxon in their orientation. Much of the work of Hymes (1972), Gumperz and Hymes (1972) and others concerned with the ethnography of speaking would resist such attempts at pan-cultural speaking norms. To cite an example, Basso's work (1970) on the place of silence among the Apache would throw a spanner into the workings of the Maxim of Manner while Irvine's research into Wolof "greetings", (cited by Coulthard, 1977 and in the collection by Bauman and Scherzer, 1974) whereby although relative rank determines who greets whom (lower greets higher), frequently higher greets lower first in order to reject the higher status which has concomitant obligations of looking after the needs of the lower status individual, would necessitate a culturally specific application of the social axes Leech proposes. Recent work into interethnic communication (Gumperz, 1977; Candlin, Bruton and Leather, 1974, 1976b) would similarly throw doubt on some of Leech's individual interpretations. To cite Gumperz (1977): "How can we be certain that our interpretation of what activity is being signalled is the same as the activity that the interlocutor has in mind, if our communicative backgrounds are not identical?" In the context of language learning across cultures they will generally not be; hence the need to focus on developing and equalizing interpretive opportunity.

Obstacle 2: Social View

Although both Leech and Labov and Fanshel rightly require social information as central factor in relating sense to force, they do not make clear whether they see the distribution of rights and duties, and the assignment of roles, as something which is independent of interaction or dependent on it. There are good grounds for believing (along with Garfinkel, 1972; Goffman, 1974) the ethnomethodological view that social knowledge emerges during interaction, and that the distribution of these social features between interlocutors is not fixed but "created" within the conversational context. Furthermore, the German research into pragmatics referred to by Leech, Wunderlich (1971) and supported by others such as Rehbein and Ehlich (1972, 1977) makes it plain that any interpretation of force from sense depends upon the interpreter's social view (whether he is a discourse analyst or an interlocutor); particular background knowledge is necessary to interpretation, and this knowledge varies *socially*.

Obstacle 3: Discoursal Context

The example from the psychiatric interview above serves also to highlight a further interpretive obstacle, undervalued in particular by Leech. It is unfortunate that he remains at the level of isolated sentences in his attempt to relate sense to force: interpretation crucially depends upon interpretations already accorded to previous utterances. Understanding as a kind of "esprit d'escalier" is a fact of discoursal life. Not only is social knowledge revealed through interaction but it also acts as a guide to the interpretation of sense. To quote an example from Turner (1975) (cited in Wootton, 1975):

A: Isn't it nice that there's such a crowd of you in the office?
B: You're asking us to leave not telling us to leave, right?

The significance of B's reply is that he is attempting to compel A to clarify his force (much in the way that analysts do when asking questions of utterances). A can reply in a number of ways:

—No, you're the guests and you only leave when you wish
or:—I didn't mean that at all
or:—Don't be so touchy
or:—I don't want you to leave . . . the others

(which replies are themselves, for the strategic conversational purposes of A, sometimes equivocal, thus throwing the obligation to mean what you say back on B). Venneman (1973) makes the point that conversation is like a pool in which utterances and their presuppositions are stored; each unchallenged force governing the interpretation of subsequent senses. Most of the work on conversational structure by the ethnomethodologists (Sacks, 1972; Schegloff, 1972; Schegloff and Sacks, 1973; Jefferson, 1972) is premissed on this cumulative, contextual view of interpreting force. Where their views need modification is in the need to accommodate culturally and ethnographically specific information to the "general principles of conversational structure" which, as erroneously as Grice's postulates, they suggest as universals. It is clear, however, that attempts at suggesting the force of individual sentences, outside a discoursal context, are unlikely to reflect an accurate picture of pragmatic meaning. Indeed, the lengths to which conversationalists go to negotiate what each other might mean (as in the example of A and B above) clearly indicate that any rule of discourse (as with Labov and Fanshel) has to have its conditions agreed upon before it can be used to interpret utterance force. If then, as the ethnomethodologists believe, even *within the context* of conversation utterances have to have their force negotiated, there is even more grounds and more necessity for enhancing learner's interpretive competence. Compelling clarification by making force overt is the language learner's principal need, and, indeed, his principal communicative weapon. Gumperz (1977) makes the point that among native speakers: "What seems to happen is that there is an introductory phase where interpersonal relationships are established/negotiated and where participants probe for common experience or some evidence for shared perception." Such tactics would seem to be a common need, whether among native speakers or second language learners.

Obstacle 4: Linguistic Realizations

In my discussion of Leech (1977) I drew attention to his assertion that *tact* is realized in English by indirectness and by circumlocution. Recent work in the realization of pragmatic value (Gumperz, 1977; Brazil, 1975; Sinclair and Coulthard, 1975 (among many others)) indicates that this can only be a very restricted example of what are likely to be a range of individual and complementary ways of signalling such value, and that it is precisely this relationship between function and form which is problematic. Gumperz's *contextualization cues*, for example, refer not only to lexical, phonetic and intonational selection, but also to code and variety switching and to choice of certain stereotypical conversational sequences, as markers of pragmatic value, and, as such, go far beyond mere syntactic choice. Furthermore, it has proved easier to assign features (whether linguistic or paralinguistic) to the hierarchical structure of discourse, rather than to individual illocutionary values. Examples of this would be Brazil's work on the connection between *key* choice and turn-taking, or investigations into lecture monologue reported in Murphy and Candlin (1976, 1979) where discoursal "chunking" is signalled by sensitive combining of syntactic, lexical, intonational and kinetic means. What seems to be the case, however, in transferring interpretive to productive associations, is that the contextual view (raised in Obstacle 3 above) is indispensable; to cite Coulthard (1977):

> . . . there is only an unlimited number of ways of making a given indirect request if one is considering it in isolation; in reality the constraints of the preceding discourse, the current topic, the facts of the situation and the current speaker's intentions for the progress of the succeeding discourse will all reduce the choice enormously.

II DISCOURSAL PATTERNING

My foregoing remarks on the essentialness of contextual reference for interpretation provide a link between discussion of the sense/force distinction and the topic of this section of the paper, the variety of discoursal patterning and its link to learner interpretation. I shall be making two points: firstly, that it is in the nature of discourse to be hierarchically structured (both linearly and dependently), and secondly, that if we can make learners aware of these structures (by outlining them, or by having them discover the outlines) we assist their ability to interpret particular values. I use the loose term "patterning" so as to be able to draw together two examples of such discourse types, which may appear dissimilar, at first sight.

Example 1 Doctor-Patient Communication
(Candlin, Bruton and Leather, 1974, 1976a)

Data
The following list of speech *FUNCTIONS* was used to make live, realtime analyses of a doctor's utterances during Casualty consultations.

Doctors' speech FUNCTIONS in Casualty

A GREET:	D: 'Hullo';
	D: 'Good morning';
	D: 'Mrs. Jones?' etc.
B ELICIT:	(to get broad description of accident with some circumstantial detail):
	D: 'Can you tell me what happened?' . . . etc.
C INTERROGATE:	(to probe circumstances of trauma relevant to diagnosis . . .):
	D: 'Do you remember if your whole weight was on the foot?!
	D: 'Did you bend right back when you fell?' . . . etc.
D QUESTION:	(to get information during examination):
	D: 'Does this hurt?!;
	D: 'Can you bend it?' etc.
E MAKESURE:	(to make sure that what Dr. understands is what P meant):
	D: 'Does it hurt here?'
	P: 'No, not really.'
	D: 'It doesn't hurt?'
	P: 'No.'

F	EXTEND:	(to test a deduction made from P's information):
		D: 'Can you walk all right?'
		P: 'Yes'
		D: 'So it doesn't hurt to put your weight on it?'
		P: 'No.'
G	ACTION-INFORM:	(to let the patient know what is being done/going to be done):
		D: 'I'm going to put in a couple of stitches.'
		D: 'I think we'd better have an X-ray, to make sure . . .' etc.
H	DIAG-INFORM:	(to let the patient know the diagnosis):
		D: 'You haven't broken anything' . . . etc.
I	PROG-INFORM:	(to let the patient know how the condition is likely to progress):
		D: 'It should heal up quite quickly.' etc.
J	TREAT-DIRECT:	(to tell the patient what to do to help the cure):
		D: 'Take plenty of rest.' etc.
K	DIRECT:	(to tell the patient what to do so that medical attention can effectively be given):
		D: 'Can you just lie down a moment.'
		D: 'Take this with you to X-ray.'
		D: 'Come back in five days.' etc.
L	APOLOGY:	(to apologise for hurting patient or otherwise inconveniencing):
		D: 'Sorry. Did that hurt?' etc.
M	TALK:	(to give information not strictly relevant to the consultation in hand):
		D: 'I've seen rather a lot of these lately.'
		D: 'Little girls tend to do that sort of thing.'
N	MED-ASK:	(to get information relevant to clinical aspects of consultation):
		D: 'Are you allergic to penicillin?'
		D: 'Have you been vaccinated against tetanus?' etc.
O	ADMIN-ASK:	(to get information not relevant to *clinical* aspects of consultation);
		D: 'Do you use this hand in your work?'
		D: 'Did you come here on foot?' etc.
P	REASSURE:	(to reassure patient)
		D: 'Nothing serious here.'
		D: 'Don't worry, it's all right.' etc.
Q	ACCEPT:	(to acknowledge receipt of communication):
		D: ' . . . Yes . . .'

P: 'I sort of twisted it round ... you know ... like ...'

D: 'Twisted it. I see.'

R LEAVETAKE: (to end the consultation):

D: 'Right, thank you Mrs. Jones.'

D: 'OK? Thank you.'

D: 'Good. See you after the X-ray then ...'

S GO-ON: (to encourage patient to continue the story):

P: 'Well, I was playing football, ...'

D: 'Mmm ...'

P: 'And ...'

T ANSWER: (to reply to query raised by patient/nurse):

P: 'Does that mean it's broken?'

D: 'Yes, I'm afraid it's broken just here.'

N: 'Shall I do an elastic bandage Doctor?'

D: 'Yes, I think that's all it needs.'

U REPEAT: (to get the patient/nurse/addressee to repeat what he/she said):

D: 'What?'

D: 'Sorry?' etc.

V RESTATE: (repeating what was said because the patient didn't catch it):

D: 'Can you swallow all right?'

P: 'Can I ...?'

D: '... Swallow all right.'

W FEED-ME-BACK: (to check that the patient/nurse/addressee has understood/is listening):

D: 'Do you follow me?'

D: 'OK?'

D: 'Is that all right?' etc.

Discoursal Patterning

Investigation of a wide range of consultations revealed that Casualty consultation discourse is highly structured, in that there are significant probabilities to the occurrence of the above FUNCTIONS, and to their distribution. The operational "phases" of a consultation, namely *information, examination, diagnosis* and *treatment/prognosis*, occurring within a general GREET/LEAVETAKE frame (FUNCTIONS A, R) were marked by high probabilities of clustering and co-occurrence of (what were termed) task-oriented FUNCTIONS (B, C, D, G, H, I, J, K), while (what were termed) metacommunicative FUNCTIONS (Q, S) were much more evenly distributed across the consultation. (For fuller discussion, see Candlin, Bruton and Leather, 1974, 1976a and b, Candlin, Bruton, Leather and Woods, 1977). There are two points to be made here concerning discoursal structuring; firstly, that the occurrence of these doctor communication values is not a random matter, but determined by a complex of general cultural conventions (beginning with A and ending with R), specific task related factors (C before I) and the exigencies of the moment (the mobility of P). Secondly, each of the FUNCTIONS enumerated above gains part of its force, interactively, from its position within the discourse. As I illustrate in another paper (Candlin, 1976), the FUNCTION INTERROGATE (C) is recognized as such within the consultation not only by its force of "seeking more detailed information" but also by its position after the general inquiry of the ELICIT (B). It is valued in relation to the ELICIT and to what follows. In terms of the pedagogic implications of this type of analysis one could not only teach the consultation language patterns as a unified sequence, as an unfolding progression of co-selected FUNCTIONS, but also make use of the discoursal distribution patterns to reproduce, for example, the highly structured opening sequence in which GREET leads to a general information-extracting FUNCTION, which in turn leads to a more specific information extractor, and so on. (For further pedagogic examples see the teaching materials in Candlin, Bruton, Leather and Woods (1977), in particular the exercises designed to reveal the essential discoursal structure of consultations and then progressively allow for learner variants.)

Example 2 Reading Text (Jones, 1975)

Data: Geography Text: Rainfall and Deserts
In the heart of desert regions, the distinctive qualities of desert climate are unmistakable. Drought, sun, wind, occasional rainstorms, and heat by day characterize the climatic year. Things are different on the desert margins.

Unless a desert region is bounded by highland, desert climate and desert scenery vanish by replacement. In such circumstances, the status of a given locality may be very doubtful, and the limits of the true desert very difficult to fix. In some areas the matter is complicated by the effects of past climatic changes—the Mediterranean borders of the Sahara were perceptibly rainier, two or three thousand years ago, than they are today. Desert climate has invaded regions which were formerly not more than semi-arid, and semi-arid climate has encroached on regions which were truly humid. Too little time has elapsed for the scenery to be fully adjusted to the changes, so that the scenic and climatic limits of the existing desert do not coincide.
Extracted from: *The Face of the Earth* by G. H. Dury
—from Biddulph, G. M. R., *Geography*,
English Studies Series 11, Oxford University
Press, 1971.

Discoursal Patterning:

I have selected an extract from a reading passage for my second example for a number of reasons: firstly, to emphasize that reading, no less than understanding the spoken discourse of doctors, is an interactive process; secondly, because written texts readily demonstrate the sequential and hierarchical discoursal patterning that I have been referring to; and thirdly, since written discourse (particularly *scientific* written discourse) has received most attention from discourse analysts, and happens to be by far the most frequent form of discourse encountered by learners in English (whether in ESP or generally), it may well be that it can be most conveniently used as one way of accessing our learners to the understanding of discoursal conventions, rules of use and realizations of value, which, as we have argued, is an essential of language learning. (It is also the case that such written scientific discourse raises fewer cases of arguable interpretation, and that is why it is suffering a little from applied linguistic overexposure.)

In his perceptive comments on this text, Jones underlines what Goodman (1967), Eskey (1973), Freedle and Carroll (1972) (inter alia) characterize as the *process* of reading; whereby the reader is involved in a "guessing game" in which he employs a "cyclic sampling technique" in predicting meanings, testing them against his own knowledge of the world, the topic and appropriate discoursal patterns, and seeing them confirmed or disconfirmed as more and more of the text in hand is revealed. Without wishing to more than hint at the extensive research literature (usefully summarized in Urquhart and Widdowson, 1976), we have a picture of reader and author interaction in which the discoursal "plan" within the text is in a constant process of "matching" with the developing "plan" in the mind of the reader, aided either by overt discoursal marking within the text (formal realizations of *exemplification, clarification, conclusion*, etc.), or by inference (as when sequential speech acts acquire interdependent values—say an *assertion* followed by an example which appears to *justify* it); the whole aided by the hierarchical structure of the discourse and premissed on an understanding of comprehension being "a provisional construct by an individual, based partly on a language text, partly on the knowledge and skills he brings to the text . . . involv(ing) accepting 'different' comprehensions" (Urquhart, 1977).

Jones argues that for the understanding of the discourse of this Geography text (much as we have argued for doctors, and have Leech and Labov) readers have available to them certain *conceptual structures* or *procedures* of science (the specifying of the *structure* of systems, the *properties* of systems and the *changes of state* such systems undergo). These constitute the "knowledge of the scientific world" against which the discourse in question is set. In this text, Jones uses the subdivision of *Regions* in paragraphs one and two as an example of system structure, the properties of the *Heart of Desert Regions* (+ brought/ + sun/ + wind/ + occasional rainstorms/ + heat by day) as examples of system properties, and the *Climatic shift* (cf. lines 8–13 of the text) from State 1 (where there is a match of climate and scenery) to State 2 (where there is less matching of climate and scenery) as an example of system change of state.

Such a match of knowledge (about deserts) with basic concepts of science needs, however, to be realized in a particular "rhetorical" (or discoursal) organization. In brief, Jones proposes that this discoursal organization is dependently structured: a basic *plan* (to delimit and characterize the system of desert climates) subsumes a series of *states* (in paragraphs one and two, *problem identification*, thereafter (though not in the extract here) *solution presentation*) each of which in turn subsumes a number of *moves*. The stage *Problem Identification*, Jones argues, is expounded by three *moves: contrastive analysis* (sentences one to four), *problem deduction* (sentences five and six), and *amplification of the problem* (remainder of paragraph two). Finally, these *moves* are themselves structured into a series of *acts*. *Contrastive analysis* (as one such *move*) subsumes the *acts* of

S1   *ascription* (of properties to a sub-system);
S2   *exemplification* (of these properties);
S3   *differentiation* (of the second sub-system, *desert margins*); and
S4   *justification* (of the differentiation)

Jones importantly stresses that each of these acts is dependent on the preceding act (and, like the doctor–patient consultation or the psychotherapeutic interview in part deriving its value from that dependence), but brings with it certain "act-specifying conditions" which characterize it. For example, Jones suggests that:
for an act of ascription to take place certain minimum conditions have to be satisfied: there needs to be:
1. a specified system or sub-system
2. a locale
3. a set of properties
4. a truth value (linking 3 with 1 at 2).
For an act of *differentiation* to occur we need the above conditions together with a previously realized *ascription*.

It is important for the purposes of the arguments in this present paper to acknowledge the link between Jones' "conditions" and those of Searle and Labov. In each case we are dealing with the conditions on the interpretation of particular forces, though here supported by the explanatory value of siting acts within discourse as when Jones extends his argument to assign ascription the *interactive* value of an "initiating" act (in contrast to differentiation which he terms a "responding" act, and exemplification and justification which he terms "supporting" acts).

Without recounting Jones' suggestions for the linguistic realizations of the acts he is isolating, we can point to the considerable impetus that similar approaches to the analysis of written discourse have had on current English language learning materials (cf. Widdowson, 1976a, Mountford, 1975, among others).

From the evidence of these examples the need for contextual reference in the establishing of sense/force relationships ought to be clear, as should the need to include discussion of the whole gamut of linguistic and paralinguistic features in the investigation of how discoursal structure is signalled. It ought also to be clear that across different types of discourse certain general patternings can be isolated and described. We may also assume that these patternings ought in principle (and by using established pedagogic techniques), to be made accessible to learners. Before we can make this leap, however, from statement of discoursal description (and underlying "rules" or conventions of discourse) to the construction of exercise material designed to assist learners in "discovering" these patterns, and in making their own interpretations of discoursal value, we should examine what psycho-sociolinguistic evidence exists to support our contentions about learners' interpretive strategies, and as a consequence be more certain than we are now that these exercises are themselves well motivated.

III EVIDENCE FOR INTERPRETIVE STRATEGIES

As we have seen from the discussion in Section I of this paper, it is possible to suggest ways of relating semantics to pragmatics by employing the machinery of inductive reasoning proper to philosophical argument. This is the methodology used by Searle (1975) (referred in Leech, 1977) in his reconstruction of the way in which "Can you pass the salt" is interpreted as a request.

Now it may be the case that one can interpret illocutionary values by appeal to general principles of human communication (though we have cast some cultural and social doubts on that) if one is pursuing a philosophical argument, but one must be careful not to assert that this is what is *actually* going on, in a psycho-sociolinguistic sense, without further evidence. It is possible to agree with Leech's comment on Searle's (1975) steps in the reasoning process:

> Obviously we need not think of such a laborious thought process going through the mind of a speaker of English whenever that speaker responds to an indirect request. The associations, through

convention, become automatic, and yet at the same time, to show that they are not arbitrary, we must, following Grice, explain how they "can be worked out".

We still need to secure psycholinguistic and sociolinguistic evidence of interpretive behaviour. This evidence is particularly necessary if we are about to suggest applied linguistic materials and methodologies for enhancing learners' interpretive strategies in confronting misunderstandable communication.

There are, I suggest, two sources of information on speaker/hearer interpretive behaviour to which we can have recourse, if we wish to have a warrant for our pedagogical suggestions. These sources ought to assist us in isolating the nature of what Widdowson has termed "procedures" (Widdowson, 1975b), where the term is used to encompass "the realizing of the communicative import of language in use", and where, clearly, he is suggesting the existence of some psycho-sociolinguistic substantiation. The sources are, firstly, evidence from actual instances of speaker/hearer interpretive behaviour, and secondly, evidence from psycholinguistic studies into perception and comprehension, some of which have a second-language-learning orientation. Let me give some brief examples from each of these sources, in order to motivate the pedagogical examples in the final section of this paper.

Source 1

The most obvious data come from studies of speaker/hearer talk, and, in particular, ethnomethodological studies of how speakers try to cope with the inexactness of utterances by a process of "remedial work". The "members methods" of ethnomethodology (by which is meant a concentration on strategies of interpretation) focus on the ways that speakers indicate (by what they say) what they understand, thus bringing out into the open as it were, the indeterminacy of meaning. Jefferson (1972) contains many such examples:

A: We stole -okay d- we'll *tell* him. We stole all the uhm
B: I stole the Mama Lisa
A: No we didn't
B: (And sold it to a pusher
A: (Well, *you* may've
A: I came in last night// and I stole all the reco(hh)rds
⧧ C: The *Mama* Lisa ⧧

where the utterance in ⧧—⧧ functions as one interpretive strategy which she terms the "questioning repeat". "This type of repeat characteristically signals that there is a problem in its product-item, and its work is to generate further talk directed to remedying this problem." What she terms "Misapprehension Sequences" produce further examples of these attempts at clarification.

> A1: Her whole room she's got it wallpapered. She just—she just got done rewallpapering it about a month ago,
> ǂⱶ B: —with the pictures of the Beatles.
> A2: No. A month ago Mom had it done in this grasscloth . . .

Jefferson's point is that this interchange is a frequent sequence in conversation, where a *statement* is made (A1), which is followed by a *misapprehension* (B), which is followed in turn by a *clarification* (A2). We could equally regard the misapprehension of B ǂⱶ — ǂⱶ as a further example of interpretive strategy by B, compelling, as it were, A, to be more clear. Here the "clarification" refers to an object (type of wall-covering); it could also refer to illocutionary force (and frequently does). Duncan's (1973) remarks on "requests for clarification" in back-channel communication give further evidence of this strategy, and add useful kinetic and paralinguistic information on the method of marking such behaviour. Silverman's (1971) paper on interview talk widens the focus of interpretive strategy by relating it to participants' variable awareness (or "attentiveness") to the transactional rules of particular types of encounter (in his case, the Interview); he argues that participants "rationalize" apparently discordant forces (at the moment of uttering) subsequently to conform to the expected force of an utterance *in that particular type of encounter.*

> For instance, what might have seemed like a trivial matter at the time (e.g. a joke that didn't come off) may now be viewed as a central contributing factor to a later outcome (e.g. creating an unfavourable impression) where that outcome *is seen as what-had-to-be.* (my italics)

This would seem to imply for us that the exercise of concurrent or posthoc interpretive strategy is directly related to the awareness of the interpreter of the particular "rules of the game"; we cannot even assume that culturally (and presuppositionally) varied interactants will be adequately aware of "what-had-to-be" even to adjust retrospectively interpretations made at the time (in the manner of Garfinkel's medical students who rationalized as plausible what were on the face of it absurd outcomes of medical interviews, simply because they were attuned to accepting any outcome from professionals as plausible, and did not want to appear "judgemental dopes" (in Silverman's phrase)). In short, the need to exercise an interpretive strategy cannot be taken for granted; it, too, depends on appreciating the conventional sequences and outcomes of the encounter. Is ignorance communicative bliss?

L2 learning situations provide frequent examples of the exercise of other interpretive strategies: those dealing with assessment of the pre-conditions on the interpretation of speech acts (see the comments on Labov in Section I of this paper) are an example. Allwright (1975), McTear (1975a and b); McLean and Castanos (1976) all provide examples where EFL/ESL learners give responses which are construed by teachers as incoherent in that they fail to match the discoursal expectation (where, for example, learners treat pattern practice interrogatives as genuine requests for information, and so answer them as such). Here the interpretive strategy of "treating utterances at their face value" or even discounting any interpretation at all and merely repeating what your interlocutor has said, is conditioned by the learner's perception of the encounter; if it is merely *mechanical* (Paulston, 1970) then different interpretive strategies are required than if it is *communicative*. To cite one example from McTear (1975a) (as one among many in this rich environment for discovering instances of interpretive strategies at work), we have the following:

> T: Where are you from? Where are you from?
> SS: We're from Venezuela . . . . .
> T: Say the sentence: "Where are you from".
> SS: Where are you from

Ionesco-like this may be, but it indicates readily enough how not only the result of a particular interpretive strategy but the exercise of it itself, depends crucially on the nature of the pre-conditions established for the to-be-interpreted utterance, in particular the mutual membershipping of the interlocutors, and the assessment of relevant position on Leech's power/solidarity axes.

Source 2

In emphasizing the need to take account of evidence for interpretive strategies from psycholinguistic experimentation, let me (very sketchily) adduce some examples from speech perception studies and from research into comprehension, which have a bearing on the understanding of discourse. I refer here extensively to discussion in Murphy and Candlin (1976, 1979).

There is a vast literature in first language perception studies (see Slobin, 1971), and therefore any small selection runs the risk of travesty: I concentrate here on a sample which bear out Fodor and Garrett's comment that "much of the decoding procedure bears no direct relationship with linguistic rules" (Fodor and Garrett, 1966). Wanner's (1973) experiments are a case in point where the identification of isolated words by native speakers is concerned. Subjects were asked to identify sample recordings, hearing the first word on the recording, then the first two words, and so on up to eight. Intelligibility for each recording was scored in terms of the percentage of words correctly identified and there were 100 eight-word samples each broken up.

> When single words were played to listeners, average intelligibility dropped as low as 30 % for some speakers . . . despite the high quality of the recordings, despite the fact that the listeners were told how many words to expect on each trial, and despite a method which provided repeated exposures to some portion of most of the speech tested. In order to achieve 90 % intelligibility, listeners had to hear recordings containing an average of 7.5 words and lasting over 1.5 seconds.
>
> (Wanner, 1973:166–7)

Clearly speech recognition does not take place in minimum units, and interpretation requires active participation by the interpreter. Wanner refers to this latter point as an "inside-out" theory of speech perception, where the hearer matches the incoming signal against an hypothesized form of the message. Lieberman (1967) has shown that when single forms with alternative readings ("light housekeeper vs lighthouse keeper") are spliced as recordings into inappropriate contexts, hearers perceived the form suggested by the context, despite differences of temporal interval between the vowel peaks which could be adduced as phonetic evidence for distinction: in short, they "heard" what they expected. This evidence for the strategies of comparison, inference and prediction will be important for subsequent comments on comprehension and the understanding of discourse, but what is important here is that perception related very clearly to a hearer's existing mastery of the phonological, syntactic, and by implication the discoursal, systems of the language in question. Slobin's comment is especially apposite:

> One cannot speak of the complexity of processing a sentence of a given grammatical form in the abstract. Sentences are used to express meanings in situations, and language allows for a range of syntactic expressions because they are called for in a range of communicative contexts . . . a passive sentence need not always be more difficult to understand than an active . . . a negative . . . than an affirmative. Rather it seems that people prefer to describe certain types of situations using certain types of sentences.
> (Slobin, 1971:33–4)

In the context of this paper, one can see here the contrast between syntactic or sense meaning and discoursal or force meaning that we have been examining. Authentic context is necessary for understanding, as is an awareness both of the lack of isomorphism between sentence-sense and utterance-force and of the range of sociolinguistic variation in the sentences themselves. We may add to the assistance provided by actually occurring context, that deriving from our capacity as hearers to exploit natural language redundancy. The much-quoted experiments by Shannon and Weaver (1949) underline our power to predict the nature of messages, given only partial information. As Greene (1975) points out: "since predictability reduces the amount of uncertainty, it follows that the more predictable or redundant a language message is, the less information it will contain and the easier it will be to perceive and memorize". If perception is not a unidirectional process but a continuous one that must be completed before the received signal fades from the primary memory system, it follows that second-language learners need to resist dwelling on the perception of individual words themselves at the cost of losing contact with the necessary interpretive relations between different parts of the larger message. Indeed, perception of these individual words themselves is dependent on a larger context of understanding a great deal about what is likely to follow in a given message. This very clearly relates not only to syntactic and discoursal awareness but also to knowledge of the topic, the speaker's/writer's "world," and his social view; all of which are key concepts in the understanding of discourse and communication. As Fry (1970) points out: "Decoding [means] determining 'what the message must have been'".

As one might expect, as soon as studies in perception value the role of what Carton (1969) refers to as *intralingual, interlingual* and *extralingual* cues, then we are firmly within the sphere of psycholinguistic studies into comprehension. Once again, there is a vast literature (see Clark, 1976; Clark and Clark, 1977; Macrae, 1977 for many sources). Let me isolate two general strategies, in summary form, supported by some more general observations which relate both to the importance of the analysis of discourse to studies of comprehension and to the design of materials and methodologies aimed at improving learners' interpretive competence. The strategies are those of *comparison*, and *inference /prediction*.

Clark (1976) suggests a four-stage comparison schema. At Stage 1, the subject is presumed to construct a semantic representation for the sentence; at Stage 2 a "representation" to which the sentence applies (say, a picture, or some item of information under query); at Stage 3 the subject *compares* his representation with that of the object/item of information under interrogation, and finally in Stage 4 "the subject takes the outcome of the Stage 3 comparison operations" and translates it into a reply/response. Clark uses propositional logic to state the representations being compared in his Stage 3 in order to achieve a necessary parity of form in the comparands. The question Macrae poses

(1977) is the need to widen Clark's reference beyond "picture descriptions": "Comprehension rarely involves the comparison of simple sentences against minimal context but requires the listener to integrate the information presented into some much larger system and to extract from it details which may have been recorded a long time before the event." This is very much the position adopted by Slobin. Macrae usefully refers to research into Artificial Intelligence to illustrate how such a model as proposed by Clark would need to include in its reference information on *action* as well as *verification*; i.e. it is not sufficient to compare representations at the level of *sense* but also at the level of force: rhetorical questions are discoursally dissimilar from commands, though both may share interrogative form. Accepting this need to determine at what "level" we are performing Clark's comparison procedure (i.e. what level of understanding) then we can agree two important consequences for devising materials and methodologies. Firstly, that we should see that comprehension involves comparison followed by action and response (a plea for integrated communication skills); and secondly, and more centrally, that comprehension involves concentrating on both the *process* and the *product*. This is what Urquhart (1977), as we have seen, refers to as comprehension being "provisional", or more exactly, a process of "analysis and synthesis" where the hearer/reader is engaged in "continuous readjustment" to the nature of the message in an active process of comprehension.

This dynamic process highlights the importance of inference or "good guessing" and its associate strategy of prediction. Carton (1969) stresses that inference is dependent on a "probabilistic" view of language, and that "comprehension is enhanced by intuitions into contingencies". We have already taken this probabilistic view of the relationship between sense and force and supported it by a general educational desire to allow materials to provide possibilities for alternative, individual learner interpretations. Carton's classification of cues into those which relate to information already provided in the text or the structure of the language in question, those which are contributed by comparisons with the interpreter's mother tongue, and those which extralinguistically refer to shared knowledge sum up the base data for the practice of inferencing.

Carton draws important pedagogic conclusions:

A language pedagogy that utilizes inferencing removes language study from the domain of mere skills to a domain that is more closely akin to the regions of complex intellectual processes. Language study becomes a matter for a kind of problem-solving and the entire breadth of the student's experience and knowledge may be brought to bear on the processing of language.

We can see this inferencing process at work precisely in the conversational data provided by the ethnomethodologists or the second-language-learning classroom research referred to earlier, and that is why such data are of central value, both as a guide for the analysis of discourse and for the construction of materials and methodologies. We can observe in such data occurrences of Goodman's cycle of *sampling, predicting, testing* and *confirming*, in his characterization of comprehension, and by careful observation of what the user attends to (and what he does not) we (like his hearer) build up a picture of his expectations and the degree of his understanding.

What we know too little about are the isolatable sub-strategies associated with this inferential process. Clark and Clark (1977) suggest some which relate to the understanding of sentence propositions, but do not indicate whether they are ordered, or even whether hearers first employ strategies which relate to the interpretation of sense before those relating to force or vice-versa. It may well be that research into the acquisition of discourse will provide more clues towards the algorithmic chaining of such strategies. Until this evidence is available it would seem sensible to combine our interpretive targets, both linguistic and discoursal, in whatever manner seems pedagogically desirable. A similar process of combination should apply to discourse and paradiscourse since we do not have evidence as to whether these are separately or integratedly decoded. What seems to be the case is that in the process of making inferences the fluent comprehender is constantly predicting and anticipating what may come; as Gardner (1977) suggests: "Meanings occur in the mind of the reader, even a beginning reader, before words are decoded". Given this, we ought not only to ensure that materials relate to text and discourse, but also that they are firmly sited in the context of an interpreter's ongoing knowledge. Texts used to have a reason for being interpreted; the degree of interpretation will depend on the particular follow-up action and the interpreter's contributory knowledge or perspective; and we would be well advised to bring out into the open the concurrent discussion of possible and plausible interpretations that continue in the hearer/reader's mind. There is a real sense in which the process of reading, for example, mirrors that of conversation; the interpreter in each case works at understanding in a dynamic fashion, seeking warrants from the immediate context of the utterances or from the outside topic or world-view, and being compelled, by the consequent remarks (or writing) of his co-conversationalist (or author) to revalue his interpretation and find alternative significance.

IV APPLIED LINGUISTIC PRACTICE

On the basis of the discussion in the first three sections of this paper, it would seem that pedagogic materials and methodologies must (at least) reflect the following assumptions about the learning of language as communication if they are to come near to developing learners' abilities to cope with problems of discoursal misunderstanding:

1. Assume that learners need to be sensitized to the cultural presuppositions which imbue particular utterances, and that this sensitivity is a prerequisite to understanding language as communication.

2. Assume that the relationship between sense and force depends on a continuing evaluation of the social view of (and by) speaker and hearer/writer and reader.

3. Assume that this sense/force relationship will be underlain by culture-specific rules of discourse (and also by some pan-cultural rules) which constitute the chief objective of language learning.

4. Assume that such rules are realized through interaction, and as a consequence the data for language learning ought to be presented in a transactional context.

5. Assume that communication is a process of applying these rules of disclosure to convey meaning via a range of linguistic and paralinguistic signs, and that these signs are culturally and socially specific.

6. Assume that deriving meaning is a process of dynamic inference.

7. Assume that (as a consequence) meanings are plural and variable in value as the communication proceeds.

8. Assume that identifying strategies of interpretation can both serve to elucidate discourse as well as act as a language-learning objective.

I am aware that this short list could easily be extended, particularly if one was to go outside the bounds of this paper and be concerned with developing learner production skills, but it can serve as one yardstick for evaluating and designing materials and teaching procedures. It would seem, moreover, that such a yardstick is necessary if only to add a note of caution to current, over-simple, applications of a loose speech act theory to language-learning materials (for further comment on this point see Candlin, 1976 and Widdowson, 1977). Certainly adopting even some of these assumptions would dramatically alter the nature of most English language teaching materials in current use (with some notable exceptions, especially in the area of ESP) and alter many of our treasured methodologies (for further comment see Allwright, 1976; Stevick, 1976; Jakobovits and Gordon, 1974; Breen and Candlin, forthcoming.

In the main body of this section I would like to suggest very briefly some example materials which go some way towards meeting these assumptions, and consequently, the goal of this paper, namely, the equalizing of interpretive opportunity among the many-cultured audience of English language speakers and learners.

Example 1 Sensitivity

(from: *Doctor–patient communication skills*, Candlin, Bruton, Leather and Woods, 1977)

> . . . the materials concentrate on the complex issues in communication that arise from the contrasting experience and expectations of the local patient and the doctor from overseas. However good the doctor's professional skills, he cannot be expected to have full knowledge of the linguistic and cultural conventions which contribute to effective communication in a consultation with a person whose background may differ so radically from his own . . . to this end there are modules (in the course) which deal with the central place of *language in the consultation*; a view of language as communication which brings together *language as form and as function*; and *the status and role of the doctor* himself. Both instructors and learners (as well as patients) need to become *sensitized* to these underlying issues, if they are to understand fully the subtle devices of oral (and gestural) communication by which speakers can give and obtain information, monitor each others' talk and indicate sympathy, reassurance and optimism . . .
> (from the *Introduction* to the course materials *Teachers' Handbook*).

Note also the *Instructional Goal* of Module 1: *The Status and Role of the Casualty Officer*:

> To make the learner objectify his experience as a doctor from overseas working in an Accident and Emergency Department of a hospital. Emphasis is on the attitudes of doctors from overseas to their status and the roles a doctor has; and on the attitudes of patients and what they expect from a doctor. The learner's attention is drawn to the role of language in the doctor–patient interview.

Note also the *Workscheme* (i.e. suggested teaching plan) from Module 2: *Language in the Consultation*:

> 1. Begin by raising the points in the first set of Discussion Notes concerning the sequence of operational phases in a consultation.
> 2. Ask the learners to view the whole *unphased* consultation recorded as Stage 3 of the videotape. Alternatively, listen to any of

the *complete* consultations recorded and transcribed in Module 24 (Transmediation).

3. Revise conclusions to 1 above on the sequence of operational phases. Aim to isolate (at least) the following:

1. Greeting	4. Diagnosis
2. Information-extracting	5. Prognosis/therapy
3. Examination	6. Leavetaking

4. Ask the learners to view the *phased* consultation recorded as Stage 4 of the videotape.

5. Move on to Recognition Exercise 1. Ask the learners to listen/view the consultation and isolate the operational phases in the transcript of the consultation. Make any amendments/suggest variants to the conclusions reached in 3 above.

6. Now introduce the points in the second set of Discussion Notes concerning the relationship between operational phases and language use in the consultation.

7. Ask the learners to view the example of extracts from consultation phases recorded as Stages 5 and 6 of the course videotape. Alternatively, listen to a variety of the consultation extracts recorded and transcribed in Modules 4–23 of the course. Aim to isolate *Cognitive, Affective* and *Meta-communicative* functions of language in the consultation.

8. Now move on to Recognition Exercise 2. Ask the learners to listen/view the consultation and suggest functional values for the underlined utterances in the light of their conclusions from 7 above.

9. Using the points in the third set of Discussion Notes, summarize the language requirements of the operational phases of the consultation, paying particular attention to the three broad functions of language you have isolated.

10. Administer the Post-Test.

Note also (from the *Teachers Handbook*):

> . . . accepting that learners will come from varying socio-cultural backgrounds, it is essential *before going on to the main part of the course* that they become aware of the particular UK socio-cultural setting in which they will be/are working. The *sensitization* modules are therefore an essential element at the outset of any course . . .

The above extracts from the DOPACS materials and Teachers Book give an idea of the central place afforded by these materials to the assumptions at the outset of this section. In addition to the three modules entirely devoted to the establishment of a cultural context for the materials and to conveying the principle of viewing language as communication, there are, in many of the FUNCTION modules, *sensitivity exercises*; these are designed to require the learner to become aware of the contextualization cues (both in terms of language and paralanguage) through which it is possible to suggest the communicative value of particular utterances.

Example 2. Integrated Interpretation Exercises

(from: *CHALLENGES* (a multimedia course in developing communication skills in English) Abbs, Candlin, Edelhoff, Moston and Sexton, Longman 1978)

Chain G encourages learners to estimate the speech act values of gestures and heard utterances, and progressively introduces (Hymesian) features of events. Chain H takes up some EIAL issues [sic] and asks learners to focus on spoken contextualization cues in communicative contexts. The Project effectively crosses the target language boundary by stressing the universality of the saying versus doing problem. Note, in particular, how the whole context of utterances is portrayed through interrelated channels of communication: film, slide, tape, printed text.

Example 3.   Discourse Chains

(Examples (a) and (b) from *CHALLENGES* op. cit., Example (c) from: *Protokoll der 7 Arbeitstagung Bundesarbeitsgemeinschaft Englisch an Gesamtschulen*, Kassel 1975.)

The objective of each of these relatively simple exercises is to encourage learners to see the way in which speech acts are "chained" interactively in discourse; using such simple diagrams they can both practise interpretive techniques, as in Example (a), leading to productive practice, as in the Task section of (a) and (b), and the open exercise in Example (c). In this way we can lead learners to analyse discourse themselves, both by employing interpretive strategies and through modelling exercises in turn-taking. From the "product-orientation" of such a model can be developed a learner interest in the "process orientation" of ongoing monitoring of the discourse linked to the choice of different conversational "routes".

I leave it to the reader to judge the appropriateness of these examples in the light of the points made at the beginning of this section, and in Sections II and III of the paper. To me they go some way towards meeting the key criteria governing materials designed to improve learners' interpretive competence, namely:
1. The provision of cultural/ethnographic/contextual information;

Saying it

STEP 1 MATCHING

Look at the pictures. What do you think the person speaking in each picture is saying? Match the number of the picture with the list of intentions. Then fill in the bubbles with what you think the people are saying.

STEP 2 LISTENING + MATCHING

Listen to the snatches of conversation. Match the scenes with the intentions in the chart.

INTENTION	PICTURE	TAPE-SCENE
ASKING FOR HELP		
APOLOGIZING		
FLATTERING		
PERSUADING		
GIVING INSTRUCTIONS		
GIVING ORDERS		
CRITICISING		
INTRODUCING		
THANKING		
REFUSING		

Card Game

STEP 3 PAIRWORK: LISTENING

Make two sets of cards: a set of 'intentions' and a set of 'language' cards. Then listen to the tape. You are walking along the street. As you walk, you overhear bits of conversation. As you hear each extract, put down the right language card, and your partner should try to cover it with the correct intention card.

STEP 4 LISTENING + NOTE-TAKING

Listen to the short extracts of people talking. Try to decide WHO is talking to WHOM, WHERE and WHEN. Make notes under these headings:

STEP 5 GROUPWORK: DISCUSSION

TASK 1

TASK 2

INTENTION

1. MAKING A SUGGESTION
2. SHOWING ENTHUSIASM
3. GREETING
4. SHOWING SYMPATHY
5. ASKING FOR INFORMATION
6. GIVING AN OPINION
7. DESCRIBING A PERSON
8. ASKING FOR AN OPINION
9. SHOWING DISAGREEMENT
10. EXPRESSING ANXIETY
11. DENYING
12. GIVING INFORMATION

LANGUAGE

A. You haven't said anything yet. What do you think?
B. What time's your train?
C. He's about your age, but a bit taller, and thinner.
D. She left school when she was fifteen.
E. Why don't you go and see a doctor?
F. Heh! That's marvellous!
G. I just don't know what to do.
H. Hello, Mike. Fancy seeing you here!
I. I think it was a very stupid thing to do.
J. No, that's not right, that's not right at all.
K. It wasn't me who did it.
L. Oh, I am sorry, I really am.

Speaker | Hearer(s) | Place | Event

Discuss your notes with the other members of your group.

SITUATION GAME

In groups write a short extract of someone talking in English. It should not be too difficult to identify WHO is talking to WHOM, WHERE and WHEN. Record the extract and see if the other groups can work out WHO is talking to WHOM, WHERE and WHEN.

ROLEPLAY

Choose one of the intentions from Step 1 or Step 3. Take one of the utterances which matches this intention (either one you have heard or one you made up for the illustrations). Make it the *first* or *last* line of a little scene. Rehearse your scene and act it out.

chain h

STEP 1 LISTENING QUIZ (1)

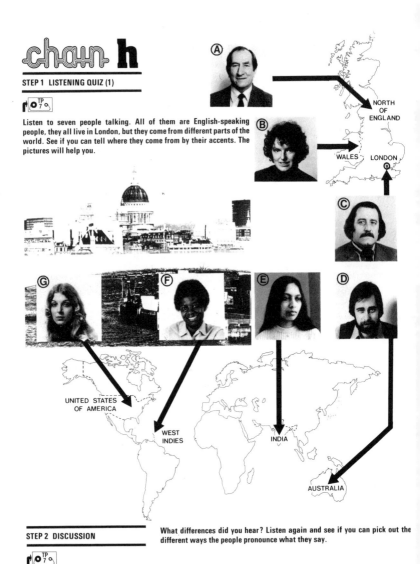

Listen to seven people talking. All of them are English-speaking people, they all live in London, but they come from different parts of the world. See if you can tell where they come from by their accents. The pictures will help you.

NORTH OF ENGLAND

WALES   LONDON

UNITED STATES OF AMERICA

WEST INDIES

INDIA

AUSTRALIA

STEP 2 DISCUSSION

What differences did you hear? Listen again and see if you can pick out the different ways the people pronounce what they say.

TEP 3 LISTENING QUIZ (2)

Here are more people from the same places talking. Write down the numbers 1–7 and then the places the speakers come from.

TEP 4 LISTENING + MATCHING

People don't only speak English in different ways if they come from different parts of the world. The *same person* speaks English in different ways too – according to the person he or she is talking to. Listen to the man asking permission to do something from 4 different people.
Who do you think he is talking to in each case? (Someone he dislikes/His boss/Someone who works under him/His son)

1. ....
2. ....
3. ....
4. ....

TEP 5 LISTENING + MATCHING

We also talk differently to people according to the situation. Listen to the same two people talking in three different situations. What do you think the situation is in each case? (Visiting friends/At a funeral/At a party)

A. ....
B. ....
C. ....

Take one of the intentions from Chain G, Step 3. Prepare two scenes based on it. Make them different. Choose different situations and different social roles. Act them out for your group.

THE WAY PEOPLE SPEAK

You have now seen that:

People can use language to get across different intentions.

When you overhear people speak you can tell WHO is talking TO WHOM, WHERE and WHEN.

People speak English differently depending on which part of the country or which English-speaking country they come from.

They speak differently according to who they are talking to.

They speak differently according to where they are.

They speak differently according to what role they are playing.

TASKS

Think about somebody learning your language.

1. Make some recordings of people with different accents in your own language. Note down where they come from.
2. Take some of the speech intentions you have met in this unit. For each one, record and note down different ways of expressing it, according to who is talking, where the person is speaking and what role he/she is playing.

Finally, get together in groups and make up a combined phrasebook for your language under your speech intention headings.

Key to Symbols

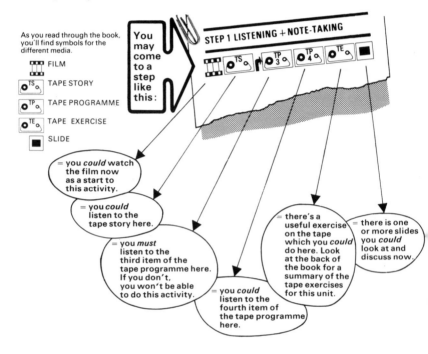

2. The provision of information on value and discoursal structure;

3. An awareness of the role of inference and prediction in the interpreting of communication;

4. The provision of particular purposes for the interpretive process; and

5. An acknowledgement of alternative outcomes to this process.

CONCLUSION

I have tried to concentrate, then, on improvements to the learner, rather than on improvements to the quality of the data which he confronts in his communication. I hope that I have, however, not minimized the problems presented by the data; indeed the concentration of much of the paper with the difficulties surrounding the analysis of discourse meaning has, if anything, heightened the problems. At the same time, the examples in Sections II and IV will, hopefully, have suggested ways in which we can begin to address them, in descriptive linguistic and

Example (a)

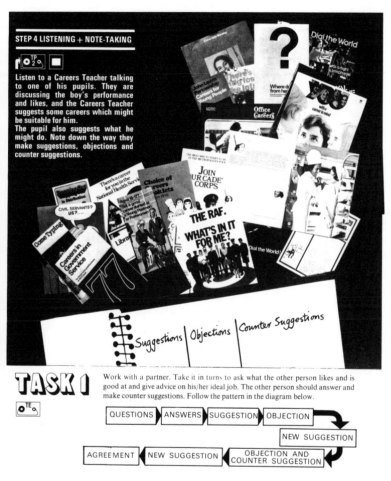

applied linguistic terms. The common ground that is beginning to emerge in the analysis of discourse is a particularly hopeful sign, as is the way in which ideas from these analyses are percolating (rather fast) into teaching materials. Notwithstanding this, however, since the paper has a strong cross-cultural implication, and, as such, constitutes an explicit challenge to the frequently ethnocentric discourse (and communicative values) of ELT, we ought to expect a little difficulty.

The equalizing of interpretive opportunity among cross-cultural learners of English is one goal which ought to unite current work in

Example (b)

STEP 5 MATCHING Now look at these expressions. Decide which expressions fit which intentions.	I put the .... near the .... I thought I needed a .... I wanted a .... I decided to buy a .... SAY IT WAS A BAD IDEA Great! SAY YOU THINK IT'S GOOD That's a good idea! You can't put it there! GIVE REASONS Not there! SAY YOU AGREE You didn't need a .... SAY YOU DISAGREE ...., did you? A .... wasn't SAY WHERE YOU PUT SOMETHING necessary, was it? SAY WHAT YOU DECIDED TO BUY Why? ASK WHY Why not? Well, I like it ASK WHY NOT I don't agree with you SAY SOMETHING WASN'T NECESSARY That's not what I think Because ....

STEP 6 DISCUSSION

When you have decided how you want your flat, discuss the arrangement with a partner or in groups. Use the chart.

Imagine you have just been shopping. Use the chart and discuss with your partner what you have bought. Simulate different kinds of situations where someone tells other people what he/she has bought.

discourse analysis, materials preparation and methodology. Certainly there will be different pedagogic paths to this goal, among different cultural and educational systems and in the face of variation in communicative challenge. Concurrently, however, with this and other related research we can take a small step to ensure that whatever types of learning materials we present to English language learners, they at least match up to my assumptions.

It may be argued that this paper has concentrated unduly on interpretation to the neglect of productive abilities. Narrowly speaking, of course, most English language learners need a reading and listening competence most, but, more generally, just as psycholinguistic experiment and discourse analysis compel us to see the comprehension and interpretation of discourse as a unity, so production and interpretation are closely related. Speaker intent and hearer uptake are two ends of a cline; communicative language learning exists to bring the poles together. To do this we shall have to make all sorts of compromises: on

Example (c)

Announce an intention, make a suggestion	Raise an objection	Counter the objection	Object again	Play down the argument	Agree
	Where is it? Oh, in Essex. That's too far.	Oh, it's not far. You can be there in under an hour.	You don't know my parents. My dad would have a fit.	Pah, you're not a kid any more.	Well, I suppose I could try.
				Say Goodbye.	
				I'll go and ask Mary, then.	
I'm going to a pop festival on Saturday. Do you fancy coming?	Agree	Express enthusiasm. Fix a date.	Fix a precise time.	All right. See you then.	
	Where is it? Oh, in Essex, that's not far. We can be there in under an hour.	That's great. Look at all these groups. When shall we meet?	Let's say on Sunday 8 p.m.		
				Make other suggestions.	Agree.
				8 is too early, 9 would be better.	Right, see you at 9 then.

occasion we may be required to "pidginize" our discourse so that our message comes over loud and clear (even at a little cost to Leech's Tact); we shall certainly have to learn particular strategies for eliciting from English-speaking interlocutors with dissimilar sociocultural presuppositions what we need to know. Devising means for making other English-speaking people plain would be a fitting adjunct to the suggestions in this paper.

12 Via-Drama: An Answer to the EIIL Problem*

Richard A. Via

For anyone, especially me, to write a paper titled *Via-Drama: An Answer to the EIIL Problem* obviously denotes either that I have a super ego or that I am a fool. I do not believe I have a super ego; however, I do not deny that I may be something of a fool. However, I would like to prevail on the community of academics to bear with me for a short time to consider some of the possibilities of incorporating drama in an EIIL context and to reflect on the possible effective results that may be obtained through its use. Like penicillin, drama may not work in every case or effect a cure for every problem, but it does have special uses that clearly classify it as a wonder drug if it is used according to directions. While wonder drugs sometimes cause adverse reactions, thus far the application of drama seems to have produced few bad side effects.

If drama—Via-Drama—is being promoted as an answer to the EIIL problem then we had best define what the problem is. Each one of us would probably suggest a different major problem; therefore, it would seem that the problem is that there are many problems. Of these, perhaps the paramount problem is the problem of change. By and large, human beings in all cultures demonstrate a certain resistance to change. We tend to be rather complacent about the way things are, and when we are faced with the prospect of change we immediately think of the problems that will be created if change ensues and in one way or another erect barriers. We wonder if change will truly result in something beneficial and more often than not conclude that it is better to maintain the status quo rather than gamble or otherwise take a risk.

The next problem is closely related to the first and that is the label—English in International and Intranational Language. EIIL! Why? We seem hesitant to add yet another acronym to the overcrowded list in the field of English teaching/learning. And yet it seems to me that we have been teaching EIIL for a long, long time. Of course, there are instances

* I am grateful to Ted Plaister for his criticisms of an earlier version of this paper.

where English is taught as an academic discipline presumably in an effort to bolster one's intellectual growth or even so perverse a use as to fill up a student's daily schedule of courses. But for the serious language students, those who are studying the language for its eventual use as a means of communication for specific needs, EIIL has been, and is, a reality.

Perhaps the next comment need not be stated, but along with a number of other English language teachers I look forward to the day when our acronym will simply be E.

Now that I have conveniently disposed of these two problems, that is, change and nomenclature, let me address teaching/learning situations directly and discuss with you exactly what is meant by Via-Drama.

Via-Drama for language teaching/learning is quite different from language learning via drama. In the past few years there have been numerous articles hailing the "new" idea of using drama for language teaching purposes (see for example, Moffett, 1967; Walker, 1977; V. Brown, 1977; Dent-Young, 1974). L. G. Kelley in his book *25 centuries of language teaching* says, "Plays have been employed to teach skill in language only since the Middle Ages" (p. 122). Yet when we look at the techniques employed in these drama *activities* we discover that rarely were there any drama *techniques* used. Instead, students were asked to memorize and recite. These rote presentations hardly qualify as successful theatre where spoken lines reflect genuine conversation. And surely all of us have at one time or another suffered through verbal exchanges with the student who rote-memorized dialogues, something which can hardly pass as legitimate conversation.

I am aware that drama terminology is likely to frighten students away and cause administrators to back off from accepting these very useful techniques. For this reason it is probably wise to refrain from using such words as drama, acting, actors, etc. and substitute terms that are more acceptable to the academic situation. I would suggest incorporating simulation exercises, language interaction, expressive communication, communicative behaviour, situational dialogues, learning through doing, activity methods and participatory interaction. The list could be greatly extended and they all represent what drama is all about.

If we are to use Via-Drama for teaching EIIL then we must abandon the idea that the use of drama for language learning requires presenting a play. I am not suggesting that a play presentation cannot be considered a useful project. But I do insist that drama techniques encompass much, much more than mere play presentation. The presenting of a play would more accurately be identified as "theatre". We can, however, incorporate theatre in our language classrooms whenever one group of students are presenting an activity for the rest of the class. Brian Way (1967) in his book *Development through drama* says: "theatre is largely concerned with communication between actors and an audience; 'drama' is concerned with experience by the participants irrespective of any function of communication to an audience" (pp. 2–3). If I expand his definition by inserting another "communication" in the drama definition portion then it will describe our needs a little better. Thus, " 'drama' is concerned with experience and communication between the participants . . .". In order to fulfil this new definition successfully the use of a number of techniques is in order.

In the process of learning and speaking a new language, students experience many of the same frustrations and inhibitions that professional actors sustain when they are preparing a new role. Still, if we incorporate some of the techniques that good actors use to overcome or control their psychological problems, we should see marked improvement in our students' linguistic performance. These techniques, some of which will be discussed later in the paper, include exercises for self-awareness, relaxation, observation, physicalization, concentration, imagination and personalization.

Everyone can act; yet no one is a born actor. And we must remember that in our use of drama for language teaching we are in the business of developing our students' language abilities, not in developing actors. By the same token all of our students can learn a new language, although none of them is born with that particular language.

Our primary concern in all language education is with the student as an individual. If ever we look at our class as a class then, in my view, we automatically and predictably minimize our chances and possibilities of success. Drama is concerned with the individual. Moreover, it is concerned with the individuality of the individual. It is the basic concern that is the key to Via-Drama.

In his writings, Constantin Stanislavski repeatedly expressed the idea that "self" was the basic of all good acting; that is, understanding one's self, understanding how one relates to others, how others react to you. From these understandings all other techniques and study can take root, grow, and ultimately flourish.

Jerome Rockwood (1966) in *The craftsmen of Dionysus* says:

> To say that the actor becomes the character is to suggest some
> sort of transformation which defies all natural laws. A person
> cannot become another person. He cannot exchange his mind and
> his limbs for those of another. He is always in possession of his
> own faculties, physical and mental . . .
>
> (p. 15)

Still another opinion in the same vein comes from *Christian and oriental philosophy of art* by Ananda Coomaraswamy (1956) who wrote, "The artist was not a special kind of man, but every man a special kind of artist." (p. 112)

To add even more emphasis to the notion of the individuality of each individual student let me emphasize that language learners are not special kinds of people, but rather that each person is a special kind of language learner.

This understanding of, use of, dependency on self is the underlying principle and foundation of all of the techniques involved in language teaching/learning using Via-Drama. It might be conceived of as the basic of basics.

According to W. Timothy Gallwey as explicated in his *The inner game of tennis*, tennis players suffer from the same obstacles as do language learners and actors in their labours to master the game of tennis. These barriers include such things as lapses in concentration, nervousness, self-doubt and self-condemnation. As Gallwey argues, it is possible for us to overcome all of these learning hurdles. All too often, however, all three of the groups of people mentioned above are suddenly thrown into a "performing" situation without having had sufficient time for them to overcome the debilitating obstacles. A student who is asked to stand in front of a class and recite a dialogue from memory is almost certain to be experiencing all four of the tortures outlined above (i.e., lapses in concentration, nervousness, self-doubt, and self-condemnation).

The solution to this whole problem area is one of relaxation. Different authors agree. For example, Gallwey says: "The player of the inner game comes to value the art of relaxed concentration above all other skills . . ." (p. 13). Rockwood states: ". . . tension is the actor's greatest enemy. When he is completely relaxed, he can command his body, his voice, and his mind to do anything of which he is capable" (p. 33). And Viola Spolin argues: "Before we can play (experience), we must be free to do so. It is necessary to become part of the world around us and make it real by touching it, seeing it, feeling it, tasting it, and smelling it— direct contact with the environment is what we seek" (1963:6), and "Very few of us are able to make the direct contact with our reality. Our simplest move out into the environment is interrupted by our need for favorable comment or interpretation by established authority."

It follows, therefore, that relaxation exercises, many of which could be language related, should be included as an integral part of each language programme. These exercises may include breathing and voice exercises (Via, 1976:12–16). With the entire group participating in a circle no one person is "up front"; thus, all students are shielded from being the focus of attention. Movement exercises can start with simple walking, having the students observe first the way they walk and then observe other students. Continue the exercise by walking on "hot sand", "through water" or "on clouds". If music can be added movement will become freer. Both Viola Spolin (1963) and Brian Way (1967) have numerous excellent movement exercises. The activities themselves may seem rather unusual for a language class and perhaps even silly, but with their application fear and shyness will gradually disappear. Students can then experience being looked at and listened to in their language learning activities in an unthreatening way. Since everyone is capable of successfully participating in these relaxation exercises, they act as a common denominator which binds the group together. By and large a classroom that has formed itself into a cohesive group does much better work. However, it is important to remember that we are still working for the individuality of each student. A good group is one that is composed of a number of individuals working interdependently to achieve their goals, with each being given the opportunity for individual participation and personal contribution.

As mentioned earlier, drama is concerned with communication between the participants. True communication must express the individuals *qua* individuals participating. Therefore, if we use accepted drama techniques we will enable our students to accomplish this. The techniques would avoid the use of such words as "memorize", "recite", "rote", and "role playing". I am aware that anything learned might be said in a sense to be memorized, but the word itself carries with it the connotation of the often-used rote learning process that results in recitation rather than communication. The term "role playing" generally denotes pretending, "acting" rather than *being*.

Through the use of drama techniques, it is possible for us to train our students to express themselves by using themselves. When we have accomplished this, we will have given them one of the greatest possible foundations for language learning. There is a price to pay, however, and that price is to change many of the accepted ideas of language teaching/learning and as I have suggested earlier in this paper, change doesn't come easy. It is encouraging, though, that many of these newer ideas have been given the nod of approval by such leaders in our field as Stevick, Jakobovits, Rivers, etc. Perhaps others will follow their lead.

One of the changes which I see a need for is to get away from the idea of modelling everything for our students, and from relating everything to the cultural context of native-speaking English cultures. There is obviously no one model of the English language. Thus, we can accept the great variety of shading, colouring or emotional feeling that each individual adds to the language. In our teaching we need to move away from the habit of asking students to say something happily, angrily, sadly or with any particular emotion because we can only feel or experience an emotion. We cannot act an emotion. An emotion is a sensing of our bodily changes. Rockwood states:

> . . . just what is an emotion? There are differing theories, but they all recognize an interplay of two factors: the mental apperception of a stimulus and a corresponding physical manifestation.

Whenever we are visited by an emotion, these two factors are always present.

(p. 44)

Thus, an emotion is a very personal thing and is something which cannot be modelled. The better approach is to let our students express their own feeling in a dialogue or in a particular situation.

An example may clarify what I am arguing and should support my contentions especially as they related to EIIL. A Peace Corps language teacher in Thailand had asked one of her students to say a particular utterance with anger. The student repeated the line but not to the teacher's satisfaction. Finally the student explained to the teacher that in her country people did not get openly angry, which ended the discussion on the matter. Now, Thais are human beings just like the rest of us and they certainly experience anger on occasion. In effect the student was saying that Thais do not get angry in this particular situation and therefore cannot express anger in any meaningful way. Thus, in order that students may express themselves honestly they need information about the content of dialogues—the who, what, why, where, when. This puts them in a position to reveal themselves so that they could then render the dialogue in a way meaningful to them.

Let me add that until I had conducted a series of workshops in Southeast Asia I had been guilty of fostering the idea that English had to fit into its native cultural context. Through my observations and experience on that tour I came to realize that we also needed to say that we can fit it into its natural context. By using *natural*, we address one problematic aspect of EIIL by allowing English to be placed wherever it is used in the natural course of events.

Wilger Rivers (1976) in an article entitled "The natural and the normal in language learning" says:

As we teach another language, or help someone learn another language, who are we to say what is a "normal" use of language for a particular individual in a particular situation? How are we to know what, to him, is the "expected order of things" at a deeper nonapparent level, since this depends on such elusive factors as personal assessment of the situation and perceived relationships? This is particularly difficult for us to divine when our student comes from a culture with which we are not intimately familiar. We must recognize that one person's "natural" may well be another person's "unnatural" or can even be disconcerting or distasteful to him.

(p. 2)

If we follow her suggestions we have automatically simplified some aspects of our teaching. We have also gone a long way towards eliminating some of the threats present in our classrooms because we have accepted and established that there are many ways of saying something. Only the individual knows if what he is saying truly expresses what he wants to express. We no longer play the game of asking our students to pretend to be, or to behave like a native speaker. Instead, we ask them to be themselves while speaking another language and possibly fitting what they say into another cultural context or its natural context.

When our students do this, they increase their mutual intelligibility because they are then much more concerned with communicating ideas and emotions than in the reproduction of words and emotions modelled by somebody else. Spoken words are merely sounds and symbols which reach full value only when individuals add themselves to those symbols. A recent television skit I observed illustrated this concept beautifully. In this skit the "English Teacher" spoke with extreme exactness and artificiality, including exaggerated facial expressions and gestures, all of which the "student" copied exactly. The result? Total lack of communication. When the "teacher" in the skit finally relaxed, out of sheer exhaustion and defeat, and began to speak normally, the "student" understood completely and gave a proper reply.

Surely the most accepted and successful of the Via-Drama activities is "talk and listen". It was developed from a technique used by many professional actors to learn their lines and to sound natural, by listening and responding to what and how something is said to them. By using "talk and listen" students will develop a conversational tone, avoid rote memorization, make their dialogues come alive, and, I have found, enjoy the experience.

A good actor, like a good conversationalist, must be a good listener. By listening an actor can judge how he/she needs to respond. The way something is said to a performer, or anyone, affects the way the other performer responds. For a language learner the same holds true. Listening provides the language learner with added opportunity to pick up a needed word or phrase to use in his/her reply.

By talking to an actor, rather than reading, the actor or conversationalist becomes more interesting—the difference between reading and talking is tremendous. Yet in most classroom situations dialogues are read aloud rather than spoken as conversation.

All too often students are asked to memorize a dialogue and recite it in class. In the real world these rote recitations cause the student to fail. The words come tumbling out, with no thought behind them, because that is the way it was memorized.

A sad but frequent consequence of this is that the speaker is not understood by the listener and thus there is no communication, no exchange of information. This isn't a problem in a classroom where dialogues are memorized because it isn't necessary to listen, nor is it necessary to communicate. The cue for the listener to begin speaking is the silence, not the message of the first speaker. With "talk and listen" students are trained to talk and listen and talk.

Perhaps the best way to start students on the "talk and listen" system is to use Talk and Listen Cards. Choose or write a simple dialogue of six to eight lines. Put the lines that A speaks on one card and those of B on another.

A: When can I see you again?	A: – – – –
B: – – – –	B: It's up to you. You're the boss.
A: How about the day after tomorrow?	
	A: – – – –
B: – – – –	B: Sure, what are your plans?
A: I'd rather not say.	A: – – – –
B: – – – –	B: Oh, then maybe I'd better think about it.

Since A speaks first, A reads his/her first line to himself/herself. B does not look at his/her card yet, but waits for A to speak to him/her. A then makes eye contact with B and says the line to B. When A has finished speaking, B then reads the first line on his/her card to himself/herself, then says it to A. The entire dialogue is done this way. Students may refer to their cards as often as necessary, but whenever someone is speaking there must be eye contact. Students should not be reading their lines planning how to say the line, they should be listening to the speaker. A proper response can be given only by listening. When using a dialogue from a textbook or play, students should be careful not to read the line that is being spoken to them. In most cases students who read the line spoken to them hear their own "inner voice" with its interpretation louder than the real voice of the speaker.

Once the students have learned to use the cards, there are other things you may do that are both fun and effective. Speaking the lines in different natural tones or speeds will show how language can be changed in meaning or feeling. The greatest change and the most fun occurs when the circumstances surrounding the situation are given. By this I mean the who, where, what, when, anything that might control the way the sentences would be spoken. Every dialogue changes according to these circumstances yet rarely do teachers think to add them. The more information we give students the more accurate and natural their conversion will be. It is important to remember that the teacher should refrain from asking them to be happy, angry, etc., but to allow the students to arrive at their own interpretations utilizes the dialogue and information given them.

How would the "talk and listen" example be spoken if:

- A is a dentist
- B is a patient who dislikes going to the dentist, and thought to-day was the last visit.

- A is a young man who loves sports, and is fond of B.
- B is a young woman who is more interested in music, dance, and theatre. She is very fond of A, but they have just returned from sailing and the boat capsized.

- A and B are thieves. Recently A has become more daring. It is now 1 a.m. and they have just completed a job.

The dialogues for "talk and listen" may be written by the teacher, taken from textbook dialogues or selected from suitable plays. The class may be divided into pairs using different cards or the same cards with each pair deciding on the given circumstances. After they have worked on them they could be presented in front of the class for all to enjoy. More than likely after working on them they will know the lines and not need the cards. In case they have not learned them, let them refer to the cards rather than memorize the lines.

What means are at our disposal for training students to cope with multicultural situations? Those of us in drama would advocate as crucial the sharpening of observation skills. Accordingly, persons who are poor observers and who resist training of their powers of observation will be poor actors, diplomats, or international persons. Extensive observation exercises are part of most creative drama and drama training. These exercises can and should complement any language programme. One way to do this is through the careful study of photographs and films as a means of increasing our students' understanding of various cultural behaviours. Those who have developed their powers of observation should be able to function in a new culture with relatively few mistakes. Through other drama study they will be able to deal with these mistakes with a minimum amount of embarrassment.

A minor, but important point—especially in large classes—is to remind ourselves and our students that mistakes are part of the learning experience, and should not be looked upon as failures. As I have repeatedly said in this paper, we learn through experience and experiencing. Brian Way (1967) says that "a basic definition of drama might be 'to practise living'". Thus, all of the exercises in the drama activities are a practice in living. Through drama our students can foster an understanding of themselves, and learn to use English in a variety of situations which are sometimes simulated, sometimes not.

There are two other problems which I would like to mention briefly before concluding. One is the problem of materials for use in the teaching of EIIL. In a great number of cases materials that we are currently using would be acceptable in the EIIL classroom if our teachers were properly trained in handling them, and if you have not guessed it by now, teacher training is the other problem.

Yes, drama does have an answer for both. In addition to the acceptable materials just mentioned, I envisage, and in fact am planning for, a series of plays, skits, and dialogues that will be in English, written by persons from various cultures. These writings should reflect their own culture, thus they would be useful tools for the language learner to become aware of and sensitive to other cultures. It is my thesis that once we become sensitive to several different cultures, we then find it easier to adapt to new environments.

In the area of teacher training I would urge that all teachers, whether they be language teachers or otherwise, have a good drama course included in their teacher training curriculum. Support for this notion may be found in a report by Jack Horn (1974) in *Psychology today* (p. 25) which related the success of the alleged "Dr Fox"; "Dr Fox" not being a medical doctor at all, but a skilled actor posing as a doctor. His audience, composed of physicians, was taken in completely. In our own field we may look to the University of Chile which has a required one-year course in drama and language learning for all student teachers of English as a foreign language. Sarah Sharim-Paz (1976) in writing of this course says:

> Our use of drama helps to achieve two goals of our language program. First, it provides an active approach to the study of English, putting students into situations that require practice in oral communication. Second, it provides an opportunity for the students to use creatively the English they have already learned, presenting them with situations that stimulate imaginative response.

In addition to the obvious benefits, such a course in drama would allow teachers to experience for themselves the many benefits that they would be giving to their students by using drama techniques in the classroom.

In conclusion, I would like to quote from *A Statement on Multi-cultural Education of the American Association of Colleges for Teacher Education* (1972). I have taken the liberty of making three changes in order that it will more closely reflect my feelings of EIIL.

> To endorse cultural pluralism is to endorse the principle that there is no one model English (American) speaker. To endorse cultural pluralism is to understand and appreciate the differences that exist among the world's (nation's) citizens. It is to see these differences as a positive force in the continuing development of a

world (society) which professes a wholesome respect for the intrinsic worth of every individual. . . . To accept cultural pluralism is to recognize that no group lives in a vacuum—that each group exists as a part of an interrelated whole.

(The words in parentheses are those used in the original.)

13 English as an International Language: an Attitudinal Approach

Gregory Trifonovitch

Cultural attitudes are manifested in many ways, but one of the most prominent means is through language communication. As English assumes the role of an international language, it is important to look at the attitudes which are transmitted by its speakers, whether they be native speakers or non-native ones, and to become aware of the dangers of some attitudes which prevail. Those involved in teaching the language need to become cognizant of its new international role and of the attitudes which develop around English. In my exploration of these attitudes, I shall draw heavily on my own personal experience in learning English (as a seventh language), in using it as an international and intranational language, and in teaching it as a second language.

I firmly believe that English has reached the status of being accepted as an international language. People long predicted this, including Fukuzawa Yukichi, who said in 1859, ". . . As certain as day, English was to be the most useful language of the future . . .".[1] I am quite sure that no one would challenge the fact that most cosmopolitan conferences that deal with international problems and concerns use English as the medium of communication. And I also firmly believe that the problems which have been reported as reasons for misunderstanding in many of these kinds of conferences, such as dialectical variations, phonological problems and other linguistic difficulties, are not as serious as they are often made out to be. Basically, these are only surface manifestations of deeper issues which cause misunderstanding, namely, cultural and psychological attitudes which we have carried over into English as it has gradually evolved into an international language.

While English is an international language, unfortunately, most of its speakers are not international persons. Let me illustrate this by an example which I draw from a conference that I recently attended. The conference included participants from Asia, Southeast Asia, the Pacific and the United States. It was very clearly evident that papers presented by native speakers of English were easily and readily accepted by the conferees. However, papers which were presented by educated non-native speakers of English were not categorized in the same area of acceptability as the native English speakers' papers. This issue came to a climax when a conferee from Japan presented her paper in educated Japanese-English. After the paper was presented, there were two comments made by native speakers of English which were completely irrelevant to the basic thesis and topic presented. These were immediately followed by two other native speakers of English who came to the rescue of the Japanese conferee by paraphrasing and explaining to the rest of the conferees the intent of the subject of the paper she presented. On the surface, this seemed to be a normal attitude for the native speakers to take and indicated an interest in elucidating in better English the paper as it was presented in non-native English. However, the reaction infuriated a conferee from Korea who immediately took the floor in a very dramatic gesture, hit the table with his fist, and exclaimed,

> We will no longer tolerate this kind of attitude! Ladies and Gentlemen, we clearly and fully understand what our colleague from Japan had to say. It was absolutely insulting when two of you made comments which were completely irrelevant to the topic of the paper. It clearly indicates to me that because our colleague spoke with a Japanese accent that immediately you thought the paper was not worthy of your attention. And then the other two gentlemen, with their condescending attitude, were trying to paraphrase for us the intent of our colleague's paper. Ladies and Gentlemen, this is an international conference. It is about time that we lay down our linguistic chauvinism and restore it with some cross-cultural tolerance.

This was my first encounter of a public denunciation of biased attitudes towards non-native English speakers. I have been at other conferences where this issue has come up, but always in private conversations rather than in the conference itself.

I began to learn my English about a quarter of a century ago, just as it was undergoing the transitional period into its present international form. As I was learning the language I was constantly reminded, in good faith, by the native speakers of English that I was a trespasser in their territory. I was always made conscious of my accent, my mispronunciation, my grammar or lack of it, my limited range of vocabulary, and most of all, my inability to "think" in English. My feelings paralleled those of Mohandas Gandhi, who on a voyage to England to attend school, wrote of his experience,

. . . But as the days passed, I became fidgety. I felt shy even in speaking to the steward. I was quite unaccustomed to talking English, and except for Sjt Mazmudar all the other passengers in the second saloon were English. I could not speak to them. For I could rarely follow their remarks when they came up to speak to me, and even when I understood I could not reply. I had to frame every sentence in my mind, before I could bring it out . . .[2]

When one discovers the need to learn another language in order to communicate, one is automatically placed in a disadvantageous position, and an attitude of inadequacy begins to grow. I have constantly noticed that non-native speakers of English apologize for their inability to speak English correctly, make excuses for their poor English, and ask for the native English speaker's indulgence and forgiveness. Others have been more subtle in making these excuses, such as in my case. Since I am Caucasian and an American, it is expected that I will speak English as a native American speaker. However, those who listen to me for the first time are immediately drawn to my accent or my way of speaking. As a result, their attention is mostly on my style, rather than on the subject which I am trying to communicate. Consequently, I have usually made it a point, before beginning any conversation with new acquaintances or before making any public addresses, to indirectly announce that I am not a native speaker of English, therefore setting the stage as early as possible for effective communication.

Another attitude which I have encountered in native speakers of English is one from those speakers who have been in contact with foreigners or have travelled to other countries and supposedly have developed a "cross-cultural sophistication". Their attitude is the overly condescending one. It was exhibited to me when I was politely asked to repeat what I had just said, or by speaking to me very slowly and distinctly or by actually tutoring and assisting me with my sentence structure and pronunciation. Usually, this attitude was manifested in a conversation such as this, "Greg, please don't misunderstand me . . . I fully understand you. However, so that you will not be misunderstood by others, since many of them have not been in contact with people from other countries, let me help you with your pronunciation." And then the lesson began with a model for me. I would repeat after them, but unfortunately, after several attempts, they would give up by saying, "Don't worry about your accent. In fact, it's rather charming to be able to speak English with a foreign accent." This type of attitude always made me conscious of the medium rather than the message. My concentration was on *speaking* rather than on communicating.

I encountered the reverse of this last attitude by those who spoke English as an official language in their country. They usually exhibited their superior attitude not by condescending or tutoring me, but by becoming very verbose and eloquent in their conversation as a demonstration of their status in the English-speaking hierarchy. Another version of this attitude is exhibited by the non-native speakers of English when they come to Hawaii and make excuses that it is very difficult for them to understand Hawaiian-English or Filipino-English Chinese or Japanese-English as spoken in Hawaii. The idea is given that their English is more closely affiliated with the native Caucasian speakers of English, and, as a result, it is very difficult for them to understand those who are not in the domain of the English-speaking world. This, of course, is a false identification with native speakers which causes them to block out non-native speakers.

Attitudes of superiority and inferiority developed very naturally as one group of people realized the need for learning another language, i.e. English, and the other group realized that since others were clamouring to learn their language, there was no need for them to learn any other language. However, as this attitude of superiority and inferiority grew, many speakers of English began to indirectly equate their ability and the degrees of speaking English to levels of intelligence. I have encountered several American teachers in Micronesia who were teaching English as a second language and who reported to me that they had no difficulty in teaching English in Micronesia since they had already had adequate training in special education and had had several years of experience in teaching the mentally handicapped. On the other hand, the Micronesian teachers of English were constantly self-deprecating themselves as bad teachers of English and as poor models.

Now these attitudes which have been developed as English was learned in order to be able to communicate with those from English-speaking countries are the same attitudes which are being transferred to English as an international language as it is being used to communicate in our global community. We must become aware of "linguacentric" attitudes, where one group believes that they are the standard native speakers of English and all others are trying to emulate that particular style, or the prejudiced attitude that good English comes from those with Caucasian features, which is actually prevalent among native as well as non-native speakers. It is the stereotyping attitude: "I really can't understand him. I know he was educated at Harvard, but he happens to come from such and such a country, and it's very difficult for me to understand him."

As educators in the field of English as an international language, we have some responsibilities:

1. Since through the medium of English we will be coming into contact with a variety of cultures, it is no longer possible for us to concentrate on the cultures of the English-speaking world as was the custom in the past. Instead it is very important for us to develop an awareness of the other cultures and, at the same time, develop a basic

cognitive awareness of our own culture. I think it is the responsibility of every person who is learning English for international communication to also develop an understanding of his own culture and to begin developing a sensitivity and awareness toward understanding other cultures, at least to understand the other person's cultural point of view.

2. It is very important for those who are learning English for international purposes to become somewhat aware of as many languages as possible by simply listening to other languages and becoming able to identify one language from another. This is an important exercise before learning to accept the different varieties of English.

3. In addition to students being exposed to the model of English presented by their teacher, it is also very important for them to listen to as many varieties of English as possible to sharpen their linguistic frequency.

4. It is imperative to be able to detect and accept various cultural styles of speaking English and to notice different styles of written English as they exhibit the cultural background of the speaker or the writer.

5. We must develop exams for English as an international language and not continue to rely only on exams that have been developed by English-speaking countries.

In conclusion, my whole aim has been to stress the psychological and cultural aspects of learning English as an international language. We must cease the over-emphasis on linguistic factors. It is extremely important for non-native speakers of English to abandon their inferiority complex and to realize that English now belongs to the world and not to an élite group only. Their variety and style is just as acceptable as any other style of English. And the native speaker of English must slowly begin to replace his linguistic chauvinism with an attitude of linguistic tolerance. Complete understanding between users of English as an international language will never be achieved. However, it is our responsibility to develop a tolerance for misunderstanding and acceptance. Possibly a linguistic tolerance could be one of our easiest first steps. Hopefully, we may soon refer to " . . . English, a language used *by* the world rather than *on* the world".[3]

NOTES TO CHAPTER 13

1. Fukuzawa Yukichi, *The Autobiography of Yukichi Fukuzawa*, trans. by Elichi Kiyooka, Tokyo, The Hokuseido Press, 1960:98.
2. Mohandas K. Gandhi, *An Autobiography*, Boston, Beacon Press, 1957:42.
3. C. J. Brumfit, *The English Language, Ideology, and International Communication: Some issues arising out of teaching for Chinese students.* Conference of IATEFL, Oxford University, January 1977.

14 Crossing the Cultural Threshold: a Challenge to Users of EIL

Mayuri Sukwiwat

We are all aware that there are affinities between linguistic and cultural manifestations, but how many of us consciously recognize the relationship between language and culture? What we think about and how we think about it are processed through our language and to a great extent influenced by our culture. In order to explain this, perhaps a definition of the word "culture" is needed. I prefer to use the term "culture" as defined by Peter S. Adler as "an intertwined system of values and attitudes, beliefs and norms that give meaning and significance to both individual and collective identity" (Adler, 1977). Understanding a language involves not only a knowledge of grammar, phonology and lexis but also a knowledge of certain features and characteristics of this so-called "intertwined system of values and attitudes, beliefs and norms," that users of that language subscribe to.

When we communicate internationally, we communicate interculturally. Can we naively assume that when we communicate interculturally what is necessary is just a knowledge of the medium of an international language? In the case of English, would fluency in English suffice? Experience indicates that when we communicate interculturally, we are likely to encounter factors of cultural differences in the connotative and denotative meanings of words that affect our ability to communicate. These factors are the main causes of solecisms that often lead to ludicrous misunderstandings, absurd consequences, embarrassment, frustration, mistrust, anger, discord, or breakdown of communication. It is concern for the cultural aspect of languages that this paper addresses.

In communicating with you I am using a detective's approach. I have divided my paper into three parts. The first part consists of a series of descriptions of events that really happened. I choose to call them "encounters" rather than "stories" or "anecdotes". The encounters which follow are the result of my personal observations on how users of

languages communicated in different cultural and international settings. They have been recorded over a period of more than 20 years.
Several of these I have experienced myself, while others have been
accounted for by most reliable sources. In short, the characters of
communicants[1] in each of these encounters are not fictitious; they were
real people.

The second part of the paper will be interpretive. It is an attempt to
find some clues and to form hypotheses to explain why communication
broke down in some encounters or why gross misunderstandings
occurred in others. As a scientist or a detective who uses theories to
explain phenomena, I will try to apply certain theories to explain the
cultural phenomena in each of the encounters.

The third part will be didactic. I think it is quite appropriate for me to
share with you some of the ways and means by which cross-cultural
misunderstanding and social blunders can be understood, if not
avoided. This last part is concerned with some of the steps by which the
cultural threshold can be crossed.

I THE ENCOUNTERS

Encounter 1
Time: 1949
Place: The southwest of England
At that time the Thai government sent a number of students to
further their studies overseas every year, mainly to Europe and the US. I
happened to be one of the students sponsored by the government to do
undergraduate studies in the United Kingdom.

After a few days in London, I was sent off to a host family in the
southwest of England. It was my first encounter with an entirely
English-speaking environment. My host family, I was told later, was
considered to belong to the upper-middle class. The head of the family
was a doctor.

The setting was a living-room. After a few greetings and welcoming
remarks, Mrs J., my hostess, asked, "On which day of the week would
you like to have your bath?"

I understood every word she said but had no idea what she meant.
Silence on my part. The lady repeated her question, and I gave her no
response. Finally she decided that I should have my bath on
Wednesdays.

Encounter 2
Time: 1957
Place: A university in the Midwest of the US.
A few days after my arrival at the university, where I was to do

218 ENGLISH FOR CROSS-CULTURAL COMMUNICATION

graduate work, I ran into an old friend, an American lecturer who had spent a year as a visiting lecturer at the institution in Thailand where I was working. Trying to reciprocate the hospitality given to him while working in Thailand, he invited me to his house, and took me out on many occasions. No doubt some of my Thai colleagues had taken notice of our friendship to which I myself attached no special importance. As a matter of routine, I would report to my colleagues what I did and where I went. One day the friendly relationship between me and my Thai colleagues came near to disruption when I gave this report to them: "We really had an enjoyable day, yesterday. We had a game of tennis, had supper and went to a drive-in theatre."

My audience giggled, looked at me disapprovingly and discontinued the conversation. I was completely in the dark and could not figure out why that sudden change of behaviour occurred.

Encounter 3
Time: 1970
Place: A city in the northeast of Thailand
An English language officer from the United Kingdom was invited to speak at a seminar. He stayed at one of the best hotels in the city. One morning he decided to have breakfast in his room. He telephoned Room Service and gave his order.

Mr U.: Omelette, please
Room Service: Large or small, sir?
Mr U. (a bit puzzled, but to save money and also to be safe): Small, please.

After a few minutes, a waiter came up to his room with a small bottle of Amarit[2] (a brand of Thai beer).

Encounter 4
Time: 1966
Place: Hong Kong
In 1966 I was invited to a conference entitled "English as a University Subject" in which many university lecturers and professors from several countries in Asia were invited to participate. Most of the participants were excellent users of English and very well versed in their academic pursuits—Shakespeare, Wordsworth, D. H. Lawrence, etc. Towards the end of a post-conference sightseeing tour we stopped for refreshments at a restaurant. At the same table I had a very distinguished professor from an Asian university, a Shakespeare scholar, sitting opposite me. As the time and place were not appropriate for a serious discussion of Shakespeare, I thought a lighter topic of conversation would be more congenial. During that week in Hong Kong I had followed the results of the first Asian Games which were held in

Thailand in the local newspapers with some interest and thought that the subject would appeal to the professor at my table.

I started the conversation by paying compliments to the athletes from the country my communicant came from. I said: "I'd like to congratulate your compatriots. They are doing great in the Asian Games. I see your country has won many gold medals in just two days." The professor looked at me and then cast his eyes down to his plate. In a very stern, professorial voice he responded: "Sorry, I don't play Mahjong."

From then on we had our tea in silence.

II THE CLUES

Analysis of each of the given Encounters will provide some clues to cross-cultural communication.

The first Encounter is a good case of perfect mutual intelligibility but total communication breakdown. I understood every word my hostess said but could not figure out the meaning implied in her question. The idea of having a day fixed for baths had no reference in my mind since I was from a water-oriented culture where one could bathe or take a bath as frequently as one wished. It was probably my fault for not learning more about the everyday life, such as hygiene habits, of the people from the culture I was to live in. But, I think, my hostess was equally guilty of assuming that the guest shared the same personal habits and expectations as herself.

Edward M. Anthony's assertion that "none of the individuals who are parties to a language agreement duplicates exactly *all* of the experiences of any of the others—but all of them duplicate *some* of one another's experience" (Anthony, 1975b) may explain why I did not understand the disapproving attitude of my colleagues in the second Encounter. As I had just arrived in the US and had fewer "differing cumulative contacts with the environment" than those of my colleagues, I only knew the denotative meaning of the expression "drive-in theatre". Many months later, from various sources of information, I came to learn the figurative or connotative meaning of "drive-in theatre", i.e. a place where activities other than viewing a film would often take place. However, complexities and miscommunication of this kind often arise among members of the same culture using the same language.

The problem in the third Encounter on the surface seems to be a phonological one. In the case of Thai speakers it is the problem of /r/ – /l/ sounds. But when I looked further into this Encounter, I came to the conclusion that this one was also a question of cultural differences. Breakfast, American or British style, is often emphasized in English textbooks found all over the world, but breakfast, Thai, Japanese,

Korean or Chinese style, is not a subject of interest to English language materials producers.[3] For a Thai it is quite normal for him to have beer with his breakfast or at any time of the day at all. Thai people, coming from a loosely structured society, have different culinary conventions from the Westerners. No description of a uniform Thai breakfast exists that would convey the same image as that of the American, the British, or the Continental breakfast. What was so shocking to Mr U. in the third Encounter would be a very normal thing for Thais. A test could be made to prove that the cause of misunderstanding was a cultural rather than a linguistic one. If the order "Amarit" were given to a room service waiter in a hotel in London or Honolulu, the cues to that stimulus would be "plain, ham, or mushroom" rather than "large or small". On the other hand, if the Thai waiter in this particular incident was given a proper orientation on what the American or British could not and would not tolerate at breakfast he would have doubted the soberness of his guest even though he was not sure whether what he heard was "Amarit", or "omelette".

My interpretation of the difficulty in Encounter 4 was that the professor did not read the newspapers and was not informed of the playing of the Asian Games. What he heard was Asian games and considered "mahjong" to be one of them. In this case, if my comment were in written form, most likely no difficulty would have arisen.

III THE STEPS TO CROSS THE CULTURAL THRESHOLD

A few words should be said concerning the levels of communication in general. To my mind there seem to be three levels. The first, which I will label the universal level, is culture free. Here I am referring to certain kinds of spiritual revelation or enlightenment, the exact communication of which can be established through non-verbal means. Though a noble subject to pursue, it is of no immediate concern here.

The second level is what I may call the professional level where communicants belonging to the same professional or academic worlds but to different cultures have to communicate internationally. We are readily in agreement that language complexities and difficulties are less critical in certain disciplines, and more critical in others. As far as the lexicon is concerned, in the realms of natural or pure sciences the cultural threshold is probably at its lowest and is easiest to cross. For instance, a group of nuclear physicists or mathematicians from the USSR, the US and Japan may communicate effectively through the medium of English while deliberating on their academic pursuits. A group of multinational doctors certainly cannot mistake anything else for a "nervous hospital". The term "computer memory" can easily lend itself to the ears of the Japanese computer scientist even though the concept of a memory-possessing machine is hard to perceive by the Japanese mind.[4] Such specialists share well-defined registers.

On the other hand, when users of English are in the social or political sciences, in business, education, psychology, or linguistics, they are likely to encounter many different variations and interpretations of words used in their respective registers. In American culture the term "human rights" is highly esteemed, but it may be viewed by another culture as another kind of American product to be sold to an international market. A constitution in one culture may be an unwritten thing, a foundation of all laws by which a nation is governed. In another it may be something that can be changed as often as women's fashions. Democracy means a way of life in one culture; in another it is merely a name given to a monument. The very word "memory" used in computer sciences is culturally neutral, but when it is used in the contexts of psychology or education it may have many different interpretations as perceived by different cultural frames of mind.

The third level may be called the mundane level. It is indeed the most difficult to deal with. It is concerned with day-to-day activities, and with the interaction between language users outside their professional circles. Before a Japanese physicist or a Thai doctor goes to his professional meetings, he has to travel on international aircraft that give him a "pleasant fright". He has to interact with a taxi-driver, or with a porter at his hotel. He orders his breakfast or lunch at a restaurant, buys some personal items at a store, makes appointments by telephone or by written messages with clerks or secretaries. During or after his business transaction or mission he may wish to act as a tourist and take bus tours with the hope that he will not be left behind. As my data indicated in Part I of this paper, it is at this level that a non-native English speaker is likely to encounter more numerous intercultural stumbling blocks than when he is interacting with his professional colleagues. If he travels well-equipped, he may try to use the best strategies to get what he needs. But if he does not, at least he should be informed that he will have to stumble over the threshold he is trying to cross.

To illustrate my point let us use names of food. My question is how many of the global travellers who resort to English as an international language realize that names of food by themselves have no meanings. How often do they (or we) blindly believe that the dishes with English labels they order will be the same they normally have in their own cultures? How many times are they disappointed because the coffee or tea or rice served at various places around the world are greatly dissimilar? They are only to be reminded that food is to be tasted to be fully understood. How can these names tell us what they actually are or taste like: Chinese doughnut, Yorkshire pudding, rice porridge, sherry ice-cream, French fries, or son-in-law eggs?

We tend to take things for granted in dealing with a language and a culture. Even the meanings of words in ordinary daily life like dinner and breakfast can be largely out of our awareness. As learners of L2 we are often reminded not to cling to one meaning of a word or phrase in the new language. Our language teachers emphasize the effectiveness of learning vocabulary in context and the fact that "vocabularies vary not only in size. They vary also in usability, and curiously enough, their usability varies with the way they are used" (Laird, 1953). Since the meanings we assign to words are partly the result of our cultural experiences, how can we then expand or widen our experiences in order to accommodate meanings in a new language? Edward M. Anthony suggests that:

In teaching new words, it is advisable to surround them with other words whose lexical meanings cluster around a certain real-world situation (or referential cluster as defined by the culture which spawns the language). Two types of contexts must thus be considered in the narrow area of vocabulary teaching: the culturally established non-language context of the referential cluster and the culturally established word context of the discourse cluster.

In material preparation, he further states that:

One is accordingly well-advised to investigate the frequency of referential clusters rather than the gross frequency of words. Even here there is the danger that a frequent referential cluster does not serve as a frequently communicated activity. Washing the face and hands, and brushing the teeth are culturally controlled activities, yet are not really discussed much, at least among adults. (Anthony, 1975a)

This is indeed a great task for materials developers for English language courses.

What needs to be emphasized is the awareness of the two different contexts of the referential cluster and the culturally established word context of the discourse cluster. In most classroom situations that I am familiar with the first context is rarely emphasized. In most teacher-training programmes; student teachers are not sufficiently equipped with relevant information, nor is resource material available to them for their own research. This may very well apply to my own case as reported in Encounter 1. If I had been given some sensitizing capsules and sufficient background information on the climatic conditions, and on the heating systems in English homes after the War years, I would have been able to give an appropriate response to my hostess and not become disillusioned by the notion that a civilized mind must be wrapped in a clean body.

It will be of great help, no doubt, if users of languages can be trained to discover relevant non-verbal cues or non-language contexts, if they can be trained to be alert to the varying interpretations of linguistic phenomena. In my view, it seems that this kind of training should first be developed in the teaching of the mother tongue. If learners of L1 have been given opportunities to explore their own linguistic world, and to examine their communicative tools, the task of making them alert to and aware of linguistic phenomena in L2 should become a much less difficult one.

It is this area where I think those who are concerned with mother tongue teaching and those who are concerned with foreign language teaching should be in close cooperation. What I consider to be a primary step and a necessary course of action is to reconstruct the overall programme of teacher education. It seems to me that we—in Thailand—are making a gross mistake by separating prospective teachers of the mother tongue from prospective teachers of foreign languages. There should be at least a series of units of courses on the nature of language, and how it relates to man's thought and action, etc., required for prospective "language teachers". It is only after the fundamental principles of language as a communicative process are firmly grasped that subsequent courses in methods and techniques pertaining to any target language can become meaningfully applicable. In my view, language teacher education is where a "deschooling" is badly needed.

However, in the area of intercultural communication, it is gratifying to discover an increasing number of works on transcultural training methods and techniques employed by various groups of people. Yet, there is room for more. As we witness the rapid growth of global communication in many areas: diplomacy, business, tourism, science and technology, and exchange of human knowledge, more resource material on intercultural communication with special focus on the English language would not only be an additional asset to the field but also a commitment and a challenge to all concerned.

CONCLUSION

In this paper I have deliberately avoided defining the term *cultural threshold* used in its title. Some may interpret it to mean cultural barriers. Personally I am allergic to the word barrier, since I usually perceive it as something which prevents one from doing something or from going somewhere. However, the term *threshold* vaguely used here, indicates a natural phenomenon already existing between two spaces. It is not fixed like a barrier. It can be transformed and changed. One can think of it in terms of money; it has currency which can rise and fall. Or one can see it as a tide which again may ebb and flow. There are variables, variations, factors and clues to predict the rise and fall of thresholds. To cross the cultural threshold in this context is perhaps to understand why the currency and the tide rise and why they fall. Once we understand these occurrences, we may be able to counter the effects of their rising and falling.

I mentioned at the beginning of this paper the importance of recognizing the relationship between culture and language. I would like to re-emphasize the understanding of this relationship. Again, allow me to quote Anthony:

> Although language may indeed be included as a feature of man's nature, *a* language is an aspect of his nurture: an indispensable, *culturally unique*, systematic agreement through which the *communicants*—all the human subscribers to the agreement—symbolically and habitually share their real, imagined, or hallucinating experience.
>   (Anthony, 1975b, my italics)

Accepting this distinction, the primary steps to cross the cultural threshold should involve knowing one's own nature and one's own nurture. This is very often a difficult goal to achieve. It seems paradoxical that one can become more sensitive and observant of one's own nature or nurture after one has experienced a strange culture through the medium of a strange language in a strange setting.

NOTES TO CHAPTER 14

1. This term is used by Edward M. Anthony in *Towards a theory of lexical meaning*.
2. *Amarit* is a Thai word derived from Sanskrit meaning nectar conferring immortality.
3. See Richard A. Via's *English in three acts*, p. 2.
4. Information obtained from a talk by Professor Kazuo Nishiyama on "Crossing the Cultural Barriers", at the Buddhist Study Center, Honolulu, 24 February 1978.

Bibliography

Achebe, C. "English and the African writer." In Mazrui, 1973. (Originally published in *Transition*, 1965, *4* (18).)

Adler, P. S. "Beyond cultural identity: Reflections upon cultural and multicultural man." In Richard W. Brislin (Ed.), *Culture learning: concepts, applications, research.* Honolulu: University Press of Hawaii, 1977.

Aiken, P. L. "Individualized language learning project." *PASAA*, 1975, *5*, (1).

Alatis, J. E. (Ed), *International dimensions of bilingual education.* George Town University Round Table on Languages and Linguistics 1978. Washington, D. C. Georgetown University Press, 1978.

Allen, J. P. B. and Widdowson, H. G. "Grammar and language teaching." In J. P. B. Allen and S. Pit Corder (Eds), *The Edinburgh course in applied linguistics*, Vol. 2, *Papers in applied linguistics.* London: Oxford University Press, 1975.

Allsopp, R. "Why a dictionary of Caribbean English usage?" Circular "A" of the Caribbean Lexicography Project. Barbados, 1972.

Allwright, R. "Problems in the study of the language teacher's treatment of learner error." In M. K. Burt and H. C. Dulay (Eds), *New directions in second language learning, teaching and bilingual education.* TESOL, 1975.

——. "Language learning through communication practice." In *ELT Documents 76/3.* London, The British Council, 1976.

Anderson, J. "Some proposals concerning the modal verbs in English." In A. J. Aitken et al. (Eds), *Edinburgh studies in English and Scots.* London: Longman, 1971.

Ansre, G. "The influence of English on West African languages." In Spencer, 1971a.

Anthony, E. M. "Lexicon and vocabulary." *RELC journal*, 1975a, *6* (1).

——. *Towards a theory of lexical meaning.* Monograph series, Regional English Language Centre. Singapore: Singapore University Press, 1975b.

Argyle, M. and Dean, J. "Eye contact, distance and affiliation." In Laver and Hutcheson, 1972.

Arumainathan, P. *Report on the census of population, 1970.* Singapore, 1973.

Austin, J. L. *How to do things with words.* Oxford: Clarendon Press, 1962.

Bacon, Francis. *Advancement of learning.* London, 1605.

Bailey, R. W. and Robinson, J. L. (Eds), *Varieties of present-day English.* New York: Macmillan, 1973.

Baker, S. J. *The Australian language*. Sydney: Angus and Robertson, 1945.

Bamgbose, A. "The English language in Nigeria." In Spencer, 1971a.

Bansal, R. K. *The intelligibility of Indian English*. Hyderabad: Central Institute of English and Foreign Languages, 1969.

Barnett, L. *The treasure of our tongue. The story of English from its obscure beginnings to its present eminence as the most widely spoken language*. New York: Alfred A. Knopf, 1964.

Basso, K. "To give up on words: Silence in Western Apache culture." *Southwestern journal of anthropology*, 1970, *26*.

Bauman, R. and Sherzer, J. (Eds.), *Explorations in the ethnography of speaking*. London: Cambridge University Press, 1974.

Bautista, M. L. S. "The noun phrase in Tagalog–English code switching." *Studies in Philippine linguistics*, 1977, *1* (1).

Bazell, C. E., et al. *In memory of J. R. Firth*. London: Longman, 1966.

Bell, R. T. *Sociolinguistics: goals, approaches and problems*. London: Batsford, 1976.

Bender, M. L., Bowen, J. D., Cooper, R. L. and Ferguson, C. A. (Eds), *Language in Ethiopia*. London: Oxford University Press, 1976.

Berry, J. 'Pidgins and creoles in Africa.' In Sebeok, 1971.

Bhatia, K. C. *A linguistic study of English loanwords in Hindi* (in Hindi). Allahabad: Hindustani Academy, 1967.

Bhattacharya, D. C. "The impact of English borrowings on the Bengali language." *Calcutta review*, July 1967, *172*.

Bialystok, E. and Frohlich, M. "Aspects of second language learning in classroom settings." *Working papers on bilingualism*, 1977, *13*.

Bibeau, G. *Report of the independent study on the language training programmes of the public service of Canada* (12 volumes). Ottawa, 1976.

Bickerton, D. *Dynamics of a creole system*. London: Cambridge University Press, 1975.

Bickley, V. C. "Cultural aspects of language imposition in Malaya, Singapore, and Indonesia." *Topics in culture learning*, 1973, *1*.

——. "Problem: The cross-cultural encounter." Paper presented at the First Annual Seminar on Pacific Prospects in Global Perspective, 15–20 January 1978, The East–West Center, Honolulu, Hawaii.

Biddulph, G. M. R. *Geography, English studies series 11*. London: Oxford University Press, 1971.

Block, J. H. (Ed.), *Mastery learning*. New York: Holt, Rinehart and Winston, 1971.

Bowen, D. "An experimental integrated test of English grammar." In *Workpapers in teaching English as a second language*. Los Angeles: UCLA, June 1975, 9.

Brazil, D. C. *Discourse intonation*. Discourses analysis monographs 1,

Birmingham English Language Research. Birmingham: University of Birmingham, 1975.

Breen, M. P. and Candlin, C. N. *The Communicative Curriculum in Language Teaching*. London: Longman. Forthcoming.

Brown, J. M. "Thai dominance over English and the learning of English by Thais." *PASAA*, October 1976, 6.

Brown, R. and Gilman, A. "Pronouns of power and solidarity." In T. Sebeok (Ed.), *Style in language*. Cambridge, Mass.: MIT Press, 1960.

Brown, R. and Levinson, S. "Universals in language usage: Politeness phenomena." Unpublished manuscript, University of Cambridge, 1974 (cited in Leech, 1977).

Brown, V. P. "The dramatic approach to the teaching of French." *Foreign language annals*, 1977, *10* (2).

Brudhiprabha, P. *The education of teachers of English as a foreign and second language in Southeast Asia: With special reference to Thailand*. Unpublished Ph. D. Dissertation, University of Toronto, 1975.

Brumfit, C. J. "The English Language, ideology, and international communication: Some issues arising out of teaching for Chinese students." Paper presented at the Ninth International Conference of IATEFL, Oxford University, January 1977.

Burt, M. K., Dulay, H. C., and Hernandez, C. E. *Bilingual syntax measure*. New York: Harcourt Brace Jovanovich, 1975.

Canada, Government of, *A national understanding: Statement of the Government of Canada on the official languages policy*. Ottawa: Ministry of Supply and Services Canada, 1977.

Candlin, C. N. "Communicative language teaching and the debt to pragmatics." In C. Ramesh (Ed.), *27th round table meeting monography series on languages and linguistics*. Washington, D. C.: Georgetown University Press, 1976.

Candlin, C. N., Bruton, C. J. and Leather, J. L. *Doctor–patient communication skills: Working papers 1–4*, Mimeo, University of Lancaster, 1974.

——. "Doctor speech functions in casualty consultations: Some quantified characteristics of discourse in a regulated setting." In G. Nickel (Ed.), *Proceedings of the IV AILA Congress 1975*. Stuttgart: Hochschulverlag, 1976 (1976a).

——. "Doctors in casualty: Applying communicative competence to components of specialist course design." *IRAL*, 1976b, *14* (3).

Candlin, C. N., Bruton, C. J., Leather, J. L. and Woods, E. *Doctor–patient communication skills* (incl. book/slides/audio/VCR). Chelmsford: Graves Medical Audiovisual Library, 1977.

Carroll, J. B. "Guide for the collection of data pertaining to the study of foreign or second languages by younger children." In H. H. Stern

(Ed.), *Languages and the young school child*. London: Oxford University Press, 1969.

Carton, A. S. "Inferencing: A process in using and learning language." In P. Pimsleur and T. Quinn (Eds), *The psychology of language learning: Papers from the II AILA Congress, Cambridge, 1969*. London: Cambridge University Press, 1971.

Catford, J. C. "The teaching of English as a foreign language." In R. Quirk and A. H. Smith (Eds), *The teaching of English*. London: Oxford University Press, 1964 (First published by Martin, Secker and Warburg, 1959).

CHALLENGES (B. Abbs, C. N. Candlin, C. Edelhoff, T. Moston, M. Sexton) (incl. book/slides/audio/film/VCR) London and Munich: Longman, BBC, Institut für Film Und Bild, 1978.

Chandraprabha, S. *Somdech phra sri savarindira* (Biography of Queen Sawangvadhana), Bangkok: Bamrungnukulkich Printing Press, 1971.

Chatterjee, R. K. *Mass communication*. New Delhi: National Book Trust, 1973.

Chia, S. H. "An investigation into language use among secondary four pupils in Singapore—Pilot project." In Crewe, 1977.

Christophersen, P. *Second-language learning: Myth and reality*. Harmondsworth: Penguin, 1973.

Chulalongkorn, H.M. King. *Klai–ban* (King Chulalongkorn's Letters from Europe). Bangkok: Praepitaya, 1965.

Chulalongkorn University. *Curriculum for the degree of Bachelor of Education*. Bangkok: Chulalongkorn University, 1976.

——. *Curriculum of the Faculty of Arts*, Bangkok: Chulalongkorn University, 1977.

Chulalongkorn University, Department of modern languages. *Grammar notes: errors in composition made by students in Thailand*. Bangkok: Chulalongkorn University, 1952.

Churchill, S. "Recherches récentes sur le bilinguisme et l'éducation des francophones minoritaires au Canada: L'example ontarien." In M. Swain (Ed.), *Bilingualism in Canadian education: Issues and research*. Yearbook of the Canadian Society for the Study of Education, 1976, *3*.

Clark, H. H. *Semantics and comprehension*. The Hague: Mouton, 1976.

Clark, H. H. and Clark, E. V. *Psychology and language: An introduction to psycholinguistics*. New York: Harcourt Brace, 1977.

Clyne, M. "Intercultural communication breakdown and its communication conflict: Towards a linguistic model and its exemplification." Paper read at the annual meeting of the Linguistic Society of Australia, Sydney, 1975a.

——. "German and English working pidgins." Paper presented at the International Congress on Pidgin and Creoles, Honolulu, Hawaii, 1975b.

Commissioner of Official Languages. *Annual Reports I–VI, 1970–76.* Ottawa: Ministry of Supply and Services Canada, 1971–7.

Conseil Scientifique pour l'Afrique (CSA) (Brazzaville Symposium). *Symposium on multilingualism.* Second Meeting of the Intra-African Committee on Linguistics, Brazzaville, 12–21 July 1962. London: CCTA/CSA Publications Bureau, 1974.

Coomaraswamy, A. K. *Christian and oriental philosophy of art.* New York: Dover Publications, 1956.

Corder, S. P. "The significance of learner's errors." In Richards, 1974.

——. "Simple codes and the source of the second language learner's initial heuristic hypothesis." In *Colloque: Theoretical Models in Applied Linguistics,* IV. Université de Neuchatel, 1975.

——. "Language continua and the interlanguage hypothesis." In *Colloque: The Notion of Simplification.* Université de Neuchatel, 1976.

——. "Language-learner language." In Richards, 1978.

Coste, D. et al. *Un niveau-seuil.* Strasbourg: Council of Europe, 1977.

Coulthard, R. M. *An introduction to discourse analysis.* London: Longman, 1977.

Crewe, W. J. (Ed.), *The English language in Singapore.* Singapore: Eastern Universities Press, 1977.

Damrong, P. Miscellaneous articles written for the Journal of the Siam Society, published for the Centenary of the Prince. Bangkok: Siam Society, 1962.

Das Gupta, H. M. *Studies in western influence on nineteenth-century Bengali poetry.* Calcutta: Semushi, 1935.

Debyasuvarn, B. M. L. (Chairman) "Report to the Ministry of Education of the National English Language Coordinating Committee, May 13, 1975." *PASAA,* 1975, *5* (2).

Dent-Young, J. "Lightening the play." *English language teaching journal,* 1974, *28* (3).

Dhabbasuta, P. "The origin and methods of teaching in Thailand." *Bulletin of the English Language Center* (Bangkok), October 1970, *1.*

Diebold, A. R. Incipient bilingualism, *Language,* 1961, *37* (1).

Duncan, S. "Towards a grammar for dyadic conversation." *Semiotica,* 1973, *9* (1).

Emmans, K., Hawkins, E. and Westoby, A. *The use of foreign languages in the private sector of industry and commerce.* York: Language Teaching Centre, 1974.

Erdmann, P. "On deriving deontic modals." *Linguistics,* 1977, *192.*

Ervin-Tripp, S. "An analysis of the interaction of language, topic and listener." In Fishman, 1968.

Eskey, D. E. "A model programme for teaching advanced reading to students of EFL." *Language learning,* 1973, *23* (2).

Ferguson, C. A. "Diglossia." *Word,* 1959, *15.*

——. C. A. "National sociolinguistics profile formulas." In W.

Bright (Ed.), *Sociolinguistics: Proceedings of the UCLA Sociolinguistic Conference, 1964*. The Hague: Mouton, 1966.

Ferguson, C. A. and De Bose, C. E. "Simplified registers, broken language and pidginization." In Valdman, 1977.

Ferguson, C. A. and Heath, S. B. *Language in the U.S.A.* To appear.

Firth, J. R. "Linguistic analysis as a study of meaning." (1952) In Palmer, 1968.

——. "Descriptive linguistics and the study of English." (1956) In Palmer, 1968.

——. "Applications of general linguistics." (1957) In Palmer, 1968.

——. "The treatment of language in general linguistics." (1959) In Palmer, 1968.

——. "The tongues of men and speech." *Language and language learning*. London: Oxford University Press, 1964.

Fishman, J. A. (Ed.), *Readings in the sociology of language*. The Hague: Mouton, 1968.

Fishman, J. et al. *Language problems in developing nations*. New York: Wiley, 1968.

——. *The Spread of English*. Rowley, Mass.: Newbury House, 1977.

Fodor, J. and Garrett, M. "Some reflections on competence and performance." In J. Lyons and C. Wales (Eds), *Psycholinguistics papers*. Edinburgh: Edinburgh University Press, 1966.

Fraser, B. "On requesting." Manuscript, 1977.

Freedle, R. O. and Carroll, J. B. *Language comprehension and the acquisition of knowledge*. Washington: Winston, 1972.

Fry, D. "Speech reception and perception." In J. Lyons (Ed.), *New horizons in linguistics*. Harmondsworth: Penguin, 1970.

Fukuzawa, Y. *The autobiography of Fukuzawa Yukichi* (translated by Eiichi Kiyooka). Tokyo: The Hokuseido Press, 1960.

Gallwey, W. T. *The inner game of tennis*. New York: Random House, 1974.

Gandhi, M. K. *An Autobiography*. Boston: Beacon Press, 1957.

Gardner, W. K. "Reading comprehension." Paper read at the BAAL Seminar on Comprehension, University of Edinburgh, 1977.

Garfinkel, H. "Studies of the routine grounds of everyday activities." In Sudnow, 1972.

Geertz, C. *The religion of Java*. New York: The Free Press, 1960.

George, H. V. *Common errors in language learning*. Rowley, Mass.: Newbury House, 1972.

Gilbert, G. G. "Indo-English" (Translation of Schuchardt, 1891). Unpublished manuscript, 1977.

Giles, H. and Powesland, P. *Speech style and social evaluation*. London: Academic Press, 1975.

Goffin, R. C. *Some notes on Indian English*. S. P. E. Tract, No. 41. Oxford, 1934.

Goffman, E. *Frame analysis.* New York: Harper and Row, 1974.

Gokak, V. K. *English in India: Its present and future.* Bombay: Asia Publishing House, 1964.

Goldenberg, T. "Memorandum to the Dean," Faculty of Arts, Silpakorn University, Nakorn Pathom, 2 January 1978 (mimeographed).

Goodman K. S. "Reading: A psycholinguistic guessing game." *Journal of the reading specialist,* 1967, *6.*

Greene, J. *Thinking and language.* London: Methuen, 1975.

Grice, H. P. "Logic and conversation." In P. Cole and J. L. Morgan (Eds), *Syntax and semantics,* Vol. 3, *Speech acts.* New York: Academic Press, 1975.

Griswold, A. B. *King Mongkut of Siam.* New York: The Asia Society, 1961.

Gumperz, J. J. "Language, communication and public negotiation." In P. Šanday (Ed.), *Anthropology and the public interest: fieldwork and theory.* New York: Academic Press, 1976.

——. "The conversational analysis of interethnic communication." In E. L. Ross (Ed.), *Interethnic Communication: Proceedings of the Southern Anthropological Society.* Atlanta: University of Georgia Press, 1977.

Gumperz, J. J. and Hymes, D. (Eds), *The ethnography of communication.* Special publication of *American anthropologist.* 1964, *66* (Part 2).

——. *Directions in sociolinguistics: The ethnography of communication.* New York: Holt, Rinehart and Winston, 1972.

Hall, R. A., Jr. "Right versus wrong: English for the world." *TESOL quarterly,* 1976, *10* (2).

Halliday, M. A. K. *Explorations in the functions of language.* London: Edward Arnold, 1973.

Halliday, M. A. K. and Hason, R. *Cohesion in English.* London: Longman, 1976.

Halliday, M. A. K., McIntosh, A. and Strevens, P. *The linguistic sciences and teaching.* London: Longman, 1964.

Hare, R. M. "Meaning and speech acts." *Philosophical review,* 1970, *79.*

Harley, B. (guest editor). "Alternative programs for teaching French as a second language in the schools of the Carleton and Ottawa School Boards." *The Canadian modern language review,* 1976, *33* (2).

Harrison, W., Prator, C. and Tucker, G. R. *English-language policy survey of Jordan: A case study in language planning.* Arlington, Va.: Center for Applied Linguistics, 1975.

Hartmann, R. R. K. and Stork, F. C. *Dictionary of language and linguistics.* New York: Wiley, 1972.

Hatch, E. "Acquisition of syntax in a second language." In Richards, 1978.

Haugen, E. *The Norwegian language in America: A study in bilingual behaviour*. Vol. I *The bilingual community*, Vol. II *The American dialects of Norwegian*. Bloomington, Indiana: Indiana University Press, 1969 (first edition published by University of Pennsylvania Press, 1953).

Heath, S. B. "A national language academy? Debate in the nation." *Linguistics*, 1977, *189*.

Henning, C. A. (Ed.), *Proceedings of the Los Angeles Second Language Research Forum*. Los Angeles: UCLA, 1977.

Herman, S. R. "Explorations in the social psychology of language choice." In Fishman, 1968.

History of Chulalongkorn University, published at the 50th Anniversary of the University's Establishment, 26 March 1967.

Horn, J. "Newsline." *Psychology today*, 1974, *8* (2).

Hymes, D. H. "The ethnography of speaking." In T. Gladwin and W. C. Sturtevant (Eds), *Anthropology and human behavior*. Washington, D.C.: The Anthropological Society of Washington, 1962 (Also in Fishman, 1968).

——. "Introduction: Toward ethnographies of communication." In Gumperz and Hymes, 1964.

——. (Ed.). *Pidginization and creolization of languages*. Cambridge: Cambridge University Press, 1971.

——. "Models of the interaction of language and social life." In Gumperz and Hymes, 1972.

——. *Foundations in sociolinguistics: An ethnographic approach*. Philadelphia: University of Pennsylvania Press, 1974.

Irvine, J. T. "Strategies of status manipulation in the Wolof greeting." In Bauman and Sherzer, 1974.

Iyengar, K. R. S. *Indian writing in English*. New York and Bombay: Asia Publishing House, 1962.

Jakobovits, L. and Gordon, B. *The context of foreign language teaching*. Rowley, Mass.: Newbury House, 1974.

James, C. "Linguistic measures for error gravity." *Audio-visual language journal*, 1974, *12* (1).

Jefferson, G. "Side sequences." In Sudnow, 1972.

Jespersen, O. *Growth and structure of the English language*, 9th ed., Garden City: Doubleday, 1938.

——. *How to teach a foreign language*. London: Allen and Unwin, 1961 (first published in 1904).

Johansson, S. "Problems in studying the communicative effect of learner's errors." *Colloque: Theoretical Models in Applied Linguistics, IV*. Université de Neuchatel, 1975.

Jones, K. "The role of discourse analysis in devising undergraduate reading programmes in English for science and technology." Unpublished paper. London: The British Council, 1975.

Kachru, B. B. "The Indianness in Indian English." *Word*, 1965, *21*.
———. "Indian English: A study in contextualization." In Bazell et al., 1966.
———. "English in South Asia." In Sebeok, 1969.
———. "Toward a lexicon of Indian English." In Kachru et al., 1973, pp. 352–76.
———. "Lexical innovations in South Asian English." *International journal of the sociology of language*, 1975, *4*.
———. "Models of English for the third world: White man's linguistic burden or language pragmatics." *TESOL quarterly*, 1976a, *10* (2).
———. "Indian English: A sociolinguistic profile of a transplanted language." *Studies in language learning*. 1976b, *1* (2).
———. "The new Englishes and old models." *English teaching forum*, July 1977a.
———. "The Englishization of Hindi: Language rivalry and language change." In Rauch et al., 1977 (1979).
———. "Toward structuring code-mixing: An Indian perspective." In Kachru and Sridhar, 1978 (1978a).
———. "Code-mixing as a verbal strategy in India." In Alatis, 1978 (1978b).
———. "Models of 'Non-native English': Origin, development and use." Paper presented at conference on progress in language planning: International perspective. New Jersey, April, 1979.
———. "American English and other Englishes." In C. Ferguson and S. Heath (Eds), *Language in the U.S.A.* To appear.
———. "Varieties of Indian English." To appear.
———. "Indian English: a history of attitudes." Forthcoming (a).
———. "South Asian English." In R. W. Bailey and M. Görlach (Eds), *English as a World Language* Berlin: Erich Schmidt, forthcoming(b).
Kachru, B. B., Lees, R. B., Malkiel, Y., Pietrangeli, A., and Sporta, S. *Issues in linguistics: Papers in honor of Henry and Renée Kahane.* Urbana: University of Illinois Press, 1973.
Kachru, B. B. and Sridhar, S. N. (Eds), *Aspects of sociolinguistics in South Asia.* Special issue of *International journal of the sociology of language*, 1978, *16*.
Kahane, H. and R. "Virtues and vices in the American language: A history of attitudes." *TESOL quarterly*, 1977, *11* (2).
Kelley, L. G. *25 centuries of language teaching.* Rowley, Mass.: Newbury House, 1969.
Kempson, R. M. *Presupposition and the delimitation of semantics.* Cambridge: Cambridge University Press, 1975.
Kendon, A. "Some functions of gaze-direction in social interaction." (1967) In J. M. Argyle (Ed.), *Social encounters.* Harmondsworth: Penguin, 1973.

Killingley, S. Y. *A phonological, grammatical, and lexical description of Malayan English.* Unpublished M.A. thesis, University of Malay, 1965.

Kindersley, A. F. "Notes on the Indian idiom of English: Style, syntax and vocabulary." *Transactions of the philological society of Great Britain,* 1938.

Kirk-Greene, A. "The influence of West African languages on English." In Spencer, 1971a.

Kloss, H. "Types of multilingual communities: A discussion of ten variables." *Sociological inquiry,* 1966, *35.*

Krashen, S. E. et al. "Testing the monitor model." Paper presented at the 1977 TESOL Convention, Miami, Florida, 1977.

Kunjara, B. M. L. and Bandhumedha, B. 'The Thai language.' In *Aspects and facets of Thailand.* Bangkok: Public Relations Department, 1959.

LaBarre, W. "The cultural basis of emotions and gestures." (1947) In Laver and Hutcheson, 1973.

Labov, W. "Rules for ritual insults." In Sudnow, 1972.

Lobov, W. and Fanshel, D. *Therapeutic discourse: psychotherapy as conversation.* Philadephia: University of Pennsylvania Press, 1977.

Ladefoged, P., Glick, R. and Criper, C. *Language in Uganda.* Nairobi: Oxford University Press, 1972.

Laird, C. *The miracle of language.* New York: Fawcett World Library, 1953.

——. *Language in America.* New Jersey: Prentice-Hall, 1970.

Lambert, W. E. "Culture and language as factors in learning and education." Paper presented at Fifth Western Symposium on Learning, Western Washington State College, 1974.

Lambert, W. E. and Tucker, G. R. *Bilingual education of children: The St. Lambert experiment.* Rowley, Mass.: Newbury House, 1972.

Larsen Freeman, D. and Strom, V. "The construction of a second language acquisition index of development." In Henning, 1977.

Latif, S. A. *The influence of English literature on Urdu literature.* Unpublished Ph.D. Thesis, University of London, 1920.

Lautamatti, L. "Suggestions for development of learning materials for reading comprehension in a foreign language." Paper given to the BAAL Seminar on Comprehension, University of Edinburgh, 1977.

Laver, J. and Hutcheson, S. (Eds). *Communication in face to face interaction.* Harmondsworth: Penguin, 1972.

Leech, G. N. "Language and Tact." *LAUT,* University of Trier, Series A, Paper 46, 1977.

Lester, M. "English as an international auxiliary language." *English teaching and learning,* 1976, *1* (2).

Lewis, E. G. *Multilingualism in the Soviet Union: Aspects of language policy and its implementation.* The Hague: Mouton, 1972.

Lewis, E. G. and Massad, C. E. *The teaching of English as a foreign language in ten countries.* New York: Wiley, 1975.

Lewis, H. E. *Learning Spanish in Jamaica: A study of errors caused by language transfer in a diglossic situation.* Unpublished Ph.D. Dissertation, University of Toronto, 1974.

Lieberman, P. "On the acoustic basis of the perception of intonation by linguists." *Word,* 1965, *21.*

——. *Intonation, perception and language.* Cambridge, Mass.: MIT Press, 1967.

Lightfoot, D. W. "The diachronic analysis of English modals." In J. M. Anderson and C. Jones (Eds), *Historical Linguistics,* Vol. I. Edinburgh: North Holland Publishing Co., 1974.

Linnarud, M. *Lexis in free production: An analysis of the lexical texture of Swedish students' written work.* Swedish-English Contrastive Studies, Report No. 6, Lund University, 1975.

Lyons, J. *Theoretical linguistics.* London: Cambridge University Press, 1968.

——. *Semantics.* London: Cambridge University Press, 1977.

McAllister, J. F. "The Philippines' tower of babel." *Bangkok post,* 25 November 1977.

——. *Language teaching analysis.* London: Longman, 1965.

Mackey, W. F. *Bilinguisme et contact des langues.* Paris: Editions Klincksieck, 1976.

McKnight, A. *Large-group conversation: Problems for discourse analysis.* Unpublished M.A. Thesis, University of Lancaster, 1976.

McLean, L. and Castanos, F. "Discourse of language learning." *MEXTESOL journal,* 1976, *1* (3).

Macrae, A. "Comprehension: The psycholinguistic view." Paper read at the BAAL Seminar on Comprehension, Edinburgh, 1977.

McTear, M. "Potential sources of confusion in foreign language classrooms: The rules of the game." Unpublished paper given at the IV AIVA Congress, Stuttgart, 1975a.

——. "Structure and categories of foreign language teaching sequences." Unpublished paper, University of Essex, 1975b.

Mafeni, B. "Nigerian pidgin." In Spencer, 1971a.

Makkai, A. et al. *Linguistics at the crossroads.* Lake Bluff, Ill.: Jupiter Press, 1977.

Malaysia Ministry of Education. *English language syllabus in Malaysian schools, tingkatan 4–5.* Kuala Lumpur: Dewan Bahasa dan Pustaka, 1975.

——. *Teachers' handbook for the post-1970 Primary school English syllabus (Items 1–64).* Kuala Lumpur: Dewan Bahasa dan Pustaka, 1971.

Marckwardt, A. H. "English as a second language or English as a foreign language." *PMLA*, 1963, *78*.

Marckwardt, A. H. and Quirk, R. *A common language: British and American English*. London: British Broadcasting Corporation, 1964.

Mathews, M. M. *The beginnings of American English: Essays and comments*. Chicago: University of Chicago Press, 1931.

Mazrui, A. A. *The political sociology of the English language: An African perspective*. The Hague: Mouton, 1973.

Mencken, H. L. *The American language*. New York: Knopf, 1919.

Misra, V. *Hindi bhasha aur sahita par angrezi prabhav* prabhav (The effect of English on Hindi language and literature) (1870–1920). Dehradan: Sahitya Sadan, 1963.

Modern Language Association of America. "Developing cultural understanding through foreign language study: A report of the MLA interdisciplinary seminar in language and culture." *PMLA*, December 1953, *3*.

Moffat, A. L. *Mongkut, King of Siam*. Ithaca, New York: Cornell University Press, 1961.

Moffett, J. *Drama: What is happening*? Champaign, Ill.: National Council of Teachers of English, 1967.

Montgomery, M. "The structure of lectures." Mimeo, University of Birmingham, 1976.

Morris, E. E. *Austral English*. London: Macmillan, 1898.

Mougeon, R., Canale, M. and Bélanger, M. "Rôle de la société dans l'acquisition et le maintien de français par les élèves franco-ontariens." *Canadian modern language review*, 1978, *34* (3).

Mountford, A. *Discourse analysis and the simplification of reading materials for ESP*, Unpublished M.Litt. thesis, University of Edinburgh, 1975.

Mukherjee, M. *The twice born fiction: Themes and techniques of the Indian novel in English*. New Delhi and London: Heinemann, 1971.

Murphy, D. F. and Candlin, C. N. *Engineering discourse and listening comprehension*. KAAU Research Project Report, University of Lancaster, 1976.

——. Revised version of 1976 Paper published in *Practical Papers in English Language Education* Vol II, 1979, University of Lancaster, Institute for English Language Education, 1979.

Naiman, N., Frohlich, M., Stern, H. H. and Todesco, A. *The good language learner*. Toronto: Ontario Institute for Studies in Education, 1978.

Nash, R. "Aspects of Spanish-English Bilingualism and language mixture in Puerto Rico." In Makkai et al., 1977.

Natividad, P. E. *The nature of a pedagogical grammar with special reference to teaching an aspect of Pilipino as a second language.*

Unpublished Ph.D. Dissertation, University of Toronto, 1975.

Noss, R., Sukwiwat, M. and Debyasuvarn, B. M. L. "Proposals for the improvement of English instruction in Thailand: Prepared at the request of the Ministry of Education, by the English Language Center of the University Development Commission, Office of the National Education Council." 1 January 1971.

O'Bryan, K. G., Reitz, J. G. and Kuplowska, O. M. *Non-official languages: A study in Canadian multiculturalism.* Ottawa: Ministry of Supply and Services, 1976.

Okara, G. "African Speech . . . English Words." *Transition,* 1963, *3* (10).

Ontario, Ministry of Education. *Report of the ministerial committee on the teaching of French* (Gillin Report). Toronto: Ministry of Education, 1974.

——. *Teaching and learning French as a second language: A new program for Ontario students.* Toronto: Ministry of Education, 1977.

Palmer, F. R. *The English verb.* London: Longman, 1974.

—— (Ed.), *Selected Papers of J. R. Firth, 1952–59.* Bloomington: Indiana University Press, 1968.

Paradis, M. (Ed.), *Aspects of bilingualism.* South Carolina: Hornbeam Press, 1978.

Paulston, C. B. "Structural pattern drills: A classification." *Foreign language annals,* 1970, *4* (2).

——. *Implications of language learning theory for language planning: Concerns in bilingual education.* Papers in Applied Linguistics: Bilingual Education Series 1. Arlington, Va.: Center for Applied Linguistics, 1974.

Perren, G. E. *Teachers of English as a second language, their training and preparation.* London: English-Teaching Information Centre, 1972.

Perren, G. E. and Holloway, M. F. *Language and communication in the Commonwealth.* London: C.E.L.C./H.M.S.O., 1965 (88.5354).

Platt, J. T. "The Singapore English speech continuum and its basilect "Singlish" as a "Creoloid"." *Anthropological linguistics,* 1975, *17* (7).

——. "The sub-varieties of Singapore English: Their sociolectal and functional status." In Crewe, 1977.

Platt, J. T. and Platt, K. K. *The social significance of speech.* Amsterdam: North-Holland, 1975.

Pramoj Na Ayudhaya, K. *An analytical study of the mistakes in writing Thai made by arts students at Chulalongkorn University 1972 and 1973.* Unpublished Master's thesis, Department of the Thai language, Graduate School, Chulalongkorn University, 1959.

Prator, C. H. "The British heresy in TESL." In Fishman et al., 1968.

Quirk, R. *The Use of English.* London: Longman, 1968.

——. *The English language and images of matter.* London: Oxford

University Press, 1972.
—— "Aspects of English as an international language." *Sproglaereren*, 1978, *9*.
Quirk, R. and Smith, A. H. *The teaching of English*. London: Oxford University Press, 1964.
Quirk, R., Greenbaum, S., Leech, G. and Svartik, J. *A grammar of contemporary English*. London: Longman, 1972.
Ramchand, K. "The language of the master?" In Bailey and Robinson, 1973.
Ramson, W. S. *Australian English: an historical study of the vocabulary 1788–1898*. Canberra: Australian National University Press, 1966.
—— (Ed.) *English transported: essays on Australasian English*. Canberra: Australian National University Press, 1970.
Rao, G. S. *Indian words in English: A study in Indo-British cultural and linguistic relations*. London: Oxford University Press, 1954.
Rao, R. *Kanthapura*. Bombay: Oxford University Press, 1947.
Rauch, I. et al., *Linguistic method: Papers in honor of Herbert Penzi*. The Hague: Mouton, 1979.
Rehbein, J. and Ehlich, K. "Zur Konstitution pragmatischer einheiten in einer Institution: das Speiserestaurant." In D. Wunderlich (Ed.), *Linguistische pragmatik*, Frankfurt/M: Athenaumverlag, 1972.
—— "Wissen, kommunikatives Handeln und die Schule." In H. M. Goeppert (Ed.), *Sprachverhalten im unterricht*. Munich: Finkverlag, 1977.
Rice, F. A. (Ed.), *Study of the role of second languages in Asia, Africa and Latin America*. Washington: Center for Applied Linguistics, 1962.
Richards, G. R. *The development of a conceptual framework for the teaching of the cultural component of second languages*. Unpublished Ph.D. Dissertation, University of Toronto, 1976.
Richards, J. C. "Social factors, interlanguage, and language learning." *Language learning*, 1972, *22* (2) (Also in Richards, 1974).
—— "Variation in Singapore English." In Crewe, 1977.
—— (Ed.), *Error analysis: Perspectives on second language acquisition*. London: Longman, 1974.
—— *Understanding second and foreign language learning: A survey of issues and approaches*. Rowley, Mass.: Newbury House, 1978.
Richards, J. C. and Kennedy, G. "Interlanguage: A review and a preview." *RELC journal*, 1977, *8* (1).
Richards, J. C. and Tay, M. W. J. "The la particle in Singapore English." In Crewe, 1977.
Rivers, W. M. 'The natural and the normal in language learning', Papers in second language acquisition, *Language learning social issues*, No. 4, 1976. Also in R. Schulz (Ed.), *Personalizing foreign language instruction: Learning styles and teaching options*. Stokie, Ill.: National Textbook Co., 1977.

Rockwood, J. *The craftsmen of Dionysus*. Gleview, Ill.: Scott Foresman, 1966.

Ross, J. R. "Auxiliaries as main verbs." In W. Todd (Ed.), *Studies in philosophical linguistics* I. Evanston: Great Expectations, 1969.

Royal Commission on Bilingualism and Biculturalism. *Report of the Royal Commission on Bilingualism and Biculturalism*. 4 vols. Ottawa: Queen's Printer, 1967.

Rustow, D. A. "Language, modernization and nationhood—An attempt at typology." In J. A. Fishman, C. A. Ferguson and J. Das Gupta (Eds), *Language problems of developing nations*. New York: Wiley, 1968, pp. 87–106.

Sachs, J. and Devin, J. "Young children's use of age-appropriate speech styles in social interaction and role-playing." *Journal of child language*, 1976, *3* (1).

Sacks, H. "An initial investigation of the usability of conversational data for doing sociology." In Sudnow, 1972.

Sacks, H., Schegloff, E. A. and Jefferson, G. "A simplest systematics for the organization of turn-taking for conversation." *Language*, 1974, *50* (4).

Samarin, W. J. "Lingua francas, with special reference to Africa." In Rice, 1962.

Samovar, L. A. and Porter, R. E. *Intercultural communication: A reader*, 2nd ed. Belmont, Ca: Wadsworth Publishing Company, 1976.

Sampson, G. P. "The strategies of Cantonese speakers learning English." In R. Darnell (Ed.), *Linguistic diversity in Canadian society*. Edmonton: Linguistic Research Inc., 1971.

Sayamanond, R. "A historical study of the teaching of foreign languages in Thailand." *Bulletin of the Faculty of Arts, Chulalongkorn University*, January 1967, *4*.

Schegloff, E. A. "Notes on a conversational practice: Formulating place." In Sudnow, 1972.

Schegloff, E. A. and Sacks, H. "Opening up closings." *Semiotica*, 1973, *8* (4).

Schneider, G. D. *West African Pidgin-English*. Unpublished Ph.D. dissertation, Harford Seminary Foundation, 1966.

Schuchardt, H. *Indo-English* (Translated into English by Gilbert, 1977). Unpublished manuscript, 1891.

Searle, J. R. *Speech acts: An essay in the philosophy of language*. London: Cambridge University Press, 1969.

——. "Indirect speech acts." In P. Cole and J. L. Morgan (Eds), *Syntax and semantics*, Vol. 3, *Speech acts*. New York: Academic Press, 1975.

Sebeok, T. A. (Ed.), *Current trends in linguistics*. Vol. 5, *South Asia*. The Hague: Mouton, 1969.

——. *Current trends in linguistics*. Vol. 7, *Linguistics in sub-Sahara*

Africa. The Hague: Mouton, 1971.

Segalowitz, N. "Communicative incompetence and the non-fluent bilingual." *Canadian journal of behavioural science*, 1976, *8*.

Selinker, L. "Interlanguage." *IRAL*, 1972, *10* (also in Richards, 1974).

Sen, P. *Western influence in Bengali literature*. Calcutta: University of Calcutta, 1932.

Seshadri, C. K. *Second language planning for a multilingual country: English language instruction in India*. Unpublished Ph.D. dissertation, University of Toronto, 1978.

Sexton, M. "Acceptance, defiance and evasion in a psychiatric meeting." Unpublished paper, University of Lancaster, 1976.

Sey, K. A. *Ghanian English: An exploratory survey*. London: Macmillan, 1973.

Shah, A. B. *The great debate*. Bombay: Lalvani Publishing House, 1968.

Shannon, C. and Weaver, W. *Mathematical theory of communication*. Urbana: Illinois University Press, 1949.

Sharim-Paz, S. "Using drama in teacher training." *English teaching forum*, 1976, *14* (1).

Sheils, M. "Why Johnny can't write." *Reader's Digest*, April 1976.

Sibayan, B. P. "Language and identity." Paper presented at the SEAMEO Regional Language Center, Twelfth Regional Seminar on Language Education in Multilingual Societies: Its Challenges and Potentials, 18–22 April 1977.

Silverman, D. "Interview talk: Bringing off a research instrument." Paper given to the British Sociological Association Conference, October 1971.

Simon, S. B., Howe, L. M. and Kirschenbaum, H. *Values clarification: A handbook of practical strategies for teachers and students*. New York: Hart Publishing Company, 1972.

Sinclair, J. M. and Coulthard, R. M. *Towards an analysis of discourse*. London: Oxford University Press, 1975.

Sitachit, K. "Modern trends in teaching English at the tertiary level." *PASAA*, 1976, *6* (1 and 2).

Sledd, J. and Ebbit, W. R. *Dictionaries and that dictionary*. Chicago: Scott, Foresman, 1962.

Slobin, D. *Psycholinguistics*. New York: Scott, Foresman, 1971.

Smith, L. E. "English as an international auxiliary language." *RELC journal*, 1976a, *7* (1).

——. "ESOL–EIAL: A position paper." *TESL Reporter*, 1976b, 10 (1).

Smudavanich, C. *Ekasarn karn-muang-karn pokrong Thai B.E. 2417–2477*. (Documents dealing with politics and administration 1870–1944), Textbooks project.

Snow, C. E. "Mother's speech to children learning language." *Child development*, 1972, *43*.

Spencer, J. W. (Ed.) *The English language in West Africa*. London:

Longman, 1971a.

———. "Colonial language policies and their legacies." In Sebeok, 1971 (1971b).

Spolin, V. *Improvisations for the theatre.* Evanston, Ill.: Northwestern University Press, 1963.

Spolsky, B., Green, J. B. and Read, J. *A model for the description, analysis, and perhaps evaluation of bilingual education.* Navajo reading study progress report No. 23. Albuquerque: The University of New Mexico, 1974.

Sridhar, K. K. "English as the language of wider communication in India." College of Education, University of Illinois (mimeo), 1978a.

———. "English in urban context: A South Indian case." Paper presented at the Conference on English in non-native context, June 30–July 2, Urbana: University of Illinois, 1978b.

Sridhar, S. N. "On the functions of code-mixing in Kannada." In Kachru et al., 1978.

Sri Nakarindara Wirodh University. *Curriculum for the degree of Bachelor of Education.* Bangkok: Sri Nakarindara Wirodh University, 1977.

Stern, H. H. "Directions in language teaching theory and research." In *Applied linguistics: Problems and solutions,* AILA Proceedings, 1972. Heidelberg: Julius Groos Verlag, 1974.

———. "What can we learn from the good language learner?" *The Canadian modern language review,* 1975, *31.*

———. "Mammoths or modules." *Times educational supplement,* 8 October 1976.

Stern, H. H., Wesche, M. B. and Harley, B. "The impact of the language sciences on second language education." In P. Suppes (Ed.), *The impact of research on education.* Los Angeles: National Academy of Education, 1978.

Stern, H. H. et al. *Three approaches to teaching French: Evaluation and overview of studies related to the federally-funded extensions of the second language learning (French) programs in the Carleton and Ottawa School Boards.* Toronto: Ontario Ministry of Education, 1976.

Stevick, E. *Memory, meaning and method.* Rowley, Mass.: Newbury House, 1976.

Stewart, W. A. "A sociolinguistic typology for describing national multilingualism." In Fishman, 1968.

Strevens, P. *British and American English.* London: Collier-Macmillan, 1972.

———. *New orientations in the teaching of English.* London: Oxford University Press, 1977.

———. *English as an international language: When is a local form of*

English a suitable target for ELT purposes? London: British Council, 1978.

——. "English for international and intranational purposes: a shift in linguistic perspectives". *Indian journal of applied linguistics*, 1978.

Sudnow, D. (Ed.), *Studies in social interaction.* New York: Macmillan, 1972.

Swain, M. (Ed.), *Bilingualism in Canadian education: Issues and research.* Yearbook of the Canadian Society for the Study of Education, 1976, *3.*

Swain, M. and Barik, H. C. "Bilingual education in Canada: French and English." In B. Spolsky and R. L. Cooper (Eds), *Case studies in bilingual education.* Rowley, Mass.: Newbury House, 1978.

Sweet, H. *The practical study of languages.* London: Oxford University Press, 1964 (first published in 1899).

Thailand, Ministry of Education. Educational Statistics. 1942–1954.

——. *An evaluative research on school broadcasting.* Report of the working group, Center of Educational Technology, 1972.

Thailand, National Council of Education. *Reports on Results of Entrance Examinations 2512–2518.* Bangkok: Thai Government Publications, 1976.

Tongue, R. K. *The English of Singapore and Malaysia.* Singapore: Eastern Universities Press, 1974.

Trifonovitch, G. J. "On cross-cultural orientation techniques." In R. W. Brislin (Ed.), *Culture learning, concepts, applications, and research.* Honolulu: University Press of Hawaii, 1977.

Turner, G. W. *The English language in Australia and New Zealand.* London: Longman, 1966.

Turner, R. (Ed.), *Ethnomethodology.* Harmondsworth: Penguin, 1975.

UNESCO *Statistical yearbook.* Paris: UNESCO Publications Centre, 1975.

Urquhart, A. "Meaning in discourse." Unpublished paper read to the BAAL Seminar on Comprehension, University of Edinburgh, 1977.

Urquhart, A. and Widdowson, H. G. *KAAU Reading Research Project. 1st Yearly Report.* Mimeo, University of Edinburgh, 1976.

Valdman, A. "On the relevance of the pidginization-creolization model for second language learning." *Colloque: Theoretical Models in Applied Linguistics, VI.* Université de Neuchatel, 1977.

——. (Ed.), *Pidgin and creole linguistics.* Bloomington, Indiana: Indiana University Press, 1977.

Valdman, A. and Phillips, J. S. "Pidginization, creolization and the elaboration of learner systems." In *Colloque: Theoretical Models in Applied Linguistics, IV.* Université de Neuchatel, 1975.

van Ek, J. A. *The threshold level for modern language learning in schools.* Strasbourg: The Council for Europe, 1976.

Venneman, T. "Topic, sentence accent, ellipse: a proposal for their formal treatment." *LAUT*, University Trier, 1973.

Via, R. *English in three acts.* Honolulu: University Press of Hawaii, 1976.

Walatara, D. "The scope and limitations of bilingualism with a second language with specific reference to the case of Ceylon." *Teaching English.* 1960, 6 (3).

Walker, T. A. "Language through drama." *English language teaching journal*, 1977, *31* (2).

Wanner, E. "Do we understand sentences from the outside-in or the inside-out?" *Daedalus*, 1973, *102*.

Warie, P. "Some aspects of code-mixing in Thai." *Studies in the linguistic sciences*, 1977, *7* (1).

Watson, K. A. "Understanding human interaction: The study of everyday life and ordinary talk." In R. W. Brislin (Ed.), *Culture learning concepts, applications, and research.* Honolulu: University Press of Hawaii, 1977.

Way, B. *Development through drama.* London: Humanities Press, 1967.

Whiteley, W. H. (Ed.), *Language in Kenya.* Nairobi: Oxford University Press, 1974.

Whitworth, G. C. *Indian English: An examination of the errors of idiom made by Indians in writing English.* Letchworth: 1907.

Widdowson, H. G. "Directions in the teaching of discourse." In S. P. Corder and E. Roulet (Eds), *Theoretical linguistic models in applied linguistics.* Brussels: AIMAV and Paris: Didier, 1973.

——. "The deep structure of discourse and the use of translation." In S. P. Corder and E. Roulet (Eds), *Linguistic insights in applied linguistics.* Brussels: AIMAV and Paris: Didier, 1974.

——. "The description of scientific language." Unpublished mimeo, 1975a.

——. "Rules and procedures in discourse analysis." Unpublished paper, Edinburgh, 1975b.

——. "The significance of simplification." In *Colloque: The Notion of Simplification.* Université de Neuchatel, 1976a.

——. "The use of simplification and the simplification of use." Unpublished paper, 1976b.

——. "The communicative approach and its application." In *English for specific purposes.* Bogota: The British Council, 1977.

——. *Teaching language as communication.* Oxford: Oxford University Press, 1978.

Wilkins, J. *An essay towards a real character.* London, 1668.

Wilson, H. H. *A glossary of judicial and revenue terms and of useful words occurring in official documents, relating to the administration of the government of British India . . .* London: W. H. Allen, 1885 (reprinted in Calcutta in 1940).

Winograd, T. "Artificial intelligence: When will computers understand people?" *Psychology today*, May 1974.

Wode, H. "Development sequences in naturalistic L2 acquisition." Englisches seminar der Universität Kiel, 1976.

Wootton, A. *Dilemmas of discourse*. London: Allen and Unwin, 1975.

Wunderlich, D. "Pragmatik, sprechsituation, deixis."*Zeitschrift für literaturwissenschaft und linguistik*, 1971, *1*.

Yearbook of statistics. 1975/76. Singapore.

Yule, Sir Henry and Burnell, A. C. *Hobson-Jobson being a glossary of Anglo-Indian words and phrases, and of kindred terms; etymological, historical, geographical and discursive*. London: Murray, 1886 (new ed. W. Crooke (Ed.), 1903).

Index

Académie Française, 8
Accents, 6, 8
Achievement tests, 70
Act of Compulsory Education (Thailand), 84
ACTFL, 58
Acting, as a teaching process, 200–10
AIR, *see* All India Radio
All India Radio (AIR), 22
American Council on the Teaching of Foreign Languages, *see* ACTFL
American English
  and Black English, 8, 12
  as nativized English, 23, 107
  spread of, xv, xix–xx, 79
Arabic language, impact on English, xix
Artificial languages, xiv, 65
Asia, use of English, 108–22
Australian English, 23, 43

Babu English, 21, 29, 35
Bahasa Malaysia, 46 *passim*, 95, 104
Basic (nuclear) English, 37, 65, 72, 151–65
Bazaar Malay, 48
Bilingualism, xiv, 26–7, 47
"Black English", 8, 12
Box-wallah English, 29–30, 35
British Council, 57
British English
  and basic (nuclear) English, 37
  and nativized English, 23, 49, 107
  dialect, 100–2
  pronunciation, 98–102
Broken English, 30
Butler English, 28

Canada
  use of English, 10, 57–73
  use of French, 58–60, 62–3, 64
Caribbean English, 30
Chee-Chee English, 28–9
Chinese language, *see* Mandarin (Chinese) language
Chulalongkorn University (Thailand), 83, 86–7
Code-mixed English, 31
Colloquial language, 43
Colonization, effect on spread of English, xiv–xv, xvi
Commissioner of Official Languages (Canada), 59
Communicative competence, 18–19, 37, 166–99
Comprehension, 123–50, 166–99, 216–20
  see also Threshold of comprehension
Context of situation, 18–19, 35–6
Conversation, *see* Verbal communication
Conversational maxims, 168–9, 170–3
Cooperative Principle, 168
Creole English, 4
Culture Learning Institute (Honolulu), xiii, xviii, 66–7, 69, 71

Dialects, 6, 7
Discoursal rules, 6–7
Drama, *see* Acting

East India Company, 94
East-West Center, Culture Learning Institute, *see* Culture Learning Institute
Engalog hybrid language, 77

English language
  as foreign language, xvii, 9–10, 40–56, 84–5
  as indication of status, 19–20
  as international language, 65
    and interlanguage, 63–5
    and intranational English, 65–9, 74–82
    bilingualism, xiv, 26–7, 47
  as intranational language, xvii–xx, 27, 37, 63–70, 74–82
  as native language, xiv–xv, xvii, 9, 52–4
  as second language, xiv–xv, xvii, xix, 211–15
    learning of, 84–5
    political aspects, 57–62
    proficiency, 40–56
  as teaching language, 11, 20, 51–2
  communication of information, xiv, xv, 2, 10–11, 21–2, 123–50
  cross-cultural communication, xiv, xxi–xxiii, 11
    proficiency necessary for, 44, 216–24
    teaching of, 62–3, 74–5
  cross-national communication, xiv, 151–65
    cultural bias, 171
    in Singapore, 48–9
    proficiency necessary for, 78
    teaching of, 74–5
  demographic distribution, xvi–xvii, 46
  expansion, xiv, xvi, 1–2
  for science students, 88–9
  geographical distribution, xiv, 17–18
  historical background, xiv, xvi, 18, 94
  impact on native languages, 32–3
  learning, 40–56, 84, 110–12, 116–17
  linguistics, 3–4
  nativization, xv, xvii, xix
    in Malaysia, 97, 104
    in Philippines, 77
    surveys, 2–14, 15–39
  political influences, 10, 12, 57–9

  status, 10, 83, 87
  structure and style, xv, xvi
  students attitudes to, 108–22
  teaching, xvii, 3–4
    aims, 54–5
    in Canada, 57–73
    in Malaysia, 98–9, 105–6
    in Philippines, 74–82
  use in Asia, 108–22
  use in Canada, 57–73
  use in India, xvi–xviii, 9, 20–30, 108–22
  use in Malaysia, 94–107
  use in the Philippines, 74–82
  use in Singapore, 46–56, 108–22
  use in Thailand, 83–93, 108–22
  users, xiv passim, 2
  vocabulary, xix–xx, 23–25
English Language Teaching Forum, 58
English Language Teaching Journal, 58
English norm, see Basic (nuclear) English
Esperanto (artificial language), xiv, 65

Fédération Internationale des Professeurs des Langues Vivantes, see FIPLV
Filipino English, 75, 80, 81
FIPLV, 58
Foreign languages (FL), 9–10
Français dans le Monde, Le, 58
Française fondamental, 65, 72
French language, impact on English, xix

Ghanian English, 23–5, 30
Greek language, impact on English, xix

Hausa language, impact on English, xix
Hindi language, impact on English, xix
Hokkien dialect, 48, 50

Ido (artificial language), xiv
Ilocano English, 79, 81
Immigrants, use of English, 43, 60

India, use of English, xvi–xvii, 9, 20–30, 108–22
Indian Bar Council, 20
Indian English, 23–5, 27–32, 34
Indigenous English, 45–6
Indo-English, 27–9, 35
Interlanguage, 42–3, 63–5
Interlingua (artificial language), xiv
International Centre for Research on Bilingualism, 61
International English, *see* Basic (nuclear) English
International French, 64
International language, 65–9
Interpretation, *see* Comprehension
Intranational language, 65–9

Language learning, 40–56, 84, 110–12, 116–17
see also English language learning, English language teaching, Language teaching
Language loss, 60
Language maintenance, 60
Language Research Group (Canada), 61
Language shift, 60
Language standardization, 34
Language teaching, xvii, 57–73
course planning, 188–99
language proficiency, 40–6
sociolinguistics, 13–14
see also English language learning, English language teaching, Language learning
Latin language, impact on English, xix
Linguistic functions, 19–22
Linguistic proficiency, 40–56
Local forms of English (LFE), 2–14

Malay language, *see* Bahasa Malaysia
Malaysia, use of English, 94–107
Malaysian English, 94–104
Mandarin (Chinese) language, 46–7, 48 *passim*
Maxim of manner, 168, 171
Maxim of quality, 168
Meaning in language, 166–99
Ministry of Education (Malaysia), 94–5

Ministry of Education (Thailand), 84
Missionaries, contribution to spread of English, 18
Modality, 161–63
Modern Language Centre (Canada), 61, 68

Native languages, impact of English, 32–3
Neo-Melanesian language, 162
New Englishes, xv, xvii, xix, 15–39
Non-standard English, 7–9
Novial (artificial language), xiv
Nuclear English, *see* Basic (nuclear) English

Occidental (artificial language), xiv
Official Languages Act (Canada), 59

Persian language, impact on English, xix
Philippines, use of English, 74–82
Pidgin English, 4, 29, 30
Pilipino language, 77
Primary languages (LI), 9, 52–4

Relaxation exercises, 203–4
Royal Commission on Bilingualism and Biculturalism (Canada), 59

School broadcasts, 85–6
Scientific English, 88–9
SEAMEO, 84
Secondary languages (L2), 9–10, 40–56, 57–73, 84–5, 211–15
Singapore English, 40, 45, 46–56
Sociolinguistics, 9–10, 13–14, 211–15
Southeast Asia Ministers of Education Organization, *see* SEAMEO
Spanish language, impact on English, xix
Speech, *see* Verbal communication
Speech communities, 32, 33–4, 35
Speech fellowship, 31–2, 35, 43
Speech patterns, 166–99
Speech recognition, *see* Comprehension
Standard English, 6, 7–9

Students, attitudes towards English, 108–22

Tact maxim, 168–9, 173
Tagalog English, 81
Tagalog language, 76, 77
Taglish hybrid language, 77
Tamil language, 46–7, 48 *passim*
Teacher education, 80–2, 88–9, 209
Teaching programmes, 89–91
TESOL Quarterly, 58
Thailand, use of English, 83–93
Threshold of comprehension, 92
    see also Comprehension

Understanding, *see* Comprehension
UNESCO, 21

United Nations Education, Scientific and Cultural Organization, *see* UNESCO
Use of language, 40–56, 123–50
USIA, 57

Variety theory, 6, 18, 26–32
Verbal communication, 41, 92, 166–99, 200–10
Visayan English, 81
Volapük (artificial language), xiv

Written communication, 43, 92, 177–80

Yoruba language, impact on English, xix